Praise for

The Performing Arts Business Encyclopedia

"Leonard DuBoff has done it again! *The Performing Arts Business Encyclopedia* is a must for anyone trying to navigate the often confusing channels of the entertainment industry. In typical fashion, DuBoff offers clear and concise explanations for both the novice and the seasoned professional. This is a resource you'll want to keep close at hand!"

—John J. Limb, Publisher, *Oregon Catholic Press* and *New Dawn Music*

"DuBoff does great service to the nonprofit performing arts with a volume that enlightens the consumer with a comprehensive view of the arts as an industry. The business of producing living art has long been underappreciated for its intricate complexities."

—Benjamin Moore, Seattle Repertory Theatre

The Performing Arts Business Encyclopedia

Leonard D. DuBoff

Allworth Press, New York

Published by Allworth Press
an imprint of Allworth Communications, Inc.
10 East 23rd Street, New York, NY 10010

Cover design by Douglas Design Associates, New York, NY

Book design by Sharp Des!gns, Holt, MI

ISBN: 1-880559-42-0

Library of Congress Catalog Card Number: 95-83003

To my mother, Millicent DuBoff,

for providing me with the necessary tools;

and to Mary Ann Crawford DuBoff,

for helping me to use those tools effectively.

Contents

reface

It has been more than a quarter century since I began practicing law, specializing in the arts. As a practicing attorney, law professor, and author, I have come to recognize the benefits of dealing with individuals who have some understanding of the disciplines in which we are involved. Pre-problem counseling and education is beneficial in order to avoid becoming embroiled in costly and time-consuming litigation. It is also quite important to understand the terms which are common in the profession in order to make informed decisions.

My earliest literary efforts focused on visual artists, though, as a lawyer, I have worked with a large number of individuals and organizations in the entertainment industry. Indeed, I was privileged to have the opportunity to work with the first Western movie company permitted to film inside the People's Republic of China, in 1982. This experience reminded me of just how complex a global transaction can be, particularly when it not only crosses geographic boundaries, but political as well as cultural ones.

When the project which now has emerged as *The Performing Arts Business Encyclopedia* was first conceived, it was recognized that the entertainment industry is extraordinarily complex and that it would be appropriate to separate out certain of its facets. While the entertainment industry clearly includes the recording, motion picture, and television industries, it is important that the reader recognize that recorded music, movies, and TV are not the focus of this publication. These industries will be covered in other volumes in this series. It also is important to understand that this text is not intended to be a lawyer's handbook but, rather, an informative resource for those involved in the performing arts, whether a performer or behind-the-scenes professional. There are a handful of entertainment law books available for attorneys, which are listed in an appendix to this volume, yet there are few nontechnical resources available for nonlawyer entertainment professionals.

It is hoped that this book will serve as a source of definitions for fundamental business, legal, and professional terms in the performing arts industry. As time goes on and the field evolves, it is likely that new terms and concepts will emerge. Future editions of this text will be revised in order to keep pace with the rapidly changing and expanding industry. New technology spurred by the computer age is likely to accelerate the industry's changes and add a myriad of new terms, though the old ones will continue to have vitality.

It is hoped that this book will function as a valauable and frequently consulted resource for you, the performing arts and entertainment professional.

LEONARD D. DuBOFF, ESQ.
Portland, Oregon

Acknowledgments

In order to survey the industry, identify key terms, and prepare a discussion of each, it was necessary to enlist the aid of numerous friends and colleagues. People were extraordinarily helpful and eager to provide me with recommendations, suggestions, and the benefit of their knowledge or experience. While it will be impossible to identify every individual or organization who contributed to the project which has emerged as *The Performing Arts Business Encyclopedia,* some deserve special recognition. I would like to thank Lynn Della, Colleen Rose DuBoff, Lora Gardner, Christy King, Harold Phillips, and Kathleen Scott; also, my publisher, Tad Crawford, for his insistence upon having this book in print as soon as possible; and, as with all of my other activities, my partner in law and in life, Mary Ann Crawford DuBoff, for all of her help, guidance, inspiration, and skill.

A special thanks to my niece, Jill Bonnie DuBoff, for her unique insights into the practical issues confronted by those who are involved in performing arts organizations. From her vantage point as an insider, she was able to aid me in identifying problems and made several useful suggestions.

LEONARD D. DUBOFF, ESQ.
Portland, Oregon

Accountant

An *accountant* is a professional qualified to practice accounting. Accountants can be found in public, private, or governmental settings. Public accountants represent a number of independent clients; management accountants are employees of particular businesses; and governmental accountants are employed by city, county, state, or federal agencies. Accountants design and maintain the recordkeeping systems of a business. (Bookkeepers may also be used for records maintenance.) Accountants may also assist with tax return preparation, business financial planning, budgeting, and, in conjunction with an attorney, personal estate planning.

Accountants are usually graduates of an accredited accounting program at a college or university, although they may have practical experience and no degree. They may or may not be certified. Certification is granted by the individual states, based on a variety of criteria including tests, experience, and continuing education. Certified public accountants are known as CPAs; certified management accountants are known as CMAs.

➤ *See also* Accounting, Budget, Estate Planning, Investment, Tax, Tax Preparer

Accounting

Accounting is a professional discipline concerned with analyzing, verifying, and reporting financial transactions. Each performing arts business is unique, so each set of books has to be created to suit the business's particular needs. Most systems include the following basic categories:

1. *Cash Receipts*: incoming cash
2. *Cash Disbursements*: outgoing cash
3. *Earnings*: the value of services rendered, or sales, such as amounts received from ticket sales
4. *Payroll*: employee wages and deductions, including taxes and Social Security
5. *Equipment*: capital assets, such as scenery for theater or an instrument for a musician, office equipment (like a computer), furniture and fixtures, a business vehicle
6. *Accounts Receivable*: what the business is owed
7. *Accounts Payable*: what the business owes

The more extensive and involved the financial records and activities become, the more necessary it is to engage the services of an accountant on a regular basis. Many businesses use an accountant on a monthly or quarterly schedule to check on the proper maintenance of its records, prepare financial statements, prepare tax returns, and furnish other accounting services.

Literally hundreds of decisions that involve money or management can benefit from an accountant's advice. For example: Should you buy that new piano in November, or can you get a tax break if you wait six weeks and buy it in the next tax year? Will a move to bigger quarters at a higher rent be justified by the expected return? Which of your activities are profitable, which are not, which can be made profitable, and which should be abandoned? Applications for business loans from a bank almost always require that the applicant furnish a financial statement prepared by an accountant.

A competent accountant is as important to a business activity as a competent lawyer, both to prevent problems from arising and to solve them if they do arise. The proper use of an accountant's services requires you to be candid and to disclose all relevant information. Your banker, lawyer, or other business acquaintances can probably recommend a good accountant, especially one who is experienced in the financial matters of a business such as yours. Choose carefully and feel free to discuss fees in advance.

ACCOUNTING METHODS

Cash Basis—A method used for tax purposes in which income and expenses are counted in the tax year in which the money actually changed hands, regardless of when the performance occurred. This is a common method used by small businesses and service-based businesses such as those in the entertainment industry. *Accrual basis* is the other type of accounting procedure; you must obtain permission from the Internal Revenue Service to switch from one method to the other.

Accrual Basis—A method in which items of income and expense are charged against the accounting period in which they are incurred, regardless of when the money was actually spent or received. For example: If you order a new sound system at the end of one year but do not receive the bill or pay for the system until the next year, the accrual basis of accounting would list the expenditure for the year in which the sound system was ordered, and the sound system would have to be *capitalized,* that is, *depreciated* (deducted) over time. Similarly, an invoice you send to another, such as the bill for the sale of a block of theater tickets is credited as *sales* on the date the invoice was sent, and carried on the books as an *account receivable.*

For most performing arts or entertainment businesses, cash basis accounting is preferable, since taxes are paid and deductions taken only when actual money is received or spent. The accrual basis of accounting is more advantageous for businesses involving inventory such as, for example, a shop selling theatrical memorabilia and posters.

COST ACCOUNTING

While financial accounting concerns itself with the accurate recording and interpretation of the financial activities of a business, *cost accounting* analyzes those records in terms of the various costs involved in the production and distribution of goods and/or services.

Most theater companies engage in some form of rudimentary cost accounting every time they determine the price to be charged for a ticket or performance. You may not know it, but whenever you take pencil in hand to break down the cost of script, talent, and the like you are engaged in cost accounting. When an accountant works with you, that process becomes much more sophisticated and serves to pinpoint problems of which you may hardly be aware. Why, for example, did it cost 10 percent more in December to produce a show than it did in May? Are you in a rut with your present suppliers, who keep raising prices? Is the talent agency you use the most cost-effective? Perhaps you should go shopping. Or do you spend more time "on call" than on productive work? Maybe you should hire a part-time helper. A good cost accounting system helps you to determine what steps must be taken to improve performance and reduce expenses.

Your profitability, in the final analysis, depends on only two factors: increasing income, and controlling costs. The only way to control costs is to know precisely what the costs are and how they are incurred. Having a professional do the cost accounting may be a luxury in a small entertainment business where the owner does all the work. But the greater and more varied the activities of the business, the more necessary it becomes to analyze the specific cost ingredients of every production.

BOOKKEEPING

Bookkeeping is an essential operation in the conduct of any business. It involves the recording of every financial transaction. It is important to every business, from the entertainer who waits on tables while waiting to be "discovered" to a large multi-national theatre organization. It may be considered the lifeblood of every entertainment business, since it involves the recording of income, expenses, profits, obligations, and the like. The results help the owner to evaluate the success of the business, as well as any reverses. The bookkeeper maintains the day-to-day records, including accounts payable and accounts receivable, and will often handle bank deposits.

Bookkeeping is not a matter of choice, but of necessity. Your financial records are the basis on which your business's financial statements are prepared and on which your business income tax returns and other taxes, such as personal property and sales taxes, are calculated. When analyzed, properly maintained financial records can reveal where your activity is profitable and where it is unprofitable, where you may be able to save money, where the price for your service needs to be adjusted, how to plan your cash flow and budget for future business, and many other factors that spell the difference between economic survival and economic disaster.

Unless you are involved in complicated credit transactions, elaborate accounts receivable operations, or other ultra-sophisticated financial dealings, you'll find that the bookkeeping mystery really boils down to this simple principle: Keep track of every penny that comes in and every penny that goes out. This can usually be done in a simple manual ledger. There are also many computer programs, such as Peachtree, Quicken, and OneWrite Plus, which provide accounting support. You and your accountant can select software that best suits your business needs.

RECORDKEEPING

Keeping good and accurate *records* serves at least three purposes: First, to comply with legal requirements, such as those related to taxation, and the like; second, for reliable business monitoring; and third, as the basis for developing a sound business plan.

Preparation of tax returns requires accurate books, which must be retained for at least three years beyond the filing date in case of an audit. Some payroll records have to be kept for as long as seven years.

Business monitoring is facilitated when you maintain complete and accurate records. For example: In order to determine which wholesalers owe you for ticket sales, you should have a complete list of your distribution network, locations, and the date of all block sales.

You can also learn a great deal about your entertainment business by analyzing your records. Is an ad in the Sunday *New York Times* cost-effective? Should you continue to attend a specific booking conference year after year, or is the cost higher than the return? It is wise to develop a *business plan* in order to establish the structure, growth pattern, and direction for your business. In addition, you should periodically review the plan and, where appropriate, revise it. Accurate recordkeeping is essential for your periodic reviews.

Recordkeeping is also necessary for you when applying for loans and other forms of credit, insurance, and the like. Businesspeople expect good record-keeping and artists must adhere to this practice when engaging in the entertainment business.

> ➤ *See also* Accountant, Appreciation, Audit, Break-Even Point, Budget, Business Plan, Cash Flow, Collection Problems, Computers, Deductions, Depreciation, Financial Statement, Net, Petty Cash, Recordkeeping, Statement, Tax, Wages, Year-End

Accrual Basis
> ➤ *See* Accounting

Adapted From
When a production is taken from a work originally produced in another medium or written by another author, the production is said to be *adapted from*

or *based on* the original work. Thus, for example, Lerner & Loewe's *My Fair Lady* was adapted from Shaw's *Pygmalion*.

There are at least two significant issues that arise when a work falls into this category. First, if the new production is adapted from a book or other copyrighted work, then the substantially similar movie, stage play, or the like is covered by the author of the original work's copyright. The adapter must, therefore, obtain permission to create the adaptation or be guilty of copyright infringement. There are questions about how similar the production must be to the original work before it is deemed "substantially similar" within the meaning of the copyright law. If, for example, the new work was merely inspired by an earlier work and does not appropriate the theme or use the principal characters, then there may not be a copyright issue. The degree of similarity which will result in a work being an infringing derivative of an original copyrighted publication is unclear. However, the closer the production parallels the theme and story line and adopts the principal characters of another work, the more likely it is to be within the scope of the original author's copyright protection.

The second issue to be considered is the credit which should be given when a work is adapted from or based on someone else's original creation. If, for example, a stage play or movie is adapted from a book, then the appropriate credit should be given in the theater program (or on the television or movie credits). This issue is typically covered in the contract or license granted by the copyright owner when the arrangement is made for the adaptation. A credit line such as "adapted from the novel by _____" is a common form of acknowledgement. If the work is not actually adapted from that novel, then claiming that it is might be considered a fraud on the public. A screenwriter might be willing to do this for the purpose of capturing some of the sensationalism surrounding a particularly controversial book. The mere use of ideas from, or inspired by, another work is not necessarily sufficient for the new work to be considered "adapted from" or "based on" the earlier work. The level or degree of appropriation of theme, story line, and principal characters will determine whether the new work was merely inspired by the original work or actually adapted from it.

➤ *See also* Contract, Copyright, Credit

Advance Man, Advance Team

When a show is scheduled to "go on the road" or travel to several locations it is common to have a person or people known as an *advance man* or *advance team* pave the way. Generally, the advance man (or woman) precedes the performance by several weeks or even months, arranges for interviews and press conferences, and works with the local contact in publicizing the performance. The advance person is likely to work closely with the company's advertising agency in an attempt to coordinate the publicity.

➤ *See also* Advertising, Publicity

Advertising

Advertising is used to create public awareness of a product or service for the purpose of stimulating sales. The entertainment business thrives on publicity. "I don't care what you say about me as long as you spell my name right" is one of the mottos of the entertainment business.

Advertising can take many forms: newspapers, magazines, radio, television, billboards, handbills, or direct mail. Within certain limitations, you are in complete control of what you want to say, how you want to say it, and to whom it is said.

Newspaper or magazine ads, and television or radio commercials are commonly purchased, but there are also free forms of advertising such as word-of-mouth, interviews, and reviews. Favorable reviews in major publications from respected critics are probably the best advertisements. In addition to being free, they establish your reputation and create or expand the market for your work. Regrettably, there is no way to control the placement or content of reviews. As an alternative, most entertainers hire publicists who are skilled in attracting media attention. A well-drafted employment contract should provide for appropriate publicity.

It may be an ego trip to advertise on television, but it is not likely to be cost-effective for a small theater company. It is worth the investment, however, when beginning your advertising program, to hire an agency experienced in the entertainment industry.

No matter how much experience you have, you should monitor your advertising. Keep track of each ad, whether it's a display ad of ten inches on two columns, a classified ad, a handbill, postcard, or whatever. It is best, in the beginning, not to run more than one type of ad at a time. Using only one makes it easier to track results. See what results each type of advertisement brings in. Does one magazine produce better results than another? Dollar for dollar, does a mailing piece produce more activity than a magazine? Some entertainers publish periodic newsletters for their fans. Try various types of advertisements, one at a time. This is not to suggest a specific sequence, but only an approach to testing various media. Since advertising is expensive, it pays to keep records of results so that you can concentrate on the more effective methods and eliminate the less effective ones.

Cost should be a factor only as it relates to results. A $100 ad that generates $1,000 worth of ticket sales is more productive than a $50 ad that generates $500 worth of ticket sales, though the ratio is identical. Your overhead and the cost of preparing the ad remain fairly constant, no matter how much or little you sell. In this hypothetical, then, it is more profitable to produce $900 above the cost of the ad than $450. On the other hand, if the $50 ad produces $800 worth of sales, it is probably wasteful to spend another $50 simply to produce another $200. Each situation is specific, and each result must be judged by the advertiser's particular needs and objectives. When noting results, take into consideration special circumstances.

A good way to record the effectiveness of ads and other promotional materials is to organize them into a book and make notes of their results right next to them. Include not only the cost of the ad and what income it produced, but also any outside influences. For example, if ticket sales were down because of inclement weather, this should be noted. Keep records of both positive and negative results so you can repeat your successes and avoid your failures.

Several factors contribute to results: (1) where the ad runs; (2) what the ad looks like (whether it will be read); and (3) the nature of the promotion.

Simplicity and visual appeal are essential. This is particularly true in small-space advertising. That small space has to stand out among all the other ads and other textual material appearing on the same page. Plenty of white space, a catchy headline that grabs the reader's attention, brief but explicit copy, and an uncomplicated illustration all contribute to readability.

The basic principle to observe is that your advertisement has to compete for attention. Everything in the ad should help achieve that goal; nothing should detract from it. Printing a headline upside down, for example, may be clever, but it usually interferes with the readability of the ad. Let's examine some of these factors.

WHITE SPACE

When you buy advertising space, whether it's two inches in a newspaper, an $8\frac{1}{2} \times 11$ inch flyer, or a billboard on the highway, what you are really buying is empty space. You now have to fill it with your message. Don't fill it too full. Keep some *white space* (breathing space) in the ad. Properly used, white space is not wasted because it helps direct the eye toward the relevant material, whether text or an illustration.

THE HEADLINE
Do you need a *headline?* Will it aid in getting your reader's attention?

COPY
Copy is the text of your advertisement. The same principle of reader benefit applies. Keep the copy brief. If you're using a very small space, don't try to tell a story. Strip it down to the bare essentials that will excite the reader's interest. You may not even need text: A picture may, indeed, be worth a thousand words.

ILLUSTRATIONS
Simplicity applies here, as well. Better to use a small, dramatic drawing that reproduces clearly than a cluttered photograph that can barely be deciphered and comes out a gray glob.

Finally, every piece of printed material, every advertisement, must include the relevant name, address, and telephone number.

THE NATURE OF THE OFFER
Advertising falls into two basic categories: *immediate response* or *long-range impact.*

Immediate-response advertising is expected to produce quick results. Included in this category are announcements of show openings and events, mail-order ads, offers of specific products, such as T-shirts and mugs bearing a performer's image, and the like. A mail-order ad is the easiest of all to measure: you simply count the responses. There's no confusion as to the source of the sale.

Immediate-response advertising is also easy to measure. It either brings results at once or it doesn't. A premier performance generally brings large crowds, though it may bring smaller profits since many of the attendees receive complimentary tickets. The size of the crowd at a premier is an extremely important factor in the success of the performance.

Long-range impact is created through advertising which is expected to bring the performer or theater company's name to the attention of the public and keep it there, so that people will remember it. This type of advertising would stress skill, talent, or whatever other attribute makes the theater company or performer distinctive and appealing.

Several other considerations should enter into advertising planning. One concerns repetition: Should you repeat the same ad again and again? That question does not arise, of course, with ads for special events, but advertising experts generally agree that an *institutional ad*—one which promotes a theater or a troupe on a long-range basis—works best when the same ad is repeated several times in the same publication. The cumulative effect often yields better results than running a different ad each time.

Even where ads are different, they should have a "family resemblance." That's best observed in theme park advertising. You could probably identify the ads of several famous theme parks even if the names were removed, simply because the ads have a similar appearance, although the specific content of each ad is different. Stick to the same style of illustrative device, the same typeface for the headline and text, the same signature for your name and address. Familiarity produces recognition.

Everything mentioned so far applies to performing arts businesses with advertising needs and budgets that are very limited. If yours are not, you may wish to retain the services of a larger, more expensive, advertising agency. Agencies come in all sizes and specialties. Their services are concentrated in two important areas: selection of the media in which you advertise, and preparation of your ad copy and illustrations.

Advertising agencies have two primary sources of income: (1) They are paid a commission by the newspapers or magazines in which the advertisements appear, and (2) they are paid fees by the advertiser for such special services as preparing artwork, making engravings for printing purposes, and so forth.

The more complicated an advertising program is, and the larger the budget becomes, the more useful it is to engage the services of advertising specialists. On a very limited budget, a small agency or a friend who works for a large agency may be enough to fill the need. A theater with an annual volume of $100,000 may spend as much as $10,000 on advertising. If you are in that category, take your business to professionals who are as experienced in creating effective advertising programs as you are in presenting first-class performances.

How to find an advertising agency? Pretty much the same way you look for any other professional service—legal, accounting, etc. Ask other business people who advertise extensively. Interview several agencies. Tell them what you hope to accomplish and what your budget estimate is. Ask them to make a proposal explaining their approach to your advertising needs. Find out what they've done for others in similar situations.

The bigger the agency, the more likely it will be to have a variety of talent and expertise to serve you. In choosing an agency, it is sometimes better to be as important to the agency as it is to you. The more important your business is to an agency's annual income, the better the service you are likely to get.

> *See also* Advance Man, Billing, Credits, Direct Mail, Internet, Marketing, Press Release, Producer, Promotion, Publicist, Publicity, Public Relations

Agent

The law defines an *agent* as one who performs services for another and is subject to the other's control. The relationship is consensual, and a fiduciary duty is imposed on both the agent and the person for whom the work is performed.

In the entertainment industry, an agent is responsible for obtaining work for an artist. Agents must be distinguished from managers, who are responsible for career development and business issues. The line of demarcation between agents and managers is blurred and, occasionally, one individual may serve in both capacities. Both California and New York have enacted laws regulating agents which require, among other things, licensure.

Agents typically receive 10–15 percent of the gross earnings of the represented artist. Frequently, the agent is entitled to his or her share of an artist's earnings regardless of whether or not the agent obtained the work. The agreement between the agent and the talent should be in writing and should be drawn up or reviewed by an experienced entertainment lawyer. The contract is usually quite complex and it is essential for both parties to understand its terms.

> *See also* Contract, Deal-Breaker, Director, Extras, Manager, One-Night Stand, Resume, Season

Alternative Dispute Resolution

There are several methods whereby a legal dispute is resolved without having a traditional trial.

Alternative dispute resolution includes *arbitration,* in which one or more independent individuals—known as *arbitrators* or *arbiters*—are selected and paid by the parties to resolve their dispute. Arbitrators need not be lawyers, although most are. Arbitration can either be binding, in which case the parties have agreed to be bound by the arbitrator's decision, or non-binding, in which case the decision of the arbitrator is merely advisory and the parties may resort to traditional litigation even after the arbitration has been conducted. In addition, arbitration may be final, in which case the decision may be appealed only if it can be established that the arbitrator was arbitrary and capricious, or nonfinal, in which case the arbitrator's decision may be appealed on the merits.

The arbitrator acts like a judge, in hearing the parties' positions and rendering a decision. Arbitration, however, is much less formal than litigation and frequently occurs in the arbitrator's or an attorney's office.

The other most common form of alternative dispute resolution is *mediation*. In this situation, an individual known as a *mediator* (not necessarily a lawyer) assists the parties in negotiating a mutually agreeable solution to their dispute, usually a compromise. Some courts require the parties to subject their dispute to mediation, which must be unsuccessful before proceeding with litigation. If the mediation is successful, litigation is unnecessary.

Mediation is usually conducted by having the parties confidentially present their positions to the mediator, who shuttles between them in an attempt to get them to present or accept a workable solution. The mediator is a go-between for the parties, rather than a decision-maker, though the mediator may make recommendations. Henry Kissinger's "shuttle diplomacy"—which resulted in his Nobel Peace Prize—was mediation on a grand scale.

There are numerous organizations which specialize in alternative dispute resolution. Probably the most well-known is the American Arbitration Association, which has offices in most large cities. Most larger communities also have public and private alternative dispute organizations. In fact, at least one Volunteer Lawyers for the Arts group, California Lawyers for the Arts, offers mediation services for arts-related disputes.

> ➤ *See also* Contract, Small Claims Court, Appendix A

Americans With Disabilities Act

The *Americans With Disabilities Act* is a federal law which requires employers to make reasonable accommodation for disabled employees in hiring, promotion, and retention. The term *reasonable accommodation* is not precisely defined, but would include, for example, access ramps, adjustable-height work areas, restrooms for wheelchairs, and Braille or vocal elevator operation instructions.

The law also requires places of public accommodation, such as theaters, museums, and even dance studios, if they are open to the public, to be reasonably accessible to the disabled. This would, for example, require wheelchair ramps, handicapped-accessible restrooms, and the like. The law is very complex and the regulations which have been promulgated are extremely technical. There are, however, severe fines for noncompliance, so a manager or producer of a theater company or other performing arts organization should consult with a lawyer knowledgeable in this area in order to determine his or her obligations.

Amortization

Amortization is an accounting concept whereby a cost is spread over the period of the supposed "useful life" of the item being amortized. It is used for purposes of calculating tax deductions, such as when a capital asset like a theater company's van is purchased. The company may deduct—or amortize—a portion of the cost of the van over its projected useful life. Amortization is also used for purposes of calculating payments on, for example, a mortgage. The mortgage is amortized—or reduced—by the regular periodic payments for its term. Capital investments, such as equipment with a useful life of more than one year, are amortized through *depreciation,* which means they are carried on the books at a predictable annual reduction in value on the assumption that they will wear out at the end of the amortization period. In simplest terms, a $5,000 lighting system with a life expectancy of ten years would be amortized at $500 a year. This is important both for tax purposes and for establishing the current value of your fixed assets at any given time. A good accountant or business adviser can assist you in determining the most appropriate time to buy an asset and the best method for depreciating it.

➤ *See also* Appreciation, Depreciation, Loans, Tax

Anticompetitive Practices

Any contract, practice, or arrangement which has the effect of inhibiting competition and adversely affecting commerce is unlawful and violative of the antitrust laws. The arrangement can be as obvious as having competitors agree to fix market prices, or as subtle as when one business engages in calculated predatory activities in order to drive competitors out of a market. Thus, if a theater chain with a significant control of the marketplace intentionally reduces ticket prices in order to undercut weaker competitors and force them out of business, this *anticompetitive practice* would likely be considered unlawful in violating the antitrust laws.

Many of the arrangements which had been common in the entertainment industry, such as block-booking, shotgun sales, and tie-in arrangements have been declared unlawful anticompetitive activities, and are now prohibited by the antitrust laws. Care should be taken to have experienced business lawyers review contracts for possible antitrust problems in order to avoid the very serious consequences that may result from antitrust violations.

➤ *See also* Antitrust Law, Blind Bidding, Block-Booking

Antitrust Law

Antitrust refers to a complex body of law which prohibits any anticompetitive activities, including, for example, price-fixing and certain combinations which affect free enterprise. This specialized area of law has been held to inhibit such things as *block-booking,* whereby prospective licensees of programs or features are required to acquire other programs or features from an identified party within a prescribed period. The arrangement was held in *United States v. Paramount Pictures, Inc.* to be a violation of the Sherman Act by restraining free trade and inhibiting commerce, as well as the Clayton Act by contractually establishing an unlawful monopoly.

Shotgun sales or *tie-in arrangements,* which are essentially the mirror image of block-booking, have also been declared unlawful and a violation of the antitrust laws. Shotgun sales occur when a purchaser has greater economic clout than the seller and uses this power to compel the weaker seller to convey more rights or properties than originally proposed. If the arrangement is such as to place the stronger purchaser in a position to dominate the market, or if the arrangement establishes an anticompetitive atmosphere, an antitrust violation occurs.

> ➤ *See also* Anticompetitive Practices, Blind Bidding, Block-Booking, Contract

Appreciation

Appreciation has at least two meanings in the entertainment world. The first is the favorable response to one's work which may lead to recognition and success. Second, in financial terms, *appreciation* refers to an increase in value. A movie may appreciate because of the star's enhanced reputation, death, or popularity of the theme. For example, the renewed interest in the Vietnam War, or the birth of rock-n-roll has resulted in a plethora of material based on these themes.

Many individuals involved in the entertainment industry insist upon receiving a royalty for the exploitation of their contributions to the entertainment project. Since the royalty is based on a percentage of earnings, the individual's actual payment from the venture will be greater when the project is successful and lower when earnings are small. Similarly, a work which has lost favor and is rediscovered will once again produce earnings for individuals who are entitled to receive royalties from exploitation. It is essential to determine the base upon which royalties are to be paid since "creative accounting" may result in a royalty fee based on an illusory number. For example, if an entertainer is to receive 1 percent of a movie's "net profits" and the amounts deductible from gross receipts are not precisely defined when calculating net profits, the ultimate royalty may be nonexistent. In the Art Buchwald/Eddie Murphy case involving the movie *Coming to America,* the court pointed out some of the questionable practices of the industry. The deductions from gross receipts, in that case, included lavish meals, vacations, fees for several future ventures, and the like. The safest course is to base any royalty payment on "gross receipts from whatever source and in whatever form." This would avoid the industry practice of obtaining "in-kind" payments such as goods or services, which may not be reflected in the calculation of net profits.

➤ *See also* Accounting, Amortization, Depreciation

Apprentice

For most of human history, before there was a system of formal education, *apprenticeship* was the only way to learn a craft or trade. Boys from ages ten to fourteen would be indentured to a journeyman, earning no more than subsistence-level room and board, doing all the unpleasant, dirty jobs around the shop at first, and learning the craftsman's trade bit by bit. Apprenticeship is still the official term used for learners in some trades, for example, printing and skilled construction work. However, many apprentices are now paid salaries and other benefits that increase according to specific formulas as they learn their trade.

Traditionally, individuals who want to become technicians in the entertainment industry have apprenticed themselves to specialists in their fields of interest. This is common practice among lighting specialists, set designers, sound technicians, and the myriad of other technical support personnel who are involved in the backstage aspects of a production. While the basic techniques and principles can be learned in the classroom, most aspiring technicians find that their technical and artistic development depends to a great extent on working with an experienced specialist. This helps them not only to refine their skills but also to understand the production methods, operational procedures, and business problems of earning a living in the entertainment business.

The old method of room and board in exchange for learning the craft is no longer common, although it does still exist. In almost all cases, money changes hands: sometimes the technician pays the apprentice a small sum, occasionally the apprentice pays the technician for the privilege of studying with him or her, and sometimes an outside source provides the funds.

A major problem encountered by some theater companies in hiring apprentices involves state and federal labor laws. Some theater companies have been required to pay their apprentices the minimum wage, withhold income taxes, and meet a variety of other requirements demanded by the labor laws. In other cases, especially where the apprentice pays a fee to the company, the apprentice may be considered a "student" and, thus, not subject to the labor laws, even though no formal curriculum exists. Still other theater companies have proposed the term *intern* for someone whose work is both productive and a learning experience, to get away from the employee connotation of *apprentice*. It is advisable to consult with state and federal labor departments about the specific conditions that would apply in each case.

The relationship between the theater company and the apprentice is a very special one. Careful thought should be given to (1) whether the craftsperson and the apprentice are personally compatible; (2) whether the craftsperson or technician is emotionally and psychologically equipped to teach his or her technique with patience and understanding; and (3) what the specific arrangements and working conditions will be.

The theater company/apprentice relationship is not a one-way street. The apprentice benefits from the learning experience; the company benefits from the apprentice's contribution to the production process. These benefits are available only if the parties select each other carefully and understand their arrangements completely before they begin.

➤ *See also* Education, Employees, Wages

Arbitration

➤ *See* Alternative Dispute Resolution

Arts Councils

There is an *arts commission* or *arts council* in every state of the Union, as well as the District of Columbia and all U.S. possessions. Many municipalities have arts councils, as well. Canada has Provincial Arts Councils in each of its provinces. Arts commissions are government agencies which receive monies from both the federal and state governments for the purpose of stimulating and supporting art in their respective jurisdictions. Arts councils may or may not be government agencies, though they customarily have the same objectives. A complete list of all state arts agencies, with addresses and telephone numbers, is available from the National Endowment for the Arts. These organizations should conduct their activities in a business-like way and counsel cultural organizations they deal with to do the same. For an excellent source of up-to-date information on important business issues for cultural organizations see the *Cultural Business Times* (Appendix B).

➤ *See also* Humanities Councils or Committees, National Endowment for the Arts, National Endowment for the Humanities

Assets

➤ *See* Financial Statement

Assignability, Assignment

Assignability is a term used in contracts to describe the ability of either contracting party to assign certain rights or obligations under the contract. Generally, performance of personal services contracts, such as the activities of a performer, is not assignable. On the other hand, the right to receive payment for those services may be. Since there can be some ambiguities in whether a right or performance is assignable, it is best to specify in the contract whether or not an assignment is permissible. In fact, lawyers consider the clause regarding assignment standard.

➤ *See also* Contract, Copyright, License

Associate Producer

➤ *See* Producer

Audit

An *audit* is an examination of a business's books, records, or other documents to determine whether they are kept properly, whether all financial transactions are entered according to accepted accounting and bookkeeping practices, whether there is legal compliance, and to ensure that the company's records comply with the applicable rules and regulations. In addition, there are operations audits which examine and evaluate the business's operations and procedures.

The type of audit with which most individuals are familiar is a financial audit. For small businesses or nonprofit organizations, an annual financial audit is usually conducted by an accountant in conjunction with the preparation of the business's tax return. A financial statement or balance sheet is drawn up following a financial audit. Corporate law usually requires corporations to periodically distribute these reports to the shareholders and most state nonprofit corporation statutes require the organization to provide copies to regulatory agencies such as the Attorney General's Office.

Operations audits are commonly conducted by experienced accountants or business advisors who evaluate the propriety of a business's practices and procedures. This is also true of the activities of nonprofit organizations.

Attorneys may also conduct a legal audit in order to determine whether the organization is complying with all applicable laws. This type of audit is less common but nonetheless important for small businesses or nonprofits which desire to avoid becoming entangled in costly litigation for noncompliance. For example, business corporations are required to hold annual meetings of the shareholders for the purpose, among other things, of electing the board of directors. Similarly, nonprofit corporations should have membership meetings for the purpose of conducting elections and performing other periodically required activities. In addition, most corporations are required to file annual reports with the state or they will be dissolved.

Audits may also be conducted by government agencies, such as the Internal Revenue Service, the Department of Labor, or the Occupational Safety and Health Administration.

➤ *See also* Accounting, Financial Statement, Recordkeeping, Statute of Limitations, Tax, Tax Preparer

Audition

When a performing artist desires a part or a position in a company, he or she must often *audition* for it. Companies which have regularly scheduled events such as Shakespearean or other festivals, publish an audition calendar which notifies the industry of the date, time, and location for regularly scheduled auditions. Companies which are beginning a new production will typically notify trade and other publications about their auditions and, in some instances, contact agents in order to target specific entertainers.

An audition can be open, like that depicted in the musical *A Chorus Line*, or more formal, involving specific appointments between the talent and the casting crew. An audition may be live or on videotape. Auditions are typically conducted by producers, directors, and/or any of the other individuals involved on the production side of a presentation. It may also involve the financial backers. Typically, the director is responsible for selecting a person for a role, though, depending upon the caliber of the production, the producer may also be involved.

➤ *See also* Casting Director, Director, Producer

Balance

For financial purposes, the word *balance* represents the difference between two amounts, or what remains after one amount is deducted from the other. In the entertainment business, it has several fundamental meanings:

1. Your checking account balance represents the amount that remains after all the checks and other deductions are subtracted from all the deposits and prior balance. If you had a balance of $250, deposited $1,000, wrote checks for $800, and were charged a $10 service charge, your new balance would be $440.

2. The balance on your account with a printer is the amount you still owe after all your payments are subtracted from your orders and all credits are taken into account. If you have overpaid, then all your orders are subtracted from all your payments, and you have a credit balance.

3. If a costume shop leaves a $100 deposit for the purchase of your company's used costumes worth $1,000, the balance owed you is $900.

➤ *See also* Bank Statement, Checking Account, Financial Statement

Balance Sheet

➤ *See* Financial Statement

Bank Loans

➤ *See* Loans

Bank Statement

Periodically, usually monthly, you should receive a *statement* from your bank which lists all the deposits that were made to the account, all the withdrawals made from your account, any bank charges, plus the opening and closing balances. You should reconcile the bank statement; that is, compare it against your own records. The bank usually provides an easy-to-use form on the back of the statement to help you do this. If you cannot reconcile your balance with the bank balance, review all the entries and totals very carefully. The error might not be yours. If it still doesn't balance, contact the customer service department of your bank. Most banks offer free assistance with account reconciliation.

The bank statement has another important value: It signals a problem if a check you wrote long ago hasn't cleared. If a check has been outstanding for more than two bank cycles, you should find out why. For example, it may have been lost in the mail, the payee may have neglected to negotiate it, or you may have forgotten to mail it. The consequences of any of these situations can be catastrophic; for example, if your theater company's lease provides that if rent is not received by the tenth of the month, the lease may be cancelled and/or the tenant must pay a late charge. Similarly, your credit with a music publisher could be jeopardized if you accidentally forgot to mail a required royalty check or it was lost in the mail.

Keep your bank statements and the cancelled checks, if any, together in a safe place. You may need this information to establish that a payment was made by you or in the event that your performing arts business is ever audited.

➤ *See also* Balance, Banks, Cancelled Check, Checking Account, Computers, Outstanding Check, Statement

Bankruptcy

When your liabilities exceed your assets and there's no other way to settle your debts, you may wish to seek protection from your creditors by filing for protection under the United States Bankruptcy Code. *Bankruptcy* is a federal procedure conducted in a specialized federal court known as *bankruptcy court* whereby the court, often through a trustee, administers your assets to pay your creditors. This usually involves selling your assets, in which case the creditors may receive only part of what is owed to them, but you are free from all further dischargeable obligations. Your debts are erased and you can start all over again.

There are some situations in which a business debtor is allowed to reorganize his or her business affairs under the court's watchful eye. This happens when creditors have reason to believe that there is a real chance that the financial difficulty can be resolved under the conditions imposed by the court. They approve a plan of reorganization in the hope that they'll collect more of the debt, even though they may have to wait longer to do it.

Bankruptcy can be either voluntary (when you petition the court to declare you bankrupt), or involuntary (when your creditors petition the court to declare you bankrupt). There are some debts which cannot be discharged in bankruptcy, for example, taxes, certain student loans, and obligations incurred for intentional wrongful acts. In some forms of personal bankruptcy, *i.e.*, a so-called Chapter 13 bankruptcy, however, some taxes and intentional wrongful acts may be dischargeable.

There had been some question about whether a theater company organized as a nonprofit corporation could take advantage of the bankruptcy laws since the bankruptcy statutes did not address the issue. In *Matter of Roundabout Theatre Co.*, Bankruptcy Judge Roy Babitt made it clear that nonprofit cultural organizations are eligible to seek protection under the Bankruptcy Code. Entertainers who are not careful about satisfying creditors may also find themselves in bankruptcy court trying to obtain a new financial start.

➤ *See also* Collection Problems

Banks

A *bank* is, essentially, a money store. Money is the product it buys, sells, and rents. The interest rate a bank charges on a loan is the price the borrower pays for the use of the bank's product. Like renting a car, sooner or later you have to bring it back and, meanwhile, you're paying rent for the use of it.

Conversely, the bank has to rent its product (money) somewhere. The depositor is the supplier, who is paid for the use of its money, just as a patron pays for theater tickets. Like all successful enterprises, banks try to buy at the lowest price and sell at the highest. That is how profits are made, and that is why it always costs more to borrow money from a bank than a depositor is paid for depositing money in that bank.

There are essentially three types of banks: *commercial banks, savings banks* and *savings and loan institutions,* and *credit unions.* Commercial banks deal primarily in business and commercial money transactions, such as checking accounts, credit cards, automobile loans, international money transactions, and the like. Savings banks and savings and loan institutions deal primarily in a variety of savings accounts and long-term loans, such as home mortgages. Credit unions are very much like savings banks but provide services only for their members, who typically must be part of an identified group, such as teachers, government workers, and the like. A number of banking services, such as safe deposit boxes, traveler's checks, Christmas and vacation clubs, education and home-improvement loans, may be offered by all types of banks.

Since banks are regulated by both state and federal agencies, the specific services which may be offered vary from state to state. In some states, for example, commercial banks may offer savings accounts and savings banks may offer checking accounts. Credit unions typically offer both savings and checking accounts, as well as consumer and other loans.

Even within the same city, however, different banks often charge widely differing fees for the same services. One government study found, for example, that home mortgage interest rates in New York were as much as .75 percent apart in different institutions. This may not seem like much of a difference, but look at the end result: a twenty-year, $50,000 mortgage costs $5,324.49 more in interest at 7 percent than at 6.75 percent. Interest rates for home-improvement loans showed an even wider spread in the study—as much as 4.5 percent.

Performing artists or entertainment businesses which write numerous checks will find that it pays to shop around. Some banks charge a fixed monthly fee plus fifteen to thirty cents per check. Others charge nothing for checks if a certain minimum amount is kept on deposit. Still others base their charges on an average monthly balance, and some banks even charge for the deposits that are made. Money market accounts permit check-writing features while paying competitive interest rates on the amount in the account.

Minimum-balance accounts are sometimes advertised as "free." While you do not pay directly for checking services, you do pay for them indirectly if you must maintain a minimum balance larger than the amount you would ordinarily keep in the checking account. If those excess funds were in a savings account they would earn interest. Even if the checking account pays interest you may be able to earn more by putting the money in a certificate of deposit (CD) or money market account.

Even the cost of maintaining a checking account varies, depending upon the services provided within the bank and from bank to bank. For example, some banks charge for providing checks while others do not. Checks may also be purchased from outside sources such as bank printing companies or other printers. The same principle applies to the extra services. Banks charge anywhere from $15 to $25 if a check bounces. One bank may charge $4 for a stop-payment order, another only 50¢. One bank will charge $2.50 to certify a check, another only 25¢.

As a savings account depositor, it is important to understand where the best returns are. Savings banks pay a wide variety of interest. The lowest rate is on accounts from which you can withdraw your money virtually at will. Certificates of deposit, which last from six months to seven years, pay different rates: customarily, the longer the term, the higher the rate. Generally, however, these cannot be converted into cash before their maturity without a penalty being assessed, except in cases of extreme emergency. Even the same interest rate may provide different returns in actual dollars, depending on what basis the interest is calculated. The "low average monthly balance" method is less favorable to the depositor than the "day of deposit to day of withdrawal" method.

Like every trade or profession, banking has its own language. Don't be afraid to ask questions, and don't hesitate to ask your banker or customer service representative to explain what a particular transaction means in actual dollars and cents.

> ➤ *See also* Bank Statement, Cancelled Check, Cashier's Check, Certified Check, Checking Account, Cleared Check, Commercial Bank, Credit Union, Deposit, Endorsement, Financial Management, Interest, Letter of Credit, Loans, Money Order, Mortgage, Savings Bank, Traveler's Checks

Based on
> ➤ *See* Adapted from

Benefit
> ➤ *See* Nonprofit Organization

Bequest
> ➤ *See* Estate Planning

Berne Copyright Convention
In 1988, the United States became a party to the *Berne Copyright Convention* and, as a result, United States copyrights may be enforced in the eighty-eight member countries.

In order to become a party to Berne, it was necessary for the United States to relax some of the formalities traditionally required for U.S. copyright protection. As a result, copyright protection now attaches whenever an original work of authorship is put in a tangible form. Notating a song, videotaping the choreography of an original dance, or filming a performance would result in protection for the tangible embodiment of the work. It is no longer necessary to use the copyright notice on the protected work, though it is still a good idea to do so. The statute provides that one who relies in good faith on the omission of notice and copies is an *innocent infringer.* Only nominal damages, if any, may be assessed against innocent infringers and they may even be permitted to continue copying after learning of the copyright owner's rights.

The U.S. legislation also permits copyright owners from other countries who are parties to the treaty to litigate their copyrights in U.S. courts without registering those copyrights in the United States. Registration is still required for U.S. copyright owners suing in U.S. courts, and there is a presumption that a copyright registered within five years of the date of publication is valid. Infringements which occur after a work is registered may give rise to statutory damages, and the infringer may have to pay the copyright owner's reasonable attorney fees. Registration is quite simple.

➤ *See also* Buenos Aires Convention, Copyright, *Droit Morale*, Universal Copyright Convention

Better Business Bureau

The *Better Business Bureau* (BBB) is a nonprofit association of businesses set up to aid both business and the consumer. It is a form of self-regulation which utilizes the power of public opinion to encourage legal and ethical business practices. Over 150 local BBBs throughout the country provide background information on local businesses. Such information is free and available to anyone. Although many consumers contact the BBB only when problems arise, the BBB can be helpful to artists and entertainment organizations before they make a purchase or sign a contract.

If a person is considering a significant purchase, such as a computer, and desires business information about the manufacturer or seller, the individual may contact the BBB in the area where the manufacturer or seller is located. The Bureau may be able to provide such information as how long the company has been in business, its record for reliability, how it deals with complaints, and other relevant information which can help the consumer make a more informed decision.

The BBB usually handles only written complaints. While a BBB has no enforcement power, it often succeeds by exerting peer pressure on the offending merchant if an investigation proves the consumer's complaint to be valid. While that may not always succeed, the Bureau will at least have the complaint on file; responses to future inquiries about that merchant will contain reference to the complaint and may discourage others from dealing with that merchant.

Most BBBs also perform a great deal of work in the area of consumer education to help people make wise buying decisions. There are several things, however, that a BBB will *not* do:

1. Handle matters that require a lawyer, such as contract violations;
2. Make collections;
3. Give recommendations or endorsements;
4. Furnish lists of companies or individuals in a particular line of business;
5. Pass judgment. The Bureau may indicate that a particular ticket outlet has had complaints about its refund policy, for example, but will not say that the outlet is disreputable.

While the vast majority of major cities and most states have a BBB, not all do. Where no BBB exists, the local chamber of commerce can often be helpful in solving problems that arise between buyers and merchants in its area. Other organizations which provide relevant information include the Consumer Protection Division of the State Attorney General's Office, licensing bureaus such as those granting real estate and insurance licenses and municipal business licenses, and associations like the BBB which confine their information to certain kinds of businesses, such as automobile dealers.

BBBs are supported by local business people who pay annual dues, which vary from one BBB to another. Theater companies which advertise extensively may find membership in a BBB helpful. Mentioning such a membership in an advertisement or program may help to establish the advertiser's reputation for integrity.

➤ *See also* Chamber of Commerce

Billing Credits

Virtually everyone involved in the entertainment industry wants to receive recognition for their contribution. The playwright, producer, director, entertainer, designers, and every other participant, through and including technical personnel such as musicians, engineers, lighting specialists, and the like, all attempt to negotiate acknowledgement in window cards, house boards, programs, playbills, advertisements, and related materials.

Each class of individuals attempts to negotiate for the placement of their name in the credits or on a marquee. There is a technical distinction between *billing* and *credit,* though the words are often used together. *Credit* is used to identify or associate the person or organization with the creative work involved, and to identify the nature of the contribution. *Billing* defines the prominence of the credit and its promotional value. Billing could involve the size, location, typeface, and prominence of the credit involved, for example, in the case of a Broadway play or musical, whether the star's name appears over or under the title of the work.

There are certain conventions which are generally followed unless there is a modification in the artist's contract. Names are customarily listed alphabetically within each of these categories: producers, associate producers, directors, associate directors, and the host of other support personnel who work on a professional production. Entertainers will usually be listed alphabetically or in order of appearance, though in some special arrangements the most prominent performer may be listed before the other company members.

➤ *See also* Advertising

Blind Bidding

Blind Bidding is an arrangement in which a retailer such as a theater is required to bid on and acquire a show before having a fair opportunity to preview it. In fact, the contract may be implemented before the project is completed. Refusing to engage in this activity could leave the theater without a production for a particular period and significantly interfere with its business.

The United States Supreme Court, in *United States v. Paramount Pictures, Inc.*, imposed restrictions on blind bidding, then known as *blind selling.* These restrictions were later removed and the practice was resumed. By 1984, however, twenty-four states and Puerto Rico had enacted legislation prohibiting this practice. Thus far, challenges to these state restrictions have been unsuccessful. In order to determine whether a blind bidding arrangement is legal in your jurisdiction, and whether a contract you or your entertainment organization is involved with contains a blind bidding type arrangement you should consult with an experienced entertainment lawyer.

➤ *See also* Anticompetitive Practices, Antitrust Law, Contract

Block-Booking

Block-booking was defined in *United States v. Paramount Pictures, Inc.* as "the practice of licensing, or offering for license, one feature or group of features on condition that the exhibitor will also license another feature or group of features released by the distributors during a given period." Although this practice has been declared unlawful in the film industry, since it violates the antitrust laws of the United States, *block-booking* has a somewhat different meaning in the presentation of live performing arts. In this context, the practice appears to be legal.

In the context of live performing arts, the term refers to the practice in which a group of presenting organizations, usually located in the same geographic region, agree to book a certain performer or group for a series of dates within a short time frame. In such cases, the performer or group is guaranteed a certain amount of work and can usually realize substantial savings in travel expenses. In exchange, the group of presenters will seek to negotiate a block-booking fee, or discounted rate that is below the usual booking fee.

Before attempting any arrangement which resembles this type of situation, it is essential to confer with an experienced entertainment lawyer to determine whether the proposed activities are within the realm of "anticompetitive activities" and unlawful, or whether the arrangement is legally permissible.

➤ *See also* Anticompetitive Practices, Antitrust Law, Booking, Contract

Bookkeeping

➤ *See* Accounting

Booking

Booking is a contract for the purpose of hiring an entertainer or arranging for a performance. Individuals who are responsible primarily for establishing these arrangements are known as *booking agents.* These individuals customarily are compensated for their work by receiving a percentage of the contract price, though the individual could be a salaried employee. It has become common for talent, agents, and theater representatives to participate in a scheduled event known as a *booking conference,* which provides an opportunity for agents to present their talent and products to the entertainment community for purposes of booking arrangements and promotion. These conferences are held regionally, nationally, and internationally. Some are segregated by artistic discipline, while others are multifaceted.

➤ *See also* Agent, Block-Booking, Contract, Promotion

Booking Agent

➤ *See* Agent, Booking

Booking Conference

➤ *See* Booking

Box Office

The term *box office* has at least two meanings in the entertainment industry. It can mean the location where tickets are actually sold or reserved. It may also mean the revenue generated by a production. Terms such as *box office draw* refer to the commercial appeal of entertainers, directors, and other key personnel involved in a particular production.

➤ *See also* Director, Producer, Robinson-Patman Act, Ticket

Break-Even Point

The point at which income and expenses match is called the *break-even point*. The business is neither making money nor losing money. The break-even point can be an important tool in proper ticket pricing, merchandising, and cost control. The break-even point is based on the assumption that a theater company will sell all of its tickets or merchandise, or that a program will obtain a high percentage of financial support.

Finding the break-even point is not complicated. Two things must be known: the price at which you plan to sell tickets or merchandise, and the cost of the production, as well as any related expenses.

For simplicity, we will consider a performance running for one month, presented on Friday, Saturday, and Sunday nights, as well as two weekend matinees, totaling twenty performances. You have two cost factors to consider: the *fixed* cost (rent, overhead, etc.), which remains pretty much the same whether you have one performance or one hundred; and the *variable* costs (the cost of talent, performance-related support staff such as ticket-takers, ushers and the like), which change in direct proportion to the number of performances.

In this example we'll set the fixed costs at $10,000 and the variable costs at $3,000 per performance. Each performance now adds $3,000 to the costs of the production. Without drawing any charts or graphs, it is apparent that you have to sell more than $10,000 worth of tickets just to cover the fixed costs. As an alternative you may be able to obtain sponsors who would pay for the right to have their name associated with a production in order to reduce the amount you would have to charge for the tickets.

Merely raising $10,000, however, does not mean that the production is profitable. Indeed, it hasn't even reached the break-even point for a single performance. In order to have this production make money, it will be necessary to raise a minimum of $70,000, *i.e.*, $10,000 of fixed costs and $3,000 per performance for twenty performances.

If, however, the production would lend itself to merchandising opportunities, such as licensing the use of the show's name, logo or other features, for use on T-shirts, mugs, key chains, sweatshirts, cast albums, souvenir programs, and the like, you may be able to augment earnings and accelerate the point at which profit will be generated. While merchandising is more common in movies, and for Broadway and touring shows, it is gaining increased acceptance in regional and local theater.

If you find that you can realistically exceed the break-even point, then your business will likely be profitable. You should, however, determine whether the return on your investment of money, time and energy is reasonable. If you can earn more by putting your money in the bank, for example, why invest in a production?

If, on the other hand, you determine that your company's ticket sales and sponsorship are such that it cannot even reach the break-even point, there are still several options: (1) remain in business, continuing to lose money, with the expectation that the production company will ultimately become profitable; (2) increase the price for tickets, though you should recognize the so-called elasticity of demand, which theorizes that, as the price increases, the demand decreases; (3) reduce the cost of producing the show, if possible; (4) be more aggressive in obtaining sponsors; (5) go out of business; (6) evaluate the marketability of your company's productions and determine whether you would be willing to produce shows which have greater market appeal, perhaps a smattering of rock musicals to augment your company's traditional Greek tragedies.

Be careful of points 2 and 4. If you cannot sell tickets at the increased price, or if you cannot obtain sponsors, you are left with only two options: (1) cut costs; or (2) go out of business.

➤ *See also* Accounting, Financial Statement

Bridge Financing, Bridge Loan

As the term implies, this financial arrangement is intended to "bridge" the gap between one form of financing and another, and is almost always of short duration. A *bridge loan* may be used, for example, to commence production while a company is engaged in obtaining permanent funding from investors or conventional lenders. Bridge loans customarily command higher interest rates than long-term financing. This is because *bridge financing* has a compound risk: *i.e.*, not only must the lender have confidence in the ultimate success of the project, but the lender must also be convinced that the take-out financing will materialize as scheduled.

➤ *See also* Business Plan, Loans

Broadway

Literally, a broad road that runs the length of Manhattan Island. Geographically, New York's theater district. Commercially (and sometimes culturally) the pinnacle for live theatrical performance.

Most of today's Broadway theaters were built in the 1920s; "Broadway" now runs from Forty-fourth to Fifty-third Streets within the single block between Broadway and Eighth Avenue, with a very few exceptions—one to the south, one to the west, and three to the east. One odd fact: the many theaters that faced directly onto Broadway some eighty years ago, have almost all vanished, leaving only the Broadway, the Winter Garden, the Palace, and the Ed Sullivan Theatre (formerly Hammerstein's Theater, still standing, but given over to television since the 1930s), plus the relatively new Minskoff and Marquis, to maintain entrances directly along the fabled way.

➤ *See also* Off-Broadway, Regional Theatre

Budget

A *budget* is a plan which outlines expected income and expenditures during a given period. It helps to anticipate needs and decide how to meet them. A wide variety of budgets exist in the business world, but two are of interest to a small enterprise such as an entertainment business.

The *capital budget* is concerned with the purchase of equipment and major outlays that are not immediately used up in a production season, such as sound and lighting systems, theater seats, curtains, a grand piano, or the like. Preparing such a plan for the coming year, for example, indicates not only what you expect to buy and when, but also how you expect to pay for it, whether through loans, savings, out of income, or by taking on an investor or sponsor.

Much more important to the success of a small business is the *cash budget*. This should indicate, on a monthly basis for at least twelve months, what you expect to take in as a result of ticket sales, sponsorship, and the like, and what you expect to pay out in order to operate. The number of entries can be as brief or as elaborate as you or your accountant feel you may need in order to forecast properly and evaluate the accuracy of your budgeting.

Under "Income," for example, it might be sufficient to have four entries: *Discounted Sales, Full Priced Sales, Sponsorship, Merchandising,* and *Other.* If you also operate a concession stand, *Concession Sales* would be another category. Under "Expenses," you may also need only a few entries: *Rent & Utilities, Sales Expenses, Rights Payments, Payroll, Taxes,* and *Miscellaneous.* Note that entries to a "miscellaneous" category should be kept to a minimum; it is better accounting to add new categories.

At the beginning, if you are not using computer software, it is useful to create two columns next to each line. In the first column, you enter the budget figure—how much you estimate the income or expense for that item will total. Leave the second column blank. When you have the actual figures, enter them in the second column. You will see at a glance where your budget has been accurate, where it needs amending for the future, and where the weak spots are. That will help to make your next budget more realistic. The use of computers for accounting, bookkeeping, and budgeting is quite common, and spreadsheet software such as Lotus 1-2-3 or Microsoft Excel is very useful for this purpose.

By pinpointing the periods of high expense versus low income which happen in almost every business, the cash budget can also help to reduce the need for borrowing money, or predict more accurately how much needs to be borrowed, obtained from sponsors, or how much should be held in reserve. Budgeting, in other words, is not simply a bookkeeping exercise. It is an indispensable tool in avoiding costly mistakes and correcting errors of judgment.

➤ *See also* Accountant, Accounting, Business Plan, Computers, Deficit, Financial Management, Financial Statement, Investment, Season

Buenos Aires Convention

The *Buenos Aires Convention* is a multilateral copyright treaty which is in effect only in the Western hemisphere and has seventeen signatories, including the United States. It is, therefore, not a global treaty such as the Berne Copyright Convention or Universal Copyright Convention.

In order to obtain international protection under the Buenos Aires Convention, a copyright owner must comply with the copyright laws of his or her own country and use the legend "All rights reserved" as a part of the copyright notice. The legend must be in Spanish, English, or Portuguese, whichever is the official language of the copyright owner's country.

➤ *See also* Berne Copyright Convention, Copyright, Universal Copyright Convention

Bus and Truck Rights

Frequently included as part of first-class live theatrical rights, *bus and truck rights* refer to the right to produce a live theatrical projects as a *bus and truck tour.*

➤ *See also* Bus and Truck Tour, First-Class Live Theatrical Production

Bus and Truck Tour

A tour of a live theatrical production in which pooled transportation, such as buses and trucks, is used for a series of consecutive engagements, is known as a *bus and truck tour.* Most bus and truck tours are shorter than one week in duration.

Business Expenses

➤ *See* Accounting, Financial Statement, Wages

Business Forms

Business forms are necessary for any business, including the entertainment and peforming arts businesses. They range from simple business letters to complex contracts, government reports, and sales documents. Businesses which have a need for large quantities of the same form contract will usually have them professionally printed. Some business publishers have commonly used forms, such as leases, security agreements, and the like available for a nominal cost. There are many useful form books available, including some which are written specifically for the entertainment industry (*See* Appendix B).

With the advent of personal computers and desktop publishing, it is becoming more common for business people to input commonly used documents and merely fill in the blanks on the computer-generated form. This may include letterhead and envelopes, production contracts, employment contracts, ticket or subscription order forms, and the like.

➤ *See also* Appendix B

Business Interruption Insurance

➤ *See* Insurance

Business Name

➤ *See* Professional Name, Trade Name

Business Plan

A *business plan* is a document which includes, among other things, a description of your business, its objectives and the methods by which you intend to achieve them, a profile of key personnel, an analysis of the market, necessary resources, and an earnings forecast.

It is extremely useful, when beginning a business, to prepare a written business plan so that you will have a road map to your ultimate business goals. Business plans are often necessary when applying for loans, attempting to obtain venture capital, or when working with an attorney in structuring your business organization. A business plan need not be a technical, complex document, but it should be as comprehensive and professional as possible. It is common for start-up businesses to work with professionals who have experience in preparing formal business plans, but this is not a necessity and many successful businesses began by having their principals create their own documents.

It may be advisable to block out a period of time, such as a weekend, and to isolate yourself and your team from outside distractions while brainstorming the issues and writing the plan. The time invested in this process is worthwhile if well spent by focusing on the issues and the goals. It may be that the development team will identify the impossibility of some aspirations and even this is an important use of your time, since you will then be in a position to redirect your energies toward objectives which can be realized.

Many nonprofit organizations, such as performing arts companies, begin their existence by preparing a "mission statement" which serves as the foundation for a business plan when it is determined to seek grants, bank financing, or the like. Individuals such as entertainers who have identified their professional goals may write a "plan of action," which is similar to a business plan. There are many books and articles about business plans and how to write them. There are consulting firms which can assist with the process. Consult your telephone directory. In addition, your attorney or accountant may be able to assist you or recommend other resources.

➤ *See also* Accounting, Bridge Financing, Budget, Financial Statement, Loans, Appendix B

Business Tax

Every business must file a federal income tax return. In addition, states, counties, cities, and other governmental entities may also impose other forms of taxation, such as income tax, inventory tax, and transfer taxes of all kinds.

➤ *See also* Income Tax—Business, Tax, Unrelated Business Income

Business Trips

When your performing arts company is on the road and you go to a distant location for a performance or engage in field research for a production, it's a *business trip* and, therefore, tax-deductible. The determining factor isn't how much you earned for the production or how successful the trip was, but only that it was for business reasons.

If the trip is primarily for business, all reasonable and necessary business-related expenses, including transportation, lodging, and 50 percent of the cost of meals, are deductible. If the trip is primarily for pleasure or personal reasons, then only the business-related expenses may be deducted.

Extending a business trip for pleasure or making a non-business side trip does not qualify for business deductions. There are many combinations, of course. If you fly to Hawaii for a production and then spend another week to work on your tan, your travel expenses are covered, as well as the allowable expenses during the business portion of the trip. Only the expenses of the vacation week are not deductible.

Expenses for your spouse and family have to be treated very carefully. If your spouse is an active participant in the business, for example another member of the company, the spouse's allowable expenses are deductible. Even if your kids run a few errands for you, however, you'll have a hard time proving to the tax auditor that they are essential to the business. Automobile expenses are usually deductible. They don't change whether you're driving alone or transporting the whole family.

You can take several precautions to be able to establish that your trip was for business purposes. First, set up an itinerary which spreads your business contacts along the whole route of the trip. This is not necessary when you travel to a booking show, because your attendance at the show is, in itself, sufficient reason to go that distance. Next, write to all the business contacts you plan to see. Tell them when you want to see them and what you want to discuss. Keep copies of the letters in your tax file. They will help document your intentions. Make a note of all the business contacts you made during the trip, who you saw, when and where, and what the results were. Finally, keep an accurate record of all expenses.

There are special rules with respect to deductibility of expenses for luxury water travel and trips abroad. When considering such business trips, consult with your tax adviser regarding the current restrictions on their deductibility, as they change frequently.

➤ *See also* Tax, Travel

Call-Back

Typically, when a show is being cast, the producer, director and others involved in the casting process will determine which of those individuals who have auditioned for various roles will be invited back for further evaluation. This invitation is known as a *call-back*. This process continues until the roles are filled. Where an agent is involved, the callback notice will typically go to the agent; where there is no agent involved, the call will go directly to the talent.

> ➤ *See also* Agent, Audition, Director, One-Night Stand

Call-Board

The term *call-board* refers to a form posted backstage which is used as a check-in sheet for rehearsals and performances. Typically, when talent arrives at the facility, they will note their presence on the call-board. This form is frequently monitored by an assistant director or stage manager.

> ➤ *See also* Stage Manager

Cancelled Check

A *cancelled check* is a check which you have issued and which your bank has paid from your account. There was a time when little holes were punched into such checks, but other forms of cancellation today accomplish the same purpose. A check that has gone through this procedure is also referred to as a check that has *cleared.*

Cancelled checks may or may not be returned to you with your monthly bank statement. Some banks do this automatically; others make it optional. Banks which do not return cancelled checks usually make copies available either free or for a nominal charge. Cancelled checks may serve at least two important purposes: (1) to enable you to double check the bank statement, and (2) as proof that you have made payment. If you mark the bills you pay with the check number and date of payment, it is easy to identify the check as proof of payment.

Conversely, when your records show an unpaid receivable which it is claimed has been paid, request copies of both the front and back of the cancelled check.

➤ *See also* Bank Statement, Banks, Checking Account, Cleared Check, Endorsement, Uniform Commercial Code

Capital

The word *capital* has at least two business meanings. The accountant's definition, which is of immediate interest, loosely refers to the investment in a business expressed in terms of money. This includes not only the cash put up by the owner(s) of the business, but such sources as loans, sponsors, backers, trade credit, equipment, or real estate, although, technically, loans and credit are not capital.

Capitalizing a new business often draws on a combination of resources. Suppose you and a partner want to open a theater. You calculate that you'll need $100,000 to get started. Where do you get that capital? Partner A invests fixtures and decorations worth $26,000, plus $10,000 in cash. Partner B puts up $40,000 in cash. You're still $24,000 short, so you go to the bank or your college roommate to borrow the balance. And you're in business.

The initial investment is not the only source of capital. The income earned by the theater increases the business's capital if some of it is reinvested. Similarly, if you borrow money in order to expand several years after you've started, that also counts as capital.

➤ *See also* Capital Gains, Financial Statement, Loans, Securities

Capital Campaign

This term can be used in at least two contexts. If a production company is structured as a nonprofit corporation, its *capital campaign* will mean an arrangement for purposes of raising operating or other capital. This may involve professional fundraisers or be confined to the organization's staff and/ or members. Capital campaigns, as used in this context, can be conducted for the purpose of funding a particular performance or production, an endowment, a building acquisition, or the like.

The term *capital campaign* may also be used to refer to the process of raising funds by a business corporation or other for-profit business entity, such as a limited partnership, limited liability company, or the like, in order to fund a given project. In this context, the capital campaign must conform to all relevant laws, including, for example, the securities laws, which regulate the fundraising process in a business context.

➤ *See also* Corporation, Limited Liability Company, Limited Liability Partnership, Nonprofit Corporation, Partnership, Securities

Capital Gains

Suppose you own a theater. You decide you want to move to some other part of the country, so you put the theater up for sale and sell it at a profit. That profit is known as a *capital gain*—your capital investment has increased in value and you realized the increase in dollars and cents. The capital gain becomes part of your income for tax purposes. The capital gains tax applies to the net profit on the sale of any capital asset, including corporate stocks, buildings, equipment, and similar capital investments.

There is a procedure whereby the proceeds from the sale of your theater can be reinvested in other commercial property having equal or greater value and having a similar function. If the proper procedure is followed, the capital gains can be avoided until the new property is sold. This "like for like" exchange, known as a *1231 exchange* (referring to the section of the Internal Revenue Code which permits it) is quite technical and should only be undertaken with the help of a skilled attorney, accountant, or other specialist.

Prior to the 1986 Tax Reform Act, capital gains were taxed at significantly lower rates than ordinary income, a practice which many believed would encourage capital investment and, thus, expansion of the economy. Under the 1986 Tax Reform Act, capital gains were taxed at the same rates as ordinary income. In 1991, legislation limited the tax on capital gains to a maximum of 28 percent, thus providing a slight tax benefit for capital gains. While capital gains tax treatment remained the same under the 1993 legislation, the relative benefit improved because of other changes in the tax laws. Stock acquired after August 10, 1993 in qualified small businesses which is held for at least five years is entitled to even more favorable treatment. In this situation, 50 percent of the gain realized on the sale of that stock may be excluded from gross income, up to the lesser of ten times the basis in the stock or $10 million. A small corporation for this purpose is defined as a *C corporation* using at least 80 percent of its assets in the conduct of a trade or business. It may not be a personal service or certain other designated businesses. In addition, the small corporation's gross assets may not exceed $50 million when the stock is first issued. Even now, many in Congress would like to amend tax laws to have even more favorable tax treatment for capital gains.

➤ *See also* Capital, Tax

Cash Basis

➤ *See* Accounting

Cash Flow

Cash flow is the stream of money which enters your business in the form of income and leaves your business in the form of expenses and compensation. It includes money from sales of theater tickets and other receivables, for example, sponsorship fees, and expenses such as labor, sets, costumes, and the like; it does not include the return on your investment or the value of your assets. It is short-term income and outgo, rather than the value of the entertainment business. Alternatively, some accountants define *cash flow* as cash in from whatever source and cash out for whatever reason. A business may have assets worth millions of dollars—such as unsold scripts—but, without sales, there is no income. Without income, expenses cannot be paid; therefore, there will be no cash flow.

➤ *See also* Financial Statement

Cashier's Check

Most checks are written by depositors against their checking accounts. A *cashier's check* is written by the bank against its own funds. It is considered more secure than a personal or business check.

Creditors often require cashier's or *certified checks*. You must provide the bank with cash in the amount of the check to be drawn; the bank may also charge for its services. Some drawbacks to using cashier's or certified checks are that, in the case of cashier's checks, you do not have a cancelled check as proof of payment (although you may have a check stub or carbon copy) and it may be difficult, if not impossible, to stop payment on either cashier's or certified checks.

A cashier's check and a certified check are similar, in that the bank is responsible for payment in both cases. As stated above, a cashier's check is drawn against the bank's own account and will be issued to anyone who pays for it. A certified check is drawn against a depositor's account; the bank merely certifies that it has isolated the funds and restricted them for payment of that check.

➤ *See also* Banks, Certified Check, Letter of Credit, Money Order

Casting Director

A person who conducts auditions of talent for purposes of selecting the performer for a particular role is known as a *casting director.* Often, the casting director is given authority to actually select the talent for a role or performance, though, in many situations, a casting director merely makes recommendations to the director. Some production companies combine the roles of casting director and director in one person.

➤ *See also* Audition, Contract, Credit, Director

Certified Check

When a check is *certified,* it means that the bank has confirmed that the person or organization writing it is a depositor in that bank and that the money has been set aside by the bank for payment of that particular check. The bank is now responsible and liable for payment. The depositor has no further access to that money. In almost all cases, payment cannot be stopped on a certified check. Certified checks will not be dishonored unless the bank fails and is uninsured.

To have a check certified, you must present it to the bank on which it is drawn. An officer stamps the certification across the face of the check and adds his or her signature. A check is normally presented for certification by the person who writes it, but it can also be done by the person who receives it, as in the case of a check which will not be cashed until some future time when the service for which it is presented has been performed. Certified checks are often required in substantial or irrevocable transactions, such as the transfer of real estate.

➤ *See also* Banks, Cashier's Check, Checking Account, Letter of Credit, Money Order

Chamber of Commerce

A *chamber of commerce* is a group of business people and companies whose purpose is to encourage commercial activity. Chambers of commerce are organized on local, state, and national levels, and occasionally even within certain industries. They are supported by dues payments from members and engage in a variety of activities. Since they represent a diversity of business interests, one of their major functions is to bring various business people together to exchange ideas and help support each other and their community.

Some chambers of commerce have given support to entertainment organizations by establishing business committees for the arts, sponsoring theater parties, and supporting local arts and humanities commissions. Others are involved in attracting tourists to their areas and, to this purpose, they may publish listings of local performances and have gone so far as to produce maps showing the location of theaters and arts businesses or organizations.

Individuals involved in the entertainment industry who consider relocating to another area of the country often find that information about business conditions, taxes, facilities, and other details from the local chamber of commerce can be very helpful in reaching a decision. In this connection, it should be remembered that a chamber of commerce rarely, if ever, mentions any negative aspect of its community.

➤ *See also* Better Business Bureau

Charitable Contributions

Charitable contributions are gifts of money or property (including literature such as plays, and the intangible right to perform them) which are made to charitable institutions. If the recipient is a "qualified charity"—that is, one which is created for the purpose of public benefit and which has obtained an appropriate ruling from the Internal Revenue Service (traditionally under Section 501(c)(3) of the Intenal Revenue Code), then the maximum charitable donation may be taken by the donor.

Prior to 1969, creators such as authors and playwrights could deduct the fair market value of their works which they donated to qualified charities. Since then, creative people have been allowed to take charitable deduction from their federal income tax for only the cost of the materials used in creating the donated work. Some states provide creative people with the right to deduct either the fair market value of their donated work or the difference between the fair market value and the amount deducted for federal income tax purposes.

Entertainers may not deduct the fair market value of their services from either state or federal income taxes. Even famous performers such as Jerry Lewis who conduct exhausting telethons may not receive any tax consideration for their charitable services. Individuals other than the creator who donate an item may deduct only the amount they paid for the donated item regardless of its fair market value, though the deduction for items donated to qualified charities will not affect the donor's alternative minimum tax. For example, if a theater company purchases a costume which was worn by Madonna in a successful production and the costume is donated to the Rock and Roll Hall of Fame (a qualified charity), the company may only deduct the cost of the costume even though it would likely have sold for much more if consigned to an auction house, or sold to a theme club such as the Hard Rock Cafe.

➤ *See also* 501(c)(3), Income Tax—Business, Income Tax—Personal, Nonprofit Organization, Tax

Checking Account

Most people are familiar with *checking accounts*. A check is a negotiable instrument which is written as an order to the bank as agent of the depositor instructing it to pay the amount specified to the named payee of the check or, if the check is written as payable to "Cash," then to the person presenting the check. Checks and checking accounts are governed by Article 3 of the Uniform Commercial Code, as well as a host of other state and federal laws and regulations.

When you begin your business, you should establish a *business checking account.* If your entertainment business is a corporation, limited liability company, or limited liability partnership, you will need to present the bank with a copy of your articles of incorporation or articles of organization and federal Taxpayer Identification Number. Businesses operated under assumed business names or trade names will have to register the assumed name with the appropriate government office and provide the bank with proof of registration, along with the appropriate taxpayer ID number.

Business checking accounts should never be used for paying personal obligations. Instead, the business should issue an appropriate check to the individual, who should then deposit it into his or her personal account before writing personal checks against it. Similarly, personal funds should never be used for directly paying business obligations. If the individual finds it necessary to advance money on behalf of the business, he or she should promptly submit a receipt for reimbursement from the business.

Checks come in a wide variety of sizes, shapes, designs, and colors. They are available from banks and from commercial printers. Generally, the printers charge less per check than the banks, so it is a good idea to shop around when ordering new checks. More important than the look of the check is how it is used. Care should be taken when writing a check. It should be properly dated—and should never be post-dated. The payee's name should be spelled correctly, and the amount, both in the numerals and the words, should be written in such as way as to preclude alteration. The first numeral should be written as close to the preprinted dollar sign as possible, and there should be little space between the numbers. The first number word should be written as close as possible to the left edge of the check and any space between the words and the preprinted word "Dollars" should be filled with a line. The check should always be signed when written.

When you receive a check, if you endorse it "for deposit only," it cannot be cashed, even if it is stolen. You can obtain an endorsement stamp from your bank or stationer which makes your entertainment business look more professional. *Never* endorse a check before you are ready to negotiate it. It is unwise to carry endorsed checks—other than those marked "for deposit only." It is very risky to sign a blank check. If you do, you should promptly ascertain the amount which was filled in. Note that amount in your check register and be certain to verify it as promptly as possible. Consider using petty cash to avoid using blank checks. Forging a check is illegal, and a forged check cannot be charged against your account. If you believe that you are being charged for a forged check, notify the bank as promptly as possible. Altered checks are treated the same way as forged checks.

When you write a check, the recipient *negotiates* it, either by depositing it in the recipient's bank or obtaining cash. The negotiating bank then transmits the check, through banking channels, to your bank, which deducts the amount of the check from your account. You will be notified of the deduction on your next statement. You should promptly reconcile your monthly bank statements to determine whether there are any irregularities. You should also keep a running balance of deposits, checks, and other deductions in your checkbook register so that you always know what your balance is.

It is unlawful to knowingly write a bad check, and the penalties can be severe. Mistakes in arithmetic do occur and, if you inadvertently write a check which results in an *overdraft* in your account, you will likely be charged by your bank and the check may not be honored. Some banks have special provisions for covering overdrafts on behalf of certain depositors, for example, those who have maintained their accounts for some time and have had a good record with the bank.

You may wish to *stop payment* on a check after it has been issued. Most banks will permit this, though there are certain rules which must be followed. It must be done promptly and before the check has been paid. There is generally a charge for the service and most banks require the stop payment order to be in writing. Some banks will limit the number of stop payments orders they will honor within a prescribed period. Care should, therefore, be taken with your use of the stop payment procedure. If a problem arises, you should immediately contact your bank to find out what its rules and policies are with respect to stopping payment.

If you make an error in writing a check, you should write "VOID" prominently across the face of the check and keep it with your register, mark the space in your register for that check number "void," and start again with the next check.

Check-writing in no longer confined to paper and pen. Today, many computer programs will write checks and some will even make the appropriate bookkeeping entries. For example, Quicken is a sophisticated bookkeeping software package which will not only provide a computer data base for bookkeeping entries, but has check-writing capabilities. Other packages available for this purpose include One Write Plus and Microsoft Money.

With the advent of electronic banking, some banks will permit regular automatic withdrawals, such as payment of your rent or mortgage. In fact, any fixed, ongoing payment which must be made monthly—such as insurance premiums—is a prime candidate for this service. The advantage of automatic withdrawal is that you save the time and cost of writing a check and mailing it. Unfortunately, the service is automatic and you may find that your account becomes overdrawn either because of cash flow problems or because you forgot to deduct the automatic payment from your checkbook balance.

➤ *See also* Balance, Bank Statement, Banks, Cancelled Check, Certified Check, Cleared Check, Endorsement, Interest, Money Order, Statement, Stop Payment, Uniform Commercial Code

Cleared Check

The term *cleared check* commonly means that the person to whom you wrote a check deposited it in his or her bank, that bank presented the check to your bank, your bank paid it from your account, and that the check has been cancelled.

➤ *See also* Banks, Cancelled Check, Checking Account

Collaboration

It is quite common in the performing arts for two or more persons to work together on a project. This is commonly referred to as a *collaboration* and it may have some important consequences. For example, when one person writes the script and another writes the music for a musical, the two individuals are said to be *collaborators*. Whether the collaborators will be joint-owners of the copyright in the work produced or whether each will individually own the copyright in the part created by him or her, depends upon whether the parties intended their contributions to form a unitary work, or whether they intended each finite part to remain separate. If the parties are joint copyright owners, then each may have the right to exploit the entire work, though there must be an accounting to the other for any profits generated. This can be important when, for example, a dispute arises between two or more collaborators and they are unable to agree on how a production is to proceed. If the copyright is jointly owned, any one may proceed without the other(s), though, there could be competitive productions utilizing the same copyrighted material.

Another important question that arises with collaborators is how the credit line is to appear. Which of the two collaborators should be acknowledged first? If one collaborator proceeds with a project without involving the other(s), must they all be acknowledged? The safest course of action is for the parties initially to work out their arrangement and reduce it to writing. They should, among other items, consider copyright ownership, credit, distribution of profits, disposition of the work after the death of one or more of the collaborators, the right to create derivative works, and which of the parties is to have decision-making authority with respect to the collaboration. A skilled entertainment lawyer should be involved in representing each of the collaborators in order to work out a viable arrangement.

➤ *See also* Advertising, Contract, Copyright

Collateral

Collateral is something of value that is pledged as security against the repayment of a loan. If the payments are not made, the lender can foreclose through a specified procedure, which may include, among other things, a sale of the collateral. For example, stage sets and costumes may be used as collateral for a line of credit. This property would likely be secured by the lender using a UCC-1 Financing Statement. House or business real estate will likely be collateral for a mortgage. The security interest in this form of collateral is *perfected* by having the mortgage recorded. Both UCC-1s and mortgages must be perfected by recording them with the appropriate government office, since subsequent lenders and others interested in your financial situation will check these offices and since the law generally allows a secured lender to enforce its security interest only if it is perfected.

➤ *See also* Creditor, Foreclosure, Installment, Loans, Mortgage, Uniform Commercial Code

Collection Problems

Collection problems fall into two principal categories: (1) bad checks; and (2) change of ownership or insolvency.

BAD CHECKS

It would be nice if everyone in this world were honest. Unfortunately, a good many checks have been known to bounce. Protect yourself by following a few simple rules:

1. Before you accept a check as payment, ask for a check guarantee card or identification that includes the person's signature and photo. Driver's licenses and major credit cards are best. Double-check the signature and address. On the check, note the driver's license or, if allowed in your state, credit card number, and the customer's address and telephone number, if different than what is pre-printed. Do not accept as proof of identity such items as business cards, bankbooks, library cards, Social Security cards, and the like.

2. Never cash a check for someone you don't know.

3. Accept a check for payment only if it is made out to you or your business and only if it is made out for the exact amount desired.

4. Don't accept third-party checks, *i.e.,* checks made out to someone else and endorsed to you. That only adds another element of potential trouble. If you don't deal directly with the person who wrote the check, it could a stolen.

5. Mark all checks "for deposit only" the moment you receive them. That makes it impossible for a thief to cash them.

None of this guarantees that a check won't bounce, but you'll at least be more likely to find the maker of the bad check. You'll also protect yourself from being known as an easy mark. Not every bad check is uncollectible. Occasionally, checks are returned marked "nonsufficient funds" ("NSF") because of an oversight or bank error. In that event, it is best to make polite contact with the drawer, who will usually ask you to redeposit the check. In almost all cases, the check clears the second time. If it bounces again, and the drawer refuses to pay in cash or with a certfied check, take legal action. Banks will rarely allow more than one redeposit.

If payment on a check issued to your business has been stopped before the tickets have been delivered, or the entertainment service rendered, it is probably best to treat the transaction as rescinded. If, however, the tickets have been delivered or work completed and payment is stopped without there being a good reason, you may have to take legal action.

CHANGE OF OWNERSHIP OR INSOLVENCY

If there is a change in ownership of a business which owes you money, or if a debtor becomes insolvent, there is a good chance that you will not be paid. There are several common ways this can happen.

1. *Bulk sale.* When a business with inventory is sold, the creditors of the selling business have a continuing claim on the sold assets, even after the buyer of the business has paid for it. Very often, the sales contract stipulates that the buyer takes over all assets and liabilities of the business. When the liabilities are not paid, the creditors must be notified.

   Bulk sales are governed by the Uniform Commercial Code (UCC), and apply to the sale of all or substantially all of a business's assets. Many states have adopted variations, but the basic requirement generally is that a ten-day notice of sale must be given to all creditors before the sale closes. This is to allow creditors to make their claims, find out when and how they will be paid, and take legal action if they are not satisfied with the terms. Prompt action is necessary. If a security interest in the inventory was perfected under the UCC prior to the sale of the business, the buyer of the business will have "constructive notice" of the obligation.

2. *Common law composition.* This is the most flexible and least formal way for a business which owes more than it can pay to liquidate in an equitable manner, or arrange to continue in business. The debtor offers a certain proportion of the amount owed to all creditors who agree to take that amount in full payment. Since the legal costs are low, there is usually no point in a creditor rejecting such an offer if it is satisfied that the debtor is acting in good faith and that no other creditors are being treated better. If a check for the proposed settlement is enclosed with the notice, however, remember that depositing, cashing, or even just keeping the check may be considered acceptance of the plan.

3. *Assignment for benefit of creditors or receivership*. This is a more formal way of liquidating a business, but it is less formal and less expensive than bankruptcy. It is a state court proceeding in which all the assets of a business are turned over to a court-appointed receiver, who sells off the assets, usually at auction. The proceeds are distributed to the creditors in proportion to their claim after such items as wages, taxes, the receiver's fee, and certain other expenses have been paid. It is important to file a claim on the proper form when you receive a notice of assignment from the court or other authority.

4. *Bankruptcy*. This is a proceeding in federal bankruptcy court and costs are usually higher than the previous methods. Once the petition is properly filed, the court clerk will begin the process of notifying creditors listed on the bankruptcy schedules of the bankruptcy filing, the date of the first meeting of creditors, and the deadline for filing proofs of claim. Prompt filing of your claim is very important. If the case has been determined to be a "no-asset case," the court will not accept proofs of claim. Certain transactions, both before and during the bankruptcy, may ultimately be disallowed or avoided, and the recipient of the "preference" may be required to return to the bankrupt estate what was received so that it can be more fairly distributed among the various creditors of the estate. This is a very technical area and you should work with an attorney experienced in bankruptcy law whenever you become involved with bankruptcy, either as a creditor or a debtor.

FOLLOW-UP

Several systems can be used for collection follow-up. First, you should keep a written record of every transaction. Your records should reflect the day payment is due and the dates you send follow-up notices. You should also note follow-up dates on your calendar.

COLLECTION AGENCIES

The services of a collection agency may be desirable. Collection agencies generally charge a percentage of the amount they collect; the smaller the bill, the larger the percentage. Collection agencies have no greater powers to collect debts than individuals, but their services may be cost-effective and save a good deal of time. It is well known that collection agencies turn their experience with bad debts over to credit bureaus. It is important to select a collection agency whose reputation is sound. Heavy-handed tactics can backfire and expose you to legal liability under the Fair Debt Collection Practices Act. Check with other organizations in your area to learn what their experience has been with particular collection agencies, or if they have other recommendations to make.

Whether you should turn the matter over to an attorney depends upon a variety of factors, including the size of the debt and whether your state has enacted a statute law which provides for the payment of attorney's fees in situations such as yours. Even in states without such laws, your contract may have an attorney's fee provision which will entitle you to recover the amount you spend on the lawyer, provided you are successful and the debtor has the means to pay the bill. Collection practice is a specialized field and you should work with an attorney who has experience in dealing with these kinds of problems.

➤ *See also* Accounting, Bankruptcy, Endorsement, Small Claims Court

Commercial Bank

A *commercial bank* is a bank whose main function is to handle checking accounts, although it also performs numerous other banking functions such as lending money and renting safe-deposit boxes. While many commercial banks also offer savings account services, the interest paid on those accounts is generally lower than that offered by savings banks or credit unions.

➤ *See also* Banks, Credit Unions, Savings Banks

Commission

Many productions are based on pre-existing works; however, occasionally a new work will be desired. The process of hiring a person or team for the purpose of creating the new work is known as *commissioning,* and involves a contract. This arrangement can be as informal as merely requesting that a particular type of piece be created or, more commonly, the agreement would specify with particularity the details of the arrangement. An experienced entertainment lawyer should be involved in drafting this agreement in order to be sure that it covers all of the appropriate issues. These might include, for example, a description of the project, completion date, amount of payment, and ownership of the rights in the work, including copyright and ancillary works such as royalties from recording and other merchandising arrangements.

➤ *See also* Composer, Contract, Copyright, Playwright, Vehicle, Work for Hire

Common Carrier

A *common carrier* is anyone, individual or company, who publicly offers to transport goods for a fee. Truck companies, bus lines, railroads, and airlines are typical examples. They are usually regulated by some government agency, operate on a franchise, and are required to charge the same fee for the same service to all customers. Common carriers have the responsibility for transporting the goods safely, speedily, and correctly, and are legally liable for the fair market value of works which are lost or damaged.

Local truckers with whom you make your own arrangements are called *private carriers*. They can charge anything the market will bear, pick and choose their customers, and their liability and responsibility are much less clearly defined. Touring groups may either ship their sets, costumes, and the like themselves or use the services of a private carrier. It is rare for them to use common carriers, except for interstate deliveries.

➤ *See also* Insurance

Community Theater

Most communities have some form of *community theater.* These organizations are generally made up of unpaid performers and technicians who gravitate toward one another because of their common interest in theater. Community theaters typically receive royalty licenses on terms more favorable than those granted to professional theater companies. While community theaters are typically structured as nonprofit corporations, their production values may be quite high. Local businesses are usually quite willing to donate goods or services to assist the companies in exchange for program credit. Entertainment professionals sometimes attend community theater productions for the purpose of scouting quality talent. Many of today's stars began their careers in community theater. Community theater should be distinguished from summer stock, which almost always utilizes union talent and technicians and is not considered to be amateur theater.

➤ *See also* Nonprofit Organization, Royalty

Company Manager

➤ *See* Manager

Composer

A *composer* is a person who writes music. Whether the composer will own the copyright in that music depends upon the circumstances surrounding the creation of the work. Some works are created under a commission arrangement while others are independently written. Some composers work independently while others collaborate and either coauthor a work or create a part, such as music or lyrics. It is rare for collaborations to be confined to music; rather, it is more common for a composer and a librettist or lyricist to work together.

➤ *See also* Commission, Contract, Copyright, Librettist, Lyricist, Playwright, Appendix A

Computers

As the name indicates, *computers* were originally invented for the purpose of performing computation tasks. Today, they have become popular for a variety of business tasks. In addition, the prices on computers have dramatically declined since the early days and, most small businesses have become computerized.

Computers can be used for bookkeeping, check-writing, retaining mailing and other lists, asset control (costumes, props, etc.), and even for the purpose of set or costume design. At one time, it was necessary to have special programs designed to accommodate each business. Today, there are numerous software programs available which can probably be used in most small businesses. Performing arts organizations which desire to have specific programs created for them can work with *systems analysts* who can evaluate the unique needs of the business. These individuals will either write the necessary software or work with software programmers to create a program which, if properly implemented, can save countless hours and perform numerous tasks necessary for the conduct of a performing arts business.

Computer technology has been improving at a rapid pace and the prices charged for both hardware and software are in constant flux. You should purchase a system that can be upgraded as the technology evolves and your business grows. Systems and prices are very competitive, and it is worthwhile for you to shop around. You may also find it cost-effective to hire a consultant to analyze your needs and make appropriate suggestions. Be sure the person is experienced—ask around for recommendations. Be sure that you purchase equipment (hardware and software) that will be able to service the needs of your business as they expand. Care should be taken to acquire compatible components. The worth of a knowledgeable adviser cannot be overemphasized. Be sure, for example, that the hardware you purchase can support the software you need.

HARDWARE

Hardware is the term used to describe the machinery that accommodates the programs known as *software* and which perform computing functions. Hardware includes the hard drive, printers, scanners, and the other ancillary components which collectively make up a computer system.

SOFTWARE

Computer programs generally come in the form of 3.5-inch or 5.25-inch floppy disks or CD-ROM, and are available to accomplish a host of business operations including word processing, desktop publishing, database management, bookkeeping, accounting, and tax preparation. In addition, specialized software has been created for the entertainment industry, including lighting and set design packages. You should consult with your accountant before purchasing accounting, bookkeeping, or tax preparation software.

> ➤ *See also* Accounting, Bank Statement, Budget, E-Mail, Equipment, Financial Statement, Internet, Resume, Security, Tax, Tax Preparer, Ticket

Conductor

A *conductor* typically is the person who *conducts* or controls an orchestra or other musical group. A conductor may also have some management responsibilities. While a conductor typically is affiliated with a particular organization, sometimes the conductor's reputation transverses the organizational relationship and stands on its own. In fact, some conductors, such as Leonard Bernstein and George Szell, have become independently recognized and are stars in their own right.

> ➤ *See also* Music Director

Contract

A *contract* is an agreement between two or more people which is enforceable and for which the law provides a remedy when it is breached. You enter into contracts all the time. Every time an organization offers tickets for sale or an actor agrees to perform in a specific production, a contract exists. Every time you buy supplies, you are entering into a contract that requires one party to deliver and the other party to pay. Your mortgage, your lease, your relations with the telephone and electric companies, employees you hire, royalty agreement, the gas you put into your car—all of these are contractual situations and they are all legally enforceable. It is important to understand that a contract, to be enforceable, must meet *all* of the following four conditions:

1. *Competence.* The parties to the contract must be competent to enter into an agreement. Convicted prisoners, the insane, and certain other people generally are not considered competent to make contracts in the legal definition of the term. Children may be able to make contracts, although they may be able to rescind them in some situations.

2. *Mutual agreement.* Both parties must agree on the terms of the contract. That's why there is often a great deal of negotiation before a contract is signed.

3. *Consideration.* The parties have to do something for each other. This is usually expressed in terms of money, although that's not necessary. It can be the performance of some kind of service. But there has to be some balance. A contract which is very obviously lopsided in favor of one party or the other may not meet the requirements of the law.

4. *Lawful purpose.* An agreement to do something illegal is not enforceable.

The following are some examples which may be useful in understanding contracts:

a. You promise your cousin that you'll include him in your next production. Somehow you don't. What can your cousin do?

b. A twelve-year-old girl purchases a ticket to your show. She comes back and says her mother won't let her attend and she wants her money back. Can you refuse to return her money?

c. You pay the building inspector fifty dollars to overlook the safety violations in your theatre. But he's an even worse crook than you are. He takes the money and reports you anyway. Can you sue?

d. Your theater company contracts to use a performance space. When you attempt to make load-in arrangements, you are informed that the space is not available to you. Can you sue?

Let's examine the answers:

a. Your cousin may be sore, but he has no legal leg to stand on. There was no consideration involved, no agreement that he would be in the play or do something else for you in return. All he can do is never speak to you again. Perhaps you win.

b. A twelve-year-old could have fulfilled the contract, although, because of her age, she may rescind it. You'd better give her back her money and sell the ticket to someone else.

c. A contract to commit a crime is not enforceable. You're probably better off to keep quiet about the whole deal and learn from your mistake.

d. Here's a perfectly good contract. Both you and the landlord are competent to enter into a contract, you both agreed on the terms, it's a perfectly legal activity, and you upheld your end of the bargain. You can sue.

A contract does not have to be in writing. Oral contracts, even contracts which are created merely through the actions of people, are legally enforceable. It is always better to put an agreement in writing to avoid misunderstanding. The law does require certain contracts to be evidenced by a writing: all real estate transactions and most contracts which extend over a long period of time (more than a year or, in some instances, more than a lifetime) or involve large sums of money ($500 or more). This is a technical area. When in doubt, consult an attorney. It is also wise to specify a starting date and a termination date under certain conditions, as in employment or personal service agreements. They can always be renewed if both parties agree.

Most ordinary, everyday contracts require no legal advice; you'd need in-house counsel to handle them all. But it is important that you read all the fine print. When you receive a contract, even an insurance policy, read it carefully, front and back, so that you understand not only the basic terms, but all the conditions that apply. When you apply for a bank loan, read every clause in the contract and ask the bank officer to explain anything you don't understand. After all, the bank's lawyer drew up the form. You have a right to read and understand what you're signing.

When you come to more complicated contracts, *i.e.,* those which may have the potential to significantly affect your rights, interests, or obligations, a lawyer's advice is absolutely essential. A real estate sale or purchase, for example, should never be undertaken without a lawyer's review, advice, and active involvement to protect your interests. A partnership agreement or financing arrangement also should be undertaken with sound legal advice. In fact, any long-term or out-of-the-ordinary contract should be signed only after consultation with a lawyer. Expensive as legal advice may seem, it is more cost-effective to hire a lawyer before you sign a contract than it is to hire one after a problem develops.

➤ *See also* Adapted from, Alternative Dispute Resolution, Antitrust Law, Assignability, Blind Bidding, Block-Booking, Booking, Collaboration, Commission, Deal-Breaker, Employees, First Option, Independent Contractor, Industry Practices and

Customs, Installment, Joint Venture, Labor, Lawyers, Lease, Letter Agreement, License, Loans, Model Release, Morals Clause, Option, Parity, Partnership, Per Diem, Performing Rights, Prior Approval, Professional Name, Securities, Sponsorship, Statute of Frauds, Uniform Commercial Code, Union, Work for Hire

Cooperatives

A *cooperative* is an organization formed by a group of people with similar interests to achieve a common goal or to accomplish one or more objectives more effectively or economically than any individual would likely be able to on his or her own. Most cooperatives are organized because their members have a need for centralized buying or marketing; some have even begun to develop technical assistance programs, obtain group insurance, and other services.

Cooperatives are customarily created as either unincorporated associations or nonprofit corporations, though some operate as business corporations. The fundamental advantage of having the cooperative conduct its activity through a nonprofit or business corporation is that the members may shield their personal assets from business liability. The distinction between these two types of corporations is that nonprofit corporations are established for the purpose of performing a public service and no individual can own an interest in the organization or receive dividends as a return on investment. Individuals may be members of a nonprofit corporation and be permitted to vote for its governing board. They may also receive salaries for work performed on behalf of the organization. Getting a return on their investment is not the major reason why people join a cooperative; obtaining goods or services at a low cost is their basic incentive. In the case of a cooperative operating as a nonprofit corporation, all profits must be used for the organization's benefit. In the case of business corporations and unincorporated associations, profit may be distributed among members according to a formula based on ownership interest, resource or labor participation, or some other basis.

A cooperative is democratically controlled by its members. Unlike a typical business corporation, in which shareholders vote according to the number of shares they own, most cooperatives operate on a basis of one vote per member. The members elect a board of directors, and hire specialists in business administration, marketing, or purchasing to conduct the business affairs of the cooperative. Since most performing arts and entertainment cooperatives have marketing and public awareness of the performing arts as their primary purpose, the activity of the members is usually in the production of performing arts. Staff specialists take care of the marketing, purchasing, and so forth.

Knowing the market conditions and what will sell, marketing specialists occasionally make useful aesthetic suggestions to members of the cooperative.

In the case of cooperatives which are engaged in the entertainment business, it is common for members to devote a specific amount of time to the cooperative's work. The membership fee structure of cooperatives, especially those in depressed areas, is very modest. Many such co-ops are launched with long-term loans and even with federal assistance under various economic development programs.

Several excellent booklets on the principle of cooperatives and how to organize them have been published by the Agricultural Cooperative Service of the U.S. Department of Agriculture.

➤ *See also* Appendix B

Copyright

Copyright is an intangible right which was deemed so fundamentally important to the United States that the founders included, in Article I, Section 8, Clause 8, of the U.S. Constitution, a provision granting Congress the power to create a copyright law. The First Congress did just that, and copyright has been a part of American law since its beginning. Today, there are three major multinational copyright treaties which, in essence, provide reciprocal copyright protection in ninety-five countries with similar copyright laws.

Copyright grants the creator of a copyrightable original work the exclusive right to reproduce, market, sell, make derivative works, publicly perform and, where appropriate, publicly display the copyrighted work. For a work to be copyrightable, it must be original and involve some degree of creativity. It may not be a work in the public domain. Simple words and phrases, such as titles or slogans, may not be copyrighted, although they may be protected as trademarks. Work on which the copyright has expired or which is not copy-rightable is in the public domain and freely copyable.

Generally, the individual who created a work will own the copyright in it. There is, however, a significant exception. If the work is created by someone who is an employee working within the scope of his or her employment, the copyright in that work will belong to the employer. If the creator is independent, the copyright in the work will belong to the person or organization commissioning the work if (a) the work is specially ordered or commissioned, (b) it falls into any of the following nine categories:

1. a contribution to a collective work
2. a part of a motion picture or other audiovisual work

67

3. a translation
4. a supplementary work, which is a work intended to accompany or illustrate another work
5. a compilation
6. an instructional text
7. a test
8. answer material for a test, or
9. an atlas; and

(c) there is a written agreement stating that the work shall be a "work made for hire." The parties can also vary copyright ownership by contract. The law provides that an assignment of a copyright must be in writing, though a nonexclusive license—or permission to use—may be oral.

The copyright law provides that, whenever an original idea embodying some creativity is put in a tangible form, it is automatically protected by the federal statute. Adding a copyright notice: "Copyright," "Copr.," or "© [owner's name] and year of first publication," will prevent others from copying a work, believing that is it not protected and claiming that they are *innocent infringers.* This is important, since innocent infringers may be held liable only for nominal damages, if any, and may even be permitted to continue copying. The notice should, if possible, be permanently affixed but may, in the case of a playwright, composer, choreographer, or set designer, the notice must appear on the tangible embodiment of the work; *i.e.*, manuscript, notation, videotape, or the like, and, in the case of performances, in the program. It is customary to announce that the work in a production is protected and to admonish those in the audience not to use audiotape, videotape, or any other means of reproduction during the production. In fact, most royalty agreements require such notice. Garments, including theatrical costumes, are generally not copyrightable, since they are considered "functional" and functional works are protectable, if at all, under the patent laws, not the copyright laws.

The copyright should also be registered. While registration does not create a copyright, it does provide the copyright owner with certain important additional remedies in the event of an infringement. If an unregistered work is infringed, the copyright owner is entitled to enjoin the infringer and to obtain any actual, provable damages. This could include the copyright owner's lost profits or the infringer's actual profits. When a work was registered before it was infringed, the owner is also entitled to recover statutory damages of between $500 and $20,000 or, if the infringement was willful, up to $100,000, in lieu of actual damages, and is eligible to receive reasonable attorneys' fees and costs for litigating the case.

Publication is a technical term, defined by the law as meaning a distribution of the original work or any copy to the public by performance, reproduction, and distribution of a script, or the like. If the copyright is registered within three months of the work's first publication, registration is retroactive to the date of publication. If, on the other hand, registration occurs after three months have elapsed, it will be effective prospectively from the date of registration.

The Copyright Office will not assist you in protecting your copyright. In fact, the Copyright Office is merely an administrative office which will register any work if the registration application is complete and in the proper form. It is, therefore, necessary for you to enforce your own copyright through private litigation.

Registration is quite simple and inexpensive. It requires submission of a prescribed form, payment of a fee (currently twenty dollars), and deposit of two of the best copies of the work. The administrator of the Copyright Office, known as the Register of Copyrights, has been granted authority to modify the deposit requirement. In the case of works of art, such as stage sets, two photographs may be used instead of original artworks. The registration forms most commonly used in the entertainment industry are Form VA, for visual art such as set designs, Form TX, for written work, including scripts, screenplays, advertising brochures, pamphlets, and the like, Form SR, for sound recordings, and Form PA for performing arts, which includes musical, dramatic, and choreographic works and motion pictures.

A copyright lasts for the life of the copyright owner, when the owner is a human being using his or her own name. For "works made for hire," works published under a pseudonym or anonymously, the period of protection is either one hundred years from creation or seventy-five years from first publication, whichever expires first. For works which were protected prior to January 1, 1978, the effective date of the present copyright law, and for which protection was still in effect on that date, is seventy-five years from the date of registration.

There are several exceptions to the copyright owner's rights under the law. The most important for the entertainment industry is the so-called *fair use doctrine.* This essentially provides a copier with a defense if the unauthorized copying is within the scope of *fair use.* In order to determine whether a use is *fair,* the courts must consider at least four factors: (1) the nature of the work, (2) the nature of the use, (3) the extent of the copying, and (4) the effect on the market. This area is quite dynamic and, before copying another's work, you should consult with an experienced copyright lawyer in order to ascertain whether you can consider any copying fair use.

Music has some unique rules associated with it with regarding to copyright. For example, once a piece has been recorded by the copyright proprietor, any subsequent recording can be made even though no deal has been struck with the copyright owner. This is by using the so-called compulsory license provision of the copyright statute and paying the appropriate licensing fee. In addition, "jukebox" licenses and other block licenses can be acquired from music clearinghouses such as ASCAP, Fox, and BMI.

For additional information about copyright protection and registration procedures, write to the United States Copyright Office or consult with an intellectual property lawyer.

> *See also* Adopted from, Assignability, Berne Copyright Convention, Buenos Aires Convention, Collaboration, Commission, Composer, Deposit, *Droit Morale*, Endorsement, Intellectual Property, Joint Venture, License, Patent, Performing Rights, Professional Name, Public Domain, Trade Dress, Trademark, Universal Copyright Convention, Appendix B

Corporation

There are two kinds of *corporations*: business corporations, which are owned by individuals, and nonprofit corporations, which are created for public benefit. This entry will consider business corporations; nonprofit corporations are discussed under "Nonprofit Corporations."

Incorporation usually provides a shield from liability for business debts, *i.e.,* the owners of the corporation will customarily not be personally liable for the obligations incurred by the corporation. In the eyes of the law, a corporation is considered a separate legal person.

A corporation can have any number of owners, who are called shareholders or stockholders. There should be a stock purchase agreement which defines what each owner gives to the business in exchange for his or her stock. If a shareholder is also an employee of the business, there should be a separate agreement spelling out the specific terms of employment. A form, usually known as Articles of Incorporation, must be filed with the Secretary of State in the state of incorporation, which will issue a charter or Certificate of Incorporation. A copy of the Charter or Certificate must be filed in every state where the corporation has a business presence, such as a permanent office. Filing fees for incorporation vary state by state, but are approximately $40 to

$900. In addition, there are annual fees, taxes, and other various reports to be filed. All this involves legal and accounting expenses.

For small businesses, *i.e.,* thirty-five or fewer individual shareholders who are U.S. citizens, an election may be made under the Internal Revenue Code, known as an *S election,* to have the corporation taxed as if it were a sole proprietorship or partnership. This means that the corporation is not a taxable entity and that the shareholder owners will have to pay tax or may deduct losses as if the business were not incorporated. For all other corporations, known as *C corporations,* the Internal Revenue Code provides that the entity must pay its own corporate income tax, though the rates charged are different from those which are levied against individual income.

If the shareholders do not treat the corporation as a separate legal entity, the courts may pierce the corporate veil and hold the owners personally liable for business obligations. Factors which have been used to enable creditors to pierce the corporate veil include commingling funds (using corporate and personal funds interchangeably) and failing to adhere to the corporate formalities (filing annual reports, keeping accurate books, filing taxes), among others.

➤ *See also* Capital Campaign, 501(c)(3), Joint Venture, Limited Liability Company, Limited Liability Partnership, Nonprofit Organization, Partnership, Securities, Sole Proprietorship

Cost Accounting

➤ *See* Accounting

Credit

Credit, in its broadest application, is based on trust and belief. Credit is the ability to borrow money based on the lender's belief that the loan will be repaid. Credit is the ability to purchase goods without cash on the seller's belief that the bill will be paid. Credit cards are issued to people considered reliable enough to pay the debt when due.

Open credit or *credit line* means that money can be withdrawn from an account, or purchases can be made, up to a specified amount. An adaptation of this principle is *revolving credit,* very common in department store charge accounts and with credit cards, where a maximum credit line is established, and the balance of available credit changes as purchases and payments are made.

Credit also has an accounting definition and refers to a bookkeeping entry. It may also refer to credit on an account; *i.e.,* an amount owed to you and carried on someone else's books. This could occur when, for example, you overpay or if you are required to prepay or when you have sold tickets and not yet been paid for it.

Credit may also have a nonfinancial meanings, such as when you are *given credit* for fine work or *credited* with a successful production, or for *program* or *screen credit.*

➤ *See also* Adapted from, Billing, Casting Director, Credits, Credit Card, Creditor, Deposit

Credit Card

A credit card is colloquially referred to as "plastic money" since it allows a purchaser to buy goods and services without paying cash at the time of purchase. For millions of credit card holders it is an easy and convenient way to shop, facilitating impulse buying. It grants the cardholders an instant loan for the credit limit established by the credit card issuer. Credit cards are not, however, without their problems.

The most widely used credit cards are those issued by banks, such as VISA and MasterCard, which are honored at thousands of stores and other business enterprises. Other cards, such as American Express and Diners Club cover primarily travel, hotel, restaurant, and entertainment expenses, although most of them are moving into expanded use. Still others, such as gasoline and department store credit cards, are even more limited, being honored only by the issuing stores or gas stations.

A bank credit card is relatively easy to obtain through a local bank, usually the branch at which one does one's other banking business, although with the volatility in interest rates, it is probably worth while to shop around for the best deal. The bank will make a quick credit check and place a top limit on the credit available on purchases with the card. There may be an application fee charged for a bank credit card. As a result of the difficulty experienced by some people in obtaining credit cards, some financial institutions have established a special type of account whereby the applicant is required to deposit a fixed amount, often $400–$600, in a special savings account with that institution, which establishes the credit limit. The cardholder is still required to make regular payments, though the savings account is frozen so long as the card account remains open.

The bank makes its money in two ways: (1) by charging the merchant a percentage of each credit card sale, and (2) by charging the credit card holder interest on the unpaid balance.

A few credit card companies, such as American Express, charge cardholders an annual fee and expect full payment of the outstanding balance each month, except for certain types of purchases, such as travel. On most credit card bills, a minimum payment amount will appear next to the total amount due. This is typically in the range of 3–10 percent of the total outstanding balance. The cardholder has a choice—to pay the total amount and clear the debt, or to pay at least the minimum amount and to continue to accrue interest on the unpaid balance. The unpaid balance is borrowed money, and the interest rates are often very high, frequently as much as 24 percent per annum. The interest rates vary according to state law and the terms of the credit account.

This annual interest rate should be taken into account when paying a credit card bill. Unless the credit card is used judiciously and bills are paid promptly, the final cost may outweigh the card's convenience. It is certainly more economical to borrow the money at a lower interest rate, or take it out of the bank account to pay a credit card bill in full, than to run up high interest payments.

The amount of money on which you pay interest is computed in various ways by different lenders. Cards such as MasterCard and VISA are issued by individual banks, each of which sets its own policies. Thus, you should read the fine print to see how the interest is computed. There are four basic methods: adjusted balance, previous balance, average daily balance excluding current transactions, and average daily balance including current transactions. It is not at all uncommon for the amount of interest charged to be twice as high under the average daily balance including current transactions method than under the adjusted balance method, even though the *rate* of interest is the same.

Credit card purchases need not be made in person. The cardholder can furnish the number and expiration date, and the merchant fills out the form and signs it with his name plus the initials "MO" (mail order) or "TO" (telephone order). One copy is sent to the customer, one to the credit card company, and the merchant's copy is attached to the original order which serves as authorization in place of the customer's signature on the charge slip.

Credit cards can also be used for actual cash borrowing. Some banks will make cash advances on presentation of a credit card or through automated teller systems (ATMs), and others may, in addition, automatically cover any overdraft on a checking account (up to a set limit) by charging it to the credit card. Cash advances begin to accrue interest from the moment they are made; there is no interest-free grace period as with purchases. In addition, some credit cards have a higher interest rate for cash advances then for purchases.

Credit card companies are very competitive and, because of the high profitability, have created incentives such as rebates. The Discover Card, for example, issues a credit to the cardholder at the end of a specified period equal to a percentage of the purchases made during that period. Other companies allow credit purchases to be counted toward airline mileage, car rental, or hotel benefit programs. Automobile manufacturers have recently entered the credit card business by issuing cards which may be used for general purchases but which provide a specific amount of credit toward the purchase of one of their vehicles at the end of a prescribed period. American Express entitles cardholders to go to any American Express office and write a personal check for up to $1,000, of which $200 can be for cash and $800 for traveler's checks. Credit cards are also often accepted as identification if you want to write a check.

Not every business is authorized to accept credit cards. In order to become a credit card merchant, you must apply (usually to the bank where you maintain your business account) and receive authorization to accept credit card transactions. Not every business will qualify and it is important to determine whether it is economical. Credit card companies charge merchants from 2 to 10 percent per annum of the charge sales, depending on the size of each sale, the total volume of charge sales, and the type of merchandise being sold. In addition, most banks require merchants to maintain a minimum deposit in their bank account for certain chargeback purposes.

The procedures vary among different credit card companies, but the basic principle is the same. The credit card merchant is provided with the card-imprinting machine and charge slips. The merchant deposits its copy of the charge slip similarly to depositing checks, using the designated deposit slip. The bank immediately credits your account. It is important for a merchant who accepts credit cards is to be sure the card is valid. The customer's signature on the back of the card should be compared with the signature on the charge slip. The expiration date should also be noted. If the card is expired, the cardholder is no longer entitled to use the card and, if a sale is made under those circumstances, the credit card company will not be able to collect from the cardholder and will charge the merchant's account.

Some credit card companies require that charges exceeding a certain amount, twenty-five dollars for example, must be pre-approved by the credit card's central office before the sale is made. It is always advisable, even when this is not required, to check the card number against the list of lost or stolen credit card numbers which the card companies furnish periodically. Some even give an award for picking up such cards. Of course, a sale should never be made on a credit card if the number shows up on that list. For the same reason, lost or stolen cards should be reported immediately by the cardholder. If the loss or theft of a card is not reported promptly, the cardholder may be held responsible for all purchases made by others; prompt reporting generally limits the cardholder's liability to fifty dollars.

➤ *See also* Credit, Interest, Loans

Credit Union

Credit unions have increased in popularity as banks and savings and loans have failed or gone out of business in alarming numbers and lost or placed in jeopardy staggering sums of depositors' money. Credit unions offer many of the same services as banks and savings banks, such as checking and savings accounts, various certificates of deposit (CDs) and time savings instruments, and loans ranging from small signature (unsecured) loans to residential second mortgages, and even first mortgage financing at some larger, stronger credit unions.

The major difference between credit unions and banks is that banks are operated as for-profit businesses, whereas credit unions are member-owned and operated not-for-profit. By operating not-for-profit, credit unions can maintain a tighter spread between the interest rates they pay their member-depositors and the rates they charge their member-borrowers. Thus, they tend to pay slightly higher interest on deposits and charge slightly lower interest on loans. Besides not having to generate a profit for its shareholder-owners, a credit union is operated for the benefit of its members via a board of directors elected from among its members. Thus, the management of a credit union tends to be more member- and service-oriented than a commercial bank. Furthermore, the constituency or membership of a given credit union tends to be comprised of individuals sharing some common interest, such as all working for the same employer or group of related employers, *e.g.,* teachers, government workers, timber industry workers, etc.

➤ *See also* Banks, Commercial Banks, Money Order, Savings Banks, Traveler's Checks

Creditor

A *creditor* is anyone to whom money is owed and who has a legal claim to payment. It may be a bank which has made a loan, a supplier which has shipped materials, an employee who has worked in expectation of being paid, or the government which will collect taxes. If someone owes you money, you are that person's creditor.

Creditors can improve their chances of being repaid in the event the debtor defaults on a loan by requiring the debtor to pledge collateral or have a co-signer or *guarantor.* If the creditor files its security interest in the collateral with the Secretary of State or other appropriate authority, the security interest is then said to be *perfected* under the Uniform Commercial Code and the creditor becomes a *secured creditor.* A security interest gives the creditor certain rights in the collateral if the debtor defaults. If you've borrowed money from a bank to buy your business van, for example, and the bank has perfected a security interest in the van, the bank can repossess the van and sell it if you default on your loan payments.

The law establishes several classes of creditors. A first mortgage, for instance, has seniority over a second mortgage. That's one reason why the interest on a second mortgage is generally higher; the lender takes more of a risk. In bankruptcy proceedings, government claims for unpaid taxes take precedence over all other claims. Employee claims on wages come next, then secured creditors and, finally, unsecured creditors.

> *See also* Collateral, Credit, Uniform Commercial Code

Crew

The term *crew* refers to the backstage personnel involved in a production. This will typically include stage managers, costumers, makeup designers and technicians, stagehands, lighting and sound designers and technicians, and the like. Some of these jobs may be subject to union contracts; however, this is not universal. Trade unions and associations are listed in Appendix A.

Curtain-Raiser

Initially, a musical or other comic piece, which preceded the featured performance and was intended to "warm up" the audience; in contemporary theater, *curtain-raisers* are less common, but still appear. Today, a curtain-raiser is typically a one-act play with a lighter theme than the featured performance.

Curtain Speech

Curtain speech, as the term implies, is a speech given in front of the curtain. It may precede a performance, but is more commonly presented at the end. Curtain speeches can be as mundane as announcing an understudy's per-formance, as practical as advising the audience of traffic difficulties, or as significant as informing the audience of the death of a director.

Customs

Customs are duties, tolls, or taxes imposed by the government on transactions across its borders. "Customs" is also the agency which administers the laws regulating these transactions.

Customs works in two directions, import as well as export. If an object being shipped out of the country will ultimately be returned—for example, costumes on loan to a museum or another theater company—this should be noted on the export declaration so that the customs officials will permit the item back into the country duty-free as "American goods returned."

If you are the recipient of a shipment from another country, you will have to clear it through customs. It is necessary to have the bill of lading, invoices, and other documents to bring the shipment into the United States. This is all a very specialized kind of activity, and most people who only occasionally do this sort of thing find that the services of a specialist are worth the cost in the time and aggravation you save. Freight forwarders who specialize in overseas shipments can handle the whole export operation. To clear an incoming shipment through customs, a *customshouse broker* is often the most knowledgeable expert to call. These specialists are listed in the telephone yellow pages. Freight forwarders can be found in cities which have major ports and international air terminals.

Works of "art" may enter the United States duty-free. There are a number of cases in which the courts have grappled with the definition of "art" for customs purposes. If the item is not functional, it is generally considered to be "art."

Even if the work is determined to be "art," however, it may still be subject to a customs duty if the purpose for which it is imported is commercial, as, for example, sets to be used in a production. The U.S. Customs Service will also prohibit the importation of works which are illegally exported from their country of origin and which have been identified by the United States Information Agency (USIA) as protected by a treaty between the U.S. and the country of origin.

There is a procedure whereby the U.S. Customs Service can prevent the importation into the U.S. of work infringing a copyright, trademark, or patent which is properly registered in the U.S.

For information about specific situations, the U.S. Customs Service can be consulted. The Service maintains offices at every point of entry into the United

States: border crossings, international air terminals, ports, and other locations. Their telephone number can be found in the white pages under U.S. Government, Treasury Department, Customs Service. Or you can write to the U.S. Customs Service (see Appendix B).

➤ *See also* Industry Practices and Customs, Intellectual Property

Damage Insurance

➤ *See* Property Insurance

Deal-Breaker

The term *deal-breaker* is slang for a provision which is deemed so important by one side and the other to a negotiation that lack of agreement will literally result in a deadlock. It is quite common for individuals in the entertainment industry to identify the issues which they consider to be deal-breakers and determine whether it is possible to reach a compromise on them or whether the arrangement is, in fact, never going to be made. Negotiating techniques differ from individual to individual. Some negotiators identify up-front all issues upon which agreement can be reached and save the the deal-breakers for last; still others initially identify the deal-breakers in order to determine whether it would be a waste of time to pursue negotiations.

Skilled negotiators will attempt to work out some acceptable middle ground to avoid allowing any issue to rise to the level of a deal-breaker, yet even the most skilled individual may not be able to negotiate a compromise when the parties are galvanized on a particular issue, such as artistic control, participation, or the like.

➤ *See also* Agent, Contract

Debt

A *debt* is an amount acknowledged as due and owing in the accounting records of a business and, as such, may be viewed as a charge to a particular entity, project, or account. It is important for performing arts organizations and businesses to have a clear understanding of and quantify the amount of organizational debt.

➤ *See also* Budget

Deductions

➤ *See* Accounting, Income Tax

Deferred Giving

Deferred giving is a method of structuring a charitable donation for the donor to obtain current tax benefits while delaying the date when the actual gift is made. This would occur only in a situation involving a (501)(c)(3) organization, since it is only donations to this kind of organization which are qualified tax deductions. If a donor provides a qualified charitable institution with money or property, the donor may be entitled to take a tax deduction for the present value of that future interest, even though the actual gift will not take place until sometime later. Thus, an individual may reserve the right to live in a house during his or her lifetime and provide that, on death, the title shall vest in the designated charity. Another example of deferred giving can occur when a individual lends an item to a qualified charity for a prescribed period and provides that the legal title will vest in the charity at the end of that time. This type of arrangement would be made in order to accord the donor maximum tax benefits by spreading donations over a period.

There are more complex forms of deferred giving which allow individuals to realize present deductions while controlling the disposition of the donation money or property. A donor could donate money to a representative with the express understanding that the representative would follow the donor's instructions in placing the funds in charitable hands sometime in the future. In this situation, the donor would be entitled to a present deduction for the full value of the money placed in the representative's hands even though the representative may delay giving some or all of the funds to the specified charity until the donor identifies the beneficiary or specifies the portion of the funds to be given. These arrangements are quite sophisticated and involve a great deal of tax and business planning. Individuals or institutions desiring to take advantage of these tax plays should consult with experienced tax lawyers or accountants.

➤ *See also* Contract, (501)(c)(3), Tax

Deficit

A *deficit* occurs when expenses exceed income. Start-up businesses often initially operate at a deficit. In the long run, this is something to be avoided.

Deficit is also used to describe any other shortage. For example, if your books show fifty costumes in your inventory, but there are only forty-eight in storage, your inventory shows a deficit. Regrettably, the performing arts business is replete with examples of deficits. It is quite common for orchestras or theater and dance companies to operate "in the red," relying on grant monies and charitable donations to reduce the deficit. In recent years, merchandising has been attempted as a means of generating additional revenues to fill the void. For some, this has worked well, but it is by no means a universal solution. In fact, merchandising start-up costs may drive the company even further into debt.

➤ *See also* Budget, Debt

Deposit

This word has several meanings for people engaged in the performing arts and entertainment business.

1. Making a payment, known as a *deposit* in order to reserve a work for performance at a future time. Deposits may or may not be refundable in full, depending upon the terms of the agreement. The parties may also establish the size of the deposit, although this is usually dictated by the licensor. As a practical matter, however, the amount of deposit will usually relate to the royalty to be paid.

2. Putting money in the bank, either by cash or check. There are two major types of bank deposits: demand and time. A *demand deposit* is one where you can withdraw your money at any time, as with most savings and checking accounts. A *time deposit* is a deposit for a fixed period of time, usually not less than six months. Time deposits include, among others, certificates of deposit and certain accounts from which money may be withdrawn only after the depositor gives the required notice of intent to withdraw. Most time deposit agreements include penalties for early withdrawal.

3. Complying with the registration requirements of the copyright law. The copyright statute requires a copyright owner to *deposit* copies of copyrighted works with the Library of Congress within three months of first publication. This deposit requirement is separate from the registration of the copyright, though the Copyright Office has stated that, if the deposit is not accompanied by an application and registration fee, an additional deposit must accompany the application for registration.

➤ *See also* Banks, Copyright, Credit

Depreciation

When you make a capital investment, such as buying a building or a piece of equipment, the assumption is that it will last a number of years. This expenditure is part of the cost of doing business and, thus, may be subtracted from gross income, along with other deductions, for purposes of determining taxable income. Since a capital investment is, in reality, however, a conversion of one type of asset (cash) into another (equipment, building, etc.), it is not realistic (nor do the tax laws permit) for you to deduct the total cost of such investments in one tax year. Instead, you are permitted to deduct a portion of the undepreciated cost (your adjusted basis) each year you use the property in business. This corresponds, in theory, to the actual diminution in value of the property as it wears out.

Depreciation is the method used to determine what portion of capital investments you can deduct from your gross income as a business expense each year. The tax laws provide for a method of depreciation known as the *modified accelerated cost recovery system* (MACRS). Under MACRS, every fixed asset is assigned to one of several property classes based on its *class life,* its expected useful life. The property classes are: three-, five-, seven-, ten-, fifteen-, and twenty-year property. In addition, most real property is classified as residential, rental, or nonresidential real property.

In calculating depreciation, it is customary to determine the *salvage value,* if any, of the asset; that is, what the asset is likely to be worth when it is no longer used in the business. If the asset is ultimately sold for an amount which exceeds that salvage value (adjusted value), then it is necessary to "recapture" the depreciation; in other words, to recognize the gain on the sale of the asset; that is, the difference between the sale price and the salvage value. The rules on recapture also apply if the asset is sold before it is fully depreciated.

In theory, two methods of calculating depreciation are used:

1. *Straight Line*. The value of an item is reduced by a fixed dollar amount

each year. For example, if a lighting system costing $50,000 is expected to last ten years, it will be depreciated by the fixed amount of $5,000 per year ($50,000 ÷ 10 years). After one year, the system has a remaining undepreciated (book) value of $45,000; after two years, $40,000; and so on, until, after ten years, the system is fully depreciated and thus has, theoretically, no remaining value (its adjusted basis is zero).

2. *Declining balance.* The value of an item is reduced by a fixed percentage each year. For example, the $50,000 lighting system with an expected life of ten years would be depreciated at the fixed percentage rate of either 15 or 20 percent per year (either are permissible under the tax laws); we shall assume 20 percent. The depreciation of the system would be $10,000 for the first year. For the second year, the adjusted basis is, therefore, $40,000 and the depreciation would be $8,000. For the third year, the adjusted basis of the system would be $32,000, which would be depreciated by an amount equal to $6,400, and so on. These calculations are arrived at by taking 20 percent of the adjusted basis. Note that, under this method, the remaining value never reaches zero, since each year's depreciation is only 20 percent of the remaining value of the item.

In practice, MACRS specifies a method that is either a modification or combination of the classic straight-line and declining balance methods. For property in the three-, five-, seven-, or ten-year class, you use the double (200 percent) declining balance method over three, five, seven, or ten years and the half-year convention. For property in the fifteen- or twenty-year class, you use the 150 percent declining balance method and the half-year convention. In other words, the classic fixed percentage is either doubled (200 percent) or multiplied by 1.5 (150 percent) to determine each year's depreciation.

MACRS also specifies another modification for these classes of property, whereby you change to the straight-line method for the first tax year for which that method, when applied to the adjusted basis at the beginning of the year, will yield a larger deduction than the declining balance method.

The half-year convention assumes that a given item of depreciable property was placed in service at the midpoint of the year (July 1, if your tax year is the calendar year), regardless of when it was actually placed in service. Consequently, the first year's depreciation is just half what the declining balance method would otherwise determine. Another consequence is that the full depreciation and corresponding tax deductibility for an item actually span a period that is one tax year longer than the class life of the item, with a partial deduction in both the first and last years.

When a fixed asset has both a business use and a personal use, for example, a building which houses a playwright's residence and office, or a vehicle which is used for family as well as business purposes, only that portion of the depreciation attributable to the business purpose can be deducted as a business expense. Owners of residential property should be particularly cautious when characterizing a portion of the property as being used for business. When the residence is sold and a replacement of greater value is purchased within two years, then no tax is due on any profit from the residential portion, though the business property sale is taxable. Home-office deductions are particularly vulnerable to IRS audits and you should consult with your tax adviser before taking such a deduction. Nonbusiness property is never depreciable for tax purposes.

If business property other than residential rental and nonresidential real property is sold for a price which exceeds its book value, any such gain must be claimed as ordinary income to the extent of depreciation previously allowed on that property.

Depreciation not only helps you more accurately calculate your cost of doing business, but also establishes the value of your fixed assets at any given time. Note, however, that different methods of depreciation may be appropriate for the same asset, one for purposes of business valuation, credit worthiness, personal net worth, etc., and a different method for tax purposes.

➤ *See also* Accounting, Appreciation, Equipment, Tax

Design Patent

➤ *See* Patent

Direct Mail

A method of advertising which uses the mails to reach the public, rather than using such media as newspapers, magazines, radio, or television, *Direct mail* is customarily sent to individuals on selective lists, such as season ticket holders, patrons, or the like. One possible disadvantage is the cost, both in terms of time and money. Theater and dance companies and symphonies commonly use season flyers, which are a form of direct mail.

➤ *See also* Advertising, Mailing Lists, Promotion

Director

The *director* is the person responsible for placing actors, interfacing music, and generally orchestrating a production. Today, directors are considered the essential conductor of any performance, yet this role is a comparatively recent one in theater history. It was not until the 1920s that directors who are not otherwise involved in a production became commonplace and, by the mid-1940s, universal. Interestingly enough, the term *producer* is used in British theater to define the role played by the directors in the United States. A *stage director* is the person who coordinates the performance and should be distinguished from, for example, a *managing director,* who is involved with the business elements of a production company.

> ➤ *See also* Agent, Box Office, Callback, Casting Director, Dress Rehearsal, Lighting Designer, Manager, Music Director, One-Night Stand, Producer, Stage Manager

Disability Income Insurance

A serious illness or accident can spell economic disaster for a performer, especially if he or she is not eligible for unemployment benefits and has no source of income other than his or her craft. While medical insurance may cover the cost of treatment, there is no provision for the loss of income. A permanent disability will likely entitle the artist covered by Social Security to certain minimum payments from that agency.

A producer or director in a successful enterprise who has partners or employees may continue to receive income even while disabled, though this puts a burden on the business. *Disability income insurance* can be a wise investment. It allows you to choose a specific weekly or monthly income for the duration of the disability or for a specified period of time. Premiums are based on the type and amount of coverage requested. Savings in premiums can be effected with a deductible clause, which provides that no benefits are paid during the first months of a disability. Most people can make it through a short disability, and the savings are worth the deductible. Disability income insurance generally cannot be bought to pay out more than 60 percent of normal income. This insurance may be obtained through certain cooperatives or performers' organizations, such as Equity.

> ➤ *See also* Cooperatives, Group Insurance, Insurance

Discounts

A *discount* is a legitimate reduction in price, based on some stated reason and deducted before payment is made. A common discount in the entertainment industry is the discount allowed when a patron subscribes to a full season's tickets. For example, if the regular ticket price is twenty-five dollars and the patron subscribes to all five season shows, he or she pay be permitted to pay only one hundred dollars.

➤ *See also* Cooperatives, Tickets

Disparagement

Disparagement is sometimes referred to as *trade libel* and is a *prima facie* tort, that is, a civil wrong. It occurs when one, without justification, disparages the work of another. This could be excessive and unjustified criticism of a living playwright's work, though mere adverse criticism would not normally be considered disparagement. A theater critic has extraordinary latitude when critiquing work. If, however, the statements are made for purposes other than comment or criticism—as, for example, when trying to force a show to close—the words may be actionable.

➤ *See also Droit Morale*

Donations

➤ *See* Charitable Contributions

Dramaturg

Taken from the German, the term *dramaturg* refers to the person responsible for the literary aspects of a theater company's activities or of a particular production. His or her duties may include script reading and selection, editing the program, and adaptation of text. The equivalent English term is *literary manager.*

Dress Rehearsal

A *dress rehearsal* is, as the name suggests, a rehearsal in full costume. It is the last chance to fine-tune the technical aspects of a production before it is presented to a paying audience. Customarily, special friends of the cast, crew or company, may be permitted to attend dress rehearsals, and certain members of the press may be allowed to preview the production. There may be one or more dress rehearsals, depending upon the needs of the production or the desires of the company.

➤ *See also* Director

Droit Morale

Droit morale recognizes that a work of art is an extension of its creator. It is a right of personality which attaches to the work. *Droit morale* originated in France, has now been adopted by eighty-one countries, and is a part of the Berne Copyright Convention. The European *droit morale* contains a number of elements. It includes protection of:

   a. The right to create or to refrain from creating;

   b. The right to decide when a work is completed and whether it should be published or performed;

   c. The right to withdraw a previously published work, provided that the withdrawal may be subject to the creator making a required payment;

   d. The right to require name attribution, including the right to prevent the use of a creator's name in some circumstances;

   e. The right to require that integrity of all the work be preserved; and

   f. The right to respond to excessive criticism.

Early American cases stated emphatically that the United States did not endorse the *droit morale,* yet there were some comparable rights found in the federal copyright and trademark laws, and state unfair competition laws. Thus, under U.S. copyright law, an artist is granted the exclusive right to publicly perform his or her creation and, therefore, the right to refrain from permitting such a performance. Trademark law grants the trademark owner the right to enjoin the use of any name, symbol, or logo which is likely to cause confusion in the marketplace. Since the copyright law grants the copyright owner the exclusive right to prepare derivative works, then an unauthorized alteration of the copyrighted work would be a violation of this right. For example, the performance rights to a recent production of *The Fantasticks* were pulled after it was discovered that the producers had added two characters to the play.

Art advocates recognized the importance of *droit morale* and realized that the American counterparts had some limitations. They, therefore, worked diligently for the U.S. to embrace the European *droit morale.* In 1990, Congress added the Visual Artists Rights Act ("VARA") to the U.S. copyright law. While VARA is not as inclusive as the European *droit morale,* it is still a major step forward and now provides some American visual artists, such as set designers, many of the benefits previously available to their European counterparts. VARA expressly excludes audiovisual works, such as motion pictures, from its protection.

Members of the entertainment industry desiring greater protection than

VARA grants may obtain it by contract. Many established members of the entertainment community, including film directors, have used contracts containing extensive protection for their works as well as their names. Unrecognized individuals in the entertainment community will likely find it more difficult to negotiate for contractual moral rights protection.

➤ *See also* Berne Copyright Convention, Copyright, Trademark

Education

Apprenticing in the entertainment industry dates back hundreds of years, and is still in use at many institutions.

Formal education in the entertainment arts is a fairly recent phenomenon. Many colleges and universities have degree programs in theater arts; in addition, there are a host of professional training institutions. It must be noted, however, that a formal education does not guarantee success for a performer (though private study may garner a performer more audition opportunities and a network of contacts). Formal training may, however, help the technician in developing an understanding of stagecraft, design, and the like.

A major gap in entertainment education is business education. While several universities have incorporated classes on business subjects of special concern to entertainers into their curricula, many have not. Workshops have begun to appear here and there at which experts discuss such subjects as taxes, bookkeeping, legal affairs, and other problems which confront members of the entertainment community. For example, the Oregon Arts Commission and other organizations periodically sponsor workshops which deal with subjects including entertainment law, marketing, auditioning, resume-writing, and the like.

Expenses for education necessary for *improvement* in your field are usually tax-deductible as business expenses. This can include the purchase of books—such as this one, and attendance at seminars and workshops (travel included), as well as formal education. Your educational expenses are tax-deductible within some guidelines if you are already working as a professional in the entertainment industry and are merely enhancing your skill. Education expenses to qualify you to *become* an entertainment professional, however, are not deductible.

➤ *See also* Apprentice, Grants

E-Mail

Electronic mail has become another communication tool. Everyone, from entertainers and theater companies to the general audience at large, may have e-mail capabilities. Users of office computers which are linked by networks can communicate by e-mail. Individual or business computers with modem capabilities are used as communication vehicles and receptors for external e-mail transmissions. Subscription services such as America Online, Compu-Serve and Prodigy are used to facilitate retention of e-mail messages. The technology is in flux and its application is expanding.

E-mail communications may be less expensive than traditional long distance telephone calls or faxes. There are, however, numerous security questions regarding e-mail communications. Skilled hackers may be able to gain access into internal e-mail systems and even intercept internal or external e-mail communications in transmission. Several companies have been attempting to develop security systems for e-mail, and the technology is rapidly expanding. There are also legal ramifications relating to e-mail.

➤ *See also* Computers, Internet, Telephone

Employees

When someone works for you, it is important to determine whether that person is an *employee* or a so-called *independent contractor.* This is because employers are obligated to comply with various state and federal laws, such as tax, labor, Social Security, workers' compensation, and the like. Independent contractors, and not the persons with whom they contract, are primarily responsible for complying with these laws for themselves and their employees. Theater companies and other entertainment businesses often deem their box office attendants, house managers, and the like to be independent contractors so that the employer is not liable for payroll withholding and employee benefit packages.

The label you attach to the worker is not conclusive, nor is the fact that the worker is full- or part-time, permanent or temporary. The labor laws, both national and state, make no distinction between payment in wages or commissions, whether the employees are paid by the hour or by the job, or even necessarily where the work is done. The U.S. Department of Labor defines the term *employee* as it relates to the enforcement of labor laws as follows:

> Generally the relationship of employer and employee exists when the person for whom services are performed has the right to control and direct the individual who performs the services, not only as to the result to be accomplished by the work, but also as to the details and means by which the result is accomplished. That is, an employee is subject to the will and control of the employer not only as to what shall be done but how it shall be done. In this connection, it is not necessary that the employer actually direct or control the manner in which the services are performed; it is sufficient if he has the right to do so.
>
> The right to discharge is also an important factor indicating that the person possessing that right is an employer. Other factors characteristic of an employer, but not necessarily present in every case, are the furnishing of tools and a place to work to the individual who performs the services.
>
> In general, if an individual is subject to the control or direction of another merely as to the result to be accomplished and not as to the means and methods for accomplishing the result, he is not an employee.

The Labor Department makes it clear that it doesn't matter what you call the worker: *employee, partner, salesperson, agent, independent contractor,* or whatever. If the relationship meets the definition given above, then the worker is legally an employee.

Two examples: If you hire a set designer to create a stage set, you are purchasing the result. How he or she does the work, what tools are used, where supplies are purchased, and so forth are the designer's decision, not yours. The designer is, therefore, not an employee.

On the other hand, if you hire a carpenter to assist you in building a set, and you buy the materials, you direct the specific work to be done, and you determine when he or she should come to work and go to lunch, then you have an employee.

In the case of a business entity like a corporation or limited liability company, the business entity is the employer, and everyone who works for it is an employee. That even includes you, the owner, if you work for the company and draw a salary. The size of a paycheck does not determine whether an employer-employee relationship exists.

Some ticklish situations have arisen in the case of stage directors, musicians, and actors, where the Labor Department and some taxing authorities have determined that an employer-employee relationship exists, regardless of a contract which usually designates the actor as an independent contractor. As an employer, it is important to keep abreast of the constantly changing labor and tax laws. Aside from tax and salary considerations, which are discussed elsewhere in this text, both federal and most state legislation expressly prohibit the employment of children under fourteen, regulate employment of children to age eighteen in certain types of occupations, and prohibit discrimination in hiring, training, promotion, or compensation, based on race, nationality, sex, age, disability, or other conditions not related specifically to the objective requirements of the job, known as *bona fide occupational qualifications.*

When you first become an employer, it is necessary to obtain an Employer Identification Number from the Internal Revenue Service and, in some states, a separate state Employer Identification Number. This number will then appear on all forms, tax payments, and other documents you file as an employer. It is advisable to obtain the services of an accountant or bookkeeper so that tax payments are made properly and on time, and payroll records and other books are kept in proper order. Be sure to consult your state labor department for applicable rules and regulations which go into effect the minute you put the first employee on the payroll.

Aside from complying with all the rules and regulations, it is important to select the right employees. The first consideration is where to look. This depends to a great extent on what you're looking for. If you want an intern, a local college may be the best place to look. If you're looking for box office personnel, a classified ad in the local newspaper may be best. It is surprising how many employers rush headlong into hiring someone without checking his or her credentials. The owner-managers of most small companies would not think of buying a piece of equipment until they had evaluated it systematically. They want to be sure that the machine meets specifications, can help pay for itself, and will last for a reasonable length of time. However, when selecting personnel to operate the equipment, some owner-managers use no system. Little, if any, time and energy are spent trying to match the applicant to the job. The result is waste. In the long run, mistakes in selecting employees may cost far more than the loss caused by selecting the wrong equipment.

It is, therefore, prudent to take these four steps:

1. Create a detailed job description and determine exactly what qualifications, experience, and attitudes you are seeking;
2. Interview a number of applicants to determine how they meet those standards;
3. Check applicants' references, if any, especially if they're going to handle money or if you have to leave them alone in your box office or scene shop;
4. Once you've hired someone, establish a probationary period, perhaps four weeks, and evaluate your decision during that time.

The first few weeks are critical. Any new employee, no matter how experienced, will need a little time to learn how to function effectively in a new situation, working with unfamiliar people and under differing circumstances. As an employer, it pays to keep a watchful eye on new employees to see how well they fit in and how well they perform. You may not get top performance the first few weeks because the new employee is learning your business. If you decide you've made a mistake, don't compound it by wasting more time and money. Find someone else.

For most employers, the only thing more difficult than hiring is firing. After all, you're holding someone else's livelihood in your hands. Try to make it gentle. Don't fire someone in the presence of others. During the probationary period, dismissal notice or severance pay is not necessary. If someone has been on your payroll for some time, however, giving two weeks' notice is common, just as you would want two weeks' notice when someone quits. Many employers prefer to give a discharged employee two weeks' pay instead of two weeks notice to avoid having a disgruntled employee around.

An employee may legally be fired for a proper reason, *e.g.*, theft or incompetence; or for no reason at all. It is unlawful, however, to fire a person for the wrong reason, *e.g.*, an employee's pregnancy, "whistleblowing," or other illegal discrimination.

Finally, be certain that all employees understand your business' rules and regulations, and that you uphold them equitably. It is not fair to allow one employee to get away with tardiness when you require others to be prompt. It is also wrong to penalize or even discharge employees for not observing rules you never told them about. Changing the rules midstream without giving employees an opportunity to reorient themselves is also poor practice. If you're going to change the working hours, for example, give sufficient notice; don't just tell everyone to show up half an hour earlier starting tomorrow. If at all possible, notify employees of anticipated overtime. How you treat your employees has a significant effect on how effectively and enthusiastically they work for you and that, in turn, has an effect on your business. Occasionally ask yourself whether *you* would want to work for a boss like you.

> ➤ *See also* Apprentice, Contract, Cooperatives, Minimum Wage, Unemployment Insurance, Union, Visa, Wages, Withholding Tax, Workers' Compensation

Employer Identification Number

> ➤ *See* Employees, Withholding Tax

Endorsement

Endorsement is the technical legal term used to define the act of signing the back of a check so that it can be cashed or deposited. The endorsement should be exactly the same as the payee on the face of the check. If that is different from the name you use on your bank account, sign it twice: first as it appears on the face of the check, then as it appears on your account. For example, if you receive a check made out to Entertainment Extravaganza but your account is under the name Arthur Smith, endorse the check first as Entertainment Extravaganza, then as Arthur Smith.

If you accept a check made out to someone else (a *two-party check*), the same principle applies. First have the other person endorse the check, then add your endorsement. If you don't know the person from whom you are accepting such a check, be sure you see satisfactory identification, preferably a driver's license or other photo identification, as well as a credit card or other document bearing a signature for comparison. If permitted in your state, note the document number on the check, as well as the person's address so you can find him or her if the check bounces. Try not to accept two-party checks.

Never endorse a check and then leave it lying around. If it is lost or stolen, it can easily be cashed by someone adding a second endorsement. Any check which is to be deposited, and any check on which you are the second endorser, should have the words "for deposit only" and your bank account number written right under your endorsement. That way it cannot be cashed.

The endorsement (reverse) side of the check can also specify other restrictions, such as making the check payable upon delivery of goods or when a certain service has been performed. When the recipient of the check endorses it, he or she accepts those restrictions. It is not clear whether endorsing a check which states that it is "payment in full" is binding when the payment is, in fact, for less than the full amount due, and there is conflicting case law. For this reason, you should either insist upon a new check or, at the very least, endorse the check "with reservation." It is also not clear whether a check endorsement will serve as a "writing" for purposes of assigning a copyright. There is some authority suggesting that it will, but the matter has not been resolved by the courts.

➤ *See also* Banks, Cancelled Check, Checking Account, Collection Problems, Copyright

Endowment

The term *endowment* refers to a fund established for a specific purpose in a nonprofit organization. Typically, endowments are *unrestricted,* meaning that the funds may be used for any legitimate purpose of the organization in fulfilling its charitable mission. Endowments are occasionally restricted to a specific project or the fulfillment of a specific objective, such as, for example, a particular production, purchase of real property, or the like. Endowments may also be for the purpose of funding a particular position, though this more commonly occurs in the academic context, when a fund is raised for the purpose of "endowing a chair." Some universities have endowed chairs specifically for theater arts, dance, or music.

➤ *See also* 501(c)(3), Nonprofit Organization

Entertainment Tax

An *entertainment tax* is typically imposed by a governmental entity such as city, county, or state on the price of tickets to arts events. The tax will likely be a percentage of the ticket price. It is purely local and the amount and applicability is governed by the laws of the jurisdiction imposing the tax. When applicable, the laws impose the obligation on the ticket seller for collection and remittance to the governmental body.

➤ *See also* Tax

Entr'acte

This literally means "between the acts" and describes the musical presentation which occurs between any two acts of a performance. It is an interlude intended both to entertain the audience and provide a transition into the next part of the presentation.

Equipment

When you go into business, it is essential to determine your needs and your financial capability to meet those needs. This should be done in conjunction with preparation of your business plan.

For any of a variety of reasons, you may decide whether to buy or lease *equipment,* but be careful: A used computer, for example, may not be compatible with the software you need. Further, you may not be able to afford an outright purchase of major equipment, or an outright purchase may not be warranted. For example, an arts company which leases performance space would typically not purchase a lighting or sound system.

Technical personnel may be required or allowed to provide their own tools; however, the contracting entity or employer should be careful to establish policies regarding responsibility for maintenance of such equipment and be aware of liability issues relating to its use.

Maintaining equipment is essential for the smooth operation of any business; breakdowns can be both costly and inconvenient. Since equipment is often a major expense, financing its purchase should be carefully evaluated. The best way, of course, is to plan ahead and save the money. That way you not only avoid paying interest on a loan, but the savings themselves earn interest. Don't save in a checking account; it usually pays lower interest than a savings account.

If you must finance the purchase out of future earnings, the best source is probably a bank loan. Shop around; interest rates and other conditions vary from institution to institution.

➤ *See also* Banks, Business Plan, Credit, Independent Contractor, Lease, Loans, Workers' Compensation Insurance

Equity

➤ *See* Financial Statement, Loans

Equity Production

The term *equity production* refers to a stage production which is subject to an Artists Equity contract.

➤ *See* Contract, Appendix A

Estate Planning

Determining what will happen to your assets after you die is known as *estate planning.* While everyone should have some sort of estate plan, even if only a simple will, it is more important for entertainers, writers, and composers, since the problems of posthumous disposition of rights in and to creative works can be quite complex. Writers, composers, choreographers, and the like should determine whether they wish to permit their work to be performed or modified after their death, and a person whose integrity, skill, and knowledge is respected should be identified as an *art* or *literary executor.* Arrangements should be made for an alternate in the event the named person is unable or unwilling to serve. This is an issue which is best addressed earlier rather than later. An experienced estate planning or intellectual property lawyer should be consulted.

Creators of entertainment arts must consider the disposition of the unpublished work in their estates. Should it be published, donated, destroyed, or retained as a collection honoring the decedent? All restrictions on post-humous disposition should be spelled out in a will or other instrument. The tax implications of the particular arrangement should also be considered. Since the date of one's death is usually impossible to predict, an estate plan should be prepared as promptly as possible and should be reviewed at least annually. Lawyers and accountants who are experienced in this area should be relied on to assist you in preparing an estate plan which is appropriate for your situation.

➤ *See also* Accountant, Income Tax—Personal, Lawyer, Posthumous

Estimated Tax

All income from which no payroll taxes are withheld is subject to *estimated tax* payments. Estimated tax payments on such income are due April 15, June 15, September 15, and January 15 for the preceding calendar quarters.

A Declaration of Estimated Tax (Form 1040ES) must be filed on or before April 15 of each year for the current calendar year and with each estimated payment. Estimated taxes must be paid even if some of your income is subject to withholding taxes. Such a combination situation is quite common among those in the the performing arts who earn part of their income from entertain-ment and the rest from traditional employment, for example, a music teacher who also plays in a symphony orchestra or an actor who also drives a taxi.

The interest imposed for underpayment of estimated taxes is based on a short-term federal rate plus 3 percent. This rate, published by the I.R.S., is known as the Applicable Federal Rate. There are two ways to avoid paying the interest charge:

1. Pay the same quarterly estimated tax this year as last, less any payroll

taxes that may have been deducted from wages or salary if you held a job this year but not last year;

2. If you pay lower estimated taxes because you expect your income to be less this year than last, your total estimated tax payments must be at least 90 percent of your final tax obligation, paid on an even quarterly basis. The balance of 10 percent or less is payable without penalty when you file the next tax return by April 15. Beginning in 1994, taxpayers with an adjusted gross income in excess of $150,000 may avoid a penalty if they pay an estimated tax at least equal to 110 percent of the prior year's tax.

Suppose things change midstream. Suppose you unexpectedly sign a contract with a large payment after you filed your estimated tax return last April and you are, therefore, likely to have more income than at first expected. In that case, you amend your return when the next estimated payment is due and increase those payments.

The reverse is also true if your self-employed income falls below what you had expected. This can happen if you switch from self-employment to a salaried job in the middle of the year, or if an illness puts you out of commission for an extended period. In that case, you may reduce your quarterly payments by amending your return.

Be careful, though, to avoid estimating too low. If your payments drop below 90 percent of what is due in any quarter, you'll owe the interest on the shortage. If they fall far below, you may be subject to extra penalties for willful failure to pay the proper estimated tax.

If you have had any income subject to withholding, the amount withheld is figured into the 90 percent determination. Here's what that means in practical terms. If, for example, from your self-employed income you owed $1,000 in estimated taxes, and your salary was subject to $1,300 in withholding taxes, your total tax obligation would be $2,300. Let's assume you paid only $800 (80 percent) of the $1,000 estimated taxes. That would seem to fall below the 90 percent requirement. However, 90 percent of the $2,300 total is $2,070. The withholding tax payment ($1,300) and the estimated tax payment ($800) total $2,100, which is above the $2,070 requirement. In this example, you're safe.

The Internal Revenue Service also assumes that withholding taxes, even if calculated for earnings of only part of the year, are spread over the entire year to meet the even quarterly payment rule.

Social Security taxes on self-employed income are required to be included in the estimated tax declaration and quarterly payments.

➤ *See also* Income Tax—Business, Income Tax—Personal, Social Security, Tax, Withholding Tax

Extras

Extra is a term most frequently used in the motion picture industry, though extras may also be involved in television or live theater as well. The terms refers to an extra person or people who do not have major roles but who are used in crowds or to otherwise populate a scene. They may or may not be paid, though it is a good idea to have a contract with the extra, regardless of payment. Extras are frequently found by advertising in local newspapers and through agents. Entertainment professionals are often willing serve as extras since it gives them an opportunity to work in the industry and add credits to their resumes. It also provides nonprofessionals with an opportunity to be involved in the entertainment industry and, often, to be around celebrities.

Because the pay is usually low (if any at all), there are few actors who make a career out of being an extra. Still, it should be noted that extra work may, under some circumstances, have an impact on an actor's SAG or AFTRA eligibility. Actors should check with their local union office for details.

➤ *See also* Agent, Contract, Release, Appendix A

Fees

Payments for such professional services as those of lawyers, accountants, and doctors are known as *fees,* as distinguished from wages and salaries. If an entertainer serves as a consultant or speaker, payment for that service is also known as a *fee,* even if it is called an *honorarium.* Other payments called fees include admissions to entertainment or sports events, art shows, some educational activities (such as seminars), official documents, licenses, registrations, and charges established by law for the services of a public official, such as a notary public. Independent contractors, such as actors, directors, and the like, are also paid fees.

➤ *See also* Wages

Financial Management

➤ *See* Accounting, Banks, Budget, Financial Statement, Gross, Investment, Loans, Tax

Financial Statement

The term *financial statement* commonly includes three types of reports: the income statement, balance sheet, and statement of cash flow. The income statement reports the income and expenses of the business during the reporting period. The balance sheet reports the assets, liabilities and equity at the end of the period. The two reports complement each other, because the income statement helps to indicate how the business got to where the balance sheet says it is.

LEDGERS AND JOURNALS

Ledgers and journals are accounting records in which the various financial transactions of a business are recorded. The journal is used to keep the day-to-day records. Many businesses keep several journals: one in which to list sales, one for cash receipts, one for payroll, one for accounts receivable, and so forth. While some businesses may keep several subsidiary ledgers for different purposes, they will always have a general ledger. An entertainment business must have a general ledger. The information recorded in the general ledger is based on the entries in the journals, and is listed side by side in columns marked *debit* and *credit,* according to the nature, type, or source of the transaction.

INCOME STATEMENT

This summary of the income and expenses during a given period is also known as a *profit-and-loss statement* or *P&L.* The most common reporting period is monthly. The income statement lists the total income and the total costs of running the business. The difference is known as *gross profit* (or *gross loss*). Gross profit is determined by deducting the cost of that which is sold from the gross sales. Operating expenses, sales costs, and taxes are deducted from the gross profit to determine the net profit (or net loss).

Entries commonly found on an income statement include sales/receipts, income, business expenses, overhead, profit, and net profit, although all of these may not appear and others not listed here may be appropriate. An examination of the income statement and a comparison with income statements of previous periods can be helpful in pinpointing improvements or shortcomings in specific areas of income and expense. Evaluating the income statement and comparing it to a proposed budget is useful for predicting business growth and expenditures. It is also useful to compare current expenses with past expenses for comparable periods (*e.g.,* first calendar quarter).

Income, generally, is money, property, or anything of value from whatever source derived, commonly thought of as the financial gain resulting from business activity, investment, labor, personal service, or other source.

Expenses. Anything you pay out money for is an expense. If it is related to the entertainment business, it is a business expense. That includes salaries, taxes, insurance, rent, dues and subscriptions, travel expenses, and a great many other items. Business expenses are generally tax-deductible.

Overhead consists of all the operating costs that are not directly related to the production. The cost of equipment, costumes, labor (including your own) and the like, change in direct proportion to the scale of the production and number of productions. Overhead, however, remains fairly constant, even if nothing is produced. That's why overhead is also known as a *general* or *fixed expense.* Rent, insurance premiums, telephone bills, and utilities have to be paid every month, whether or not you are involved in a production. Overhead must be included in the formula you use to determine the cost of admission.

Profit. For accounting purposes, there are several categories of profit: *gross profit* (the sale of goods or services less the cost of producing the goods or services); *net profit* (total income less the cost of production and other expenses in running the entertainment business); *paper profits* (profits not yet realized, as represented, for example, by a production in rehearsal before the opening); and a number of others.

Most people are concerned only with net profit. Some people call it the "bottom line"—the last line in the financial statement which indicates what's ultimately left over for the business owner.

It is a common misconception that "the more tickets you sell, the more profit you'll make." To sell $3000 worth of tickets to a performance which costs $1000 to produce is usually more profitable than to sell $4000 worth of tickets to a performance which costs $2500 to produce. In the first case, you have $2000 above the cost of production; in the second, only $1500, even though sales dollars were higher.

Since profits are so directly tied to both sales and costs, any change in either of those factors affects the bottom line. Increasing sales can increase profits, as long as costs don't rise out of proportion. Profits can also be increased if costs are cut even if sales don't go up. Indeed, this is the part of the equation customarily focused on by business consultants. The ideal situation, of course, is to increase sales while reducing costs. An ongoing analysis of your entertainment business operations is essential for maximizing profit.

BALANCE SHEET

Unlike an income statement, which summarizes the income and expense activity over a given period, the balance sheet reflects the financial condition of a business at any given time. The balance sheet reports the assets (everything your business owns) and the liabilities (everything your business owes).

$$ASSETS = LIABILITIES + OWNERS' EQUITY$$

The owners' equity is the net worth of the business.

A balance sheet is prepared by an accountant and is used to inform the owners or stockholders of the condition of the business. It is also required with most applications for a bank loan. If the business is conducted in the form of a nonprofit corporation then there will not be any owners' equity.

Assets are all the things your business owns, but accountants give them a slightly more restricted meaning, namely all the things your business owns that can be measured in terms of money. Assets include real estate, personal property, costumes, cash in the bank, lighting and sound equipment, scripts and rights, and even the money others owe you. You may think that your business's own good name is its most valuable asset but, unless the business purchased it, neither it nor the goodwill associated with it can be carried on the books as an asset. From an accounting perspective, there is a whole host of assets. For entertainment businesses the following are the most common:

- *Fixed Assets*: Such items as real estate, personal property, costumes, sound and lighting equipment.
- *Liquid Assets*: Such items as bank accounts, accounts receivable, and tickets for future performances; in short, the kind of assets that can readily be turned into cash. The most liquid asset is cash itself.
- *Tangible Assets*: An asset which has physical properties. Equipment, tools, and costumes are all tangible assets.
- *Intangible Assets*: Assets which have value but are not tangible. These include intellectual property rights, subscriber lists, a business name, a unique process, or rights to a show or musical composition.
- *Accounts Receivable*: A balance due from a debtor on a current account. This includes short-term obligations such as installment credit payments and receipts from ticket sales. As these receivables "age" (or become past-due), they become less collectible. Banks and other lenders will rarely—if ever—lend money against receivables which are more than ninety days old.

Liabilities are what you owe others, in terms of money, goods, or services. Unpaid bills and mortgages are liabilities. So is the obligation to deliver a script which has been commissioned. Liabilities fall into two categories: *current* and *long-term.*

103

Current liabilities include all obligations that are due in the current fiscal year. Long-term liabilities are obligations that stretch over a number of years: a mortgage, a bank loan, or the payout on a piece of equipment such as a van.

Liabilities and assets appear together on the balance sheet. In a profitable business, assets are greater than liabilities. The difference represents profit plus the owner's equity in a business corporation. In this situation profit may be withdrawn by the owners.

Nonprofit corporations do not have owner's equity and profits may not be taken out of the business. They can, however, be used for the purpose of paying bonuses to certain employees who have performed exceptional tasks, so long as those bonuses are reasonable and customary in that kind of entertainment venture. These funds may also be used for purposes of expanding the nonprofit organization's projects.

Equity. The *value* of an owner's interest in a "for profit" business is called *equity.* This value is determined by subtracting the total liabilities of the business from its total assets. Equity is rarely equal to the owner's capital investment. In practical terms, the total equity of a business is equal to the liquidation value of the business. In the case of a mortgage, *equity* is used to describe the owner's (borrower's) share of the total value of the property. As the mortgage loan is paid off, the owner's equity increases, provided the value of the real estate does not decrease. Thus, if you buy a $100,000 building with $20,000 in cash and an $80,000 mortgage, your initial equity is $20,000. After you've paid off $4,000 of the principal, your equity has grown to $24,000 (plus any appreciation in the value of the building since the loan was initiated), and so forth, until finally your equity is 100 percent.

Dividend. In the literal sense, the dividing of profits. The most common dividends are those paid on the basis of stock ownership, insurance policies, and other investments. A dividend is the investor's share of the profits in proportion to the size of the investment. Dividends are generally paid on a regular basis: annually on insurance policies, quarterly on many stocks. Preferred stock will customarily have a fixed dividend which should be stated on the stock certificate, but dividends on common stock and insurance policies will vary from period to period according to the profits of the company. Dividends must be declared as income by the recipient for tax purposes; IRS Form 1099-DIV is required to be sent to the taxpayer by the payor.

> ➤ *See also* Accounting, Audit, Balance, Break-Even Point, Budget, Business Expenses, Business Plan, Capital, Cash Flow, Computers, Financial Management, Gross, Loans, Net, Petty Cash, Statement, Year-End

Fire Insurance

➤ *See* Fire Prevention, Insurance, Property Insurance

Fire Prevention

Few disasters are as tragic or as costly as a fire, and most such disasters can be prevented with proper attention to safety precautions. Consider not only that a fire can pose a serious threat to your life and the lives of those who live or work with you, but that it can also destroy your life's work, your prized possessions, your business records, and your means of earning a living. Moreover, fire is a special hazard in a performance space, where audience members are also at risk.

The following recommendations for safety in five major areas of fire danger are based on information from the National Fire Protection Association, which publishes electrical and fire codes, maintains statistics, and conducts investigations.

HAZARDS

Smoking Hazards. Smoking is one of the most common causes of fires, especially around vapors and dusty areas. Post *No Smoking* signs in potential danger areas, and be sure the signs are observed. It is common for offices and theaters to be designated smoke-free. If you must smoke, be sure to use an ashtray. Do not rest cigarettes on window sills, edges of a table, or other surfaces. Do not throw matches, cigarettes, or pipe dottle into waste baskets, even if you think the smoking matter is out.

Of all the fire hazards, those caused by smoking are the easiest to prevent. For stagehands who work with flammable materials, smoking while working is particularly dangerous. You should either designate a smoking area or permit smoking only outside of the work premises.

Electrical Hazards. Never hang electrical wiring over nails, around metal pipes, near heat or oil, across passageways, or run wiring across the floor. Frayed insulation, broken plugs, loose connections, and defective switches or outlets must be repaired or replaced promptly. Keep hot bulbs away from liquids and flammable materials. Overloading electrical equipment or bypassing the safe amperage of the fuse box creates a real fire danger. Never use electrical equipment near sinks or bathtubs. If a motor emits sparks or gets wet, it needs attention. A spark can cause a fire. The small amount saved on delay or skimping can easily become thousands of dollars of fire loss. If you must use electrical equipment near flammable liquids, gas, or dust, be sure it is designed for that purpose, *i.e.*, is explosion-proof, and that proper ventilation is maintained at all times. Electrical hazards are of particularly concern in stage and film productions, where the wiring for lights and other effects are often in close proximity to curtains, set pieces, and may even be under foot.

Cutting and Welding Hazards. All torch cutting and welding should be done in a safe place, away from flammable materials or explosives. Walls, ceilings, and floors can catch fire from flying sparks. It is always best to have a fire watcher on hand to extinguish flying sparks that land anywhere, including cracks or crevices. Don't allow workers to immediately walk away when they are through; examine the work area and stand watch for a while to be certain no sparks are smoldering anywhere. Use a fireproof apron to protect yourself and your clothing; use covers and shields to contain sparks.

Flammable Liquid Hazards. Don't ever allow flammable liquids to accumulate. Use them only outdoors or in a well-ventilated area. This is particularly true for painters and scene designers who commonly use a variety of flammable solvents. Clean up spilled liquids immediately, and keep only a small amount in a clearly-marked metal safety container (never glass) in your storage facility. Never use gasoline as a cleaning fluid, as it is among the most flammable liquids available. Don't take the chance. Gasoline is a fuel, not a cleaner. Keep flammable liquids away from all sources of flame or sparks (torches, heaters, candles, electric tools). Oil- or turpentine-soaked rags should be kept only in tightly-covered metal containers, if at all. Get rid of them as soon as you can.

Housekeeping Hazards. Neatness counts! If the work area is littered with cartons, scraps, and leftover materials, you're inviting a fire. Ditto with accumulations of chips, cuttings, oil drippings, dust, and other trash. Keep such debris in covered metal containers and dispose of it regularly and properly, recycling whenever possible. Don't let it accumulate.

Be sure that exit doors, stairways, and fire escapes are not blocked, and that the sprinkler system is in good working order. Ensure than all staff know the location of fire curtains and smoke traps and are instructed in their use. Establish a fire escape plan and have periodic fire drills. Be sure that theater personnel know the fire escape procedures. Make a fire safety fact sheet available (see Appendix B).

FIRE EXTINGUISHERS
Every commercial building and home should have one or more fire extinguishers, depending on the size of the premises and the potential type of

fire. Different types of fire require different types of fire extinguishers:

- TYPE A (water type) is used for ordinary combustible fires such as paper, cloth, wood, or trash;
- TYPE B (dry chemical or foam type) is used for flammable-liquid fires such as gasoline, paint, turpentine, lacquer, or oil;
- TYPE C (carbon dioxide type) is used for electrical-equipment fires, such as for motors or wiring;
- TYPE D (dry powder type) is used for combustible metal fires, such as certain metal chips, shavings, etc.;
- TYPE A-B-C (multipurpose chemical type) can be used for any of the various types of fire created by combustible materials, flammable liquid, or electrical equipment.

Never use a fire extinguisher on a fire for which it is not intended. Using TYPE A (water) on an electrical fire can cause an electric shock and may cause the fire to spread. Read the instructions on the fire extinguisher carefully. Be sure you know how to use it before you need it and be sure that the extinguisher is properly charged. Have the extinguisher inspected on a regular basis.

Place the fire extinguishers in strategic locations and be sure they are always easily accessible.

WHAT TO DO IF A FIRE STARTS

If you see smoke or fire, the *first* thing to do is to turn in a fire alarm. In the case of a fire occurring during a live performance, one person (usually the stage manager) should be designated to make an announcement to the audience to exit the theater calmly, and should direct that the fire curtain be dropped and smoke traps opened. Theater managers should be trained to orchestrate a calm and orderly evacuation in such an emergency. If the fire is small, such as in a wastebasket, fight it properly while you wait for the firemen; but stay low and be sure you have an escape route available. Those first few minutes are vital, but remember that personal safety is essential. There are many volatile and toxic substances present in the entertainment industry, in scenery and the like. If the fire grows and gets out of hand, get out fast! Start fire retardant procedures (sprinklers, sand traps) and close doors behind you to further retard the spread of the fire.

For information, fire standards, and statistics, contact the National Fire Prevention Association (see Appendix A).

➤ *See also* Insurance, Safety, Appendix A, Appendix B

First-Class Live Theatrical Production

For collective bargaining purposes, a particular type of live theatrical production with higher pay scales than for other types of live theatrical productions such as off-Broadway, regional theater, or stock theater productions. A *first-class production* is defined in one basic agreement as "a play (dramatic play, revue, musical, or a combination thereof) presented on the speaking stage under a Producer's management in a first-class theater, in a first-class manner with a first-class cast."

➤ *See also* Bus and Truck Rights

First Option

First option is a contractual term which provides that the owner or person controlling a property must first offer it to the holder of the option before the property may be offered to any other party. The terms of the option may be specific, such as requiring payment of a particular price, delineating a period of time within which the option must be exercised, etc., or the option may be very general. First options which are not well defined can present the parties with some problems; for example, if a playwright grants a backer the first option to produce a given work without specifying the terms of the arrangement, the backer could delay making any decision for so long a period as to make it impossible for the playwright to obtain any other arrangement. Similarly, the backer could agree to produce the work and the production could be so inferior as to render the property worthless or impair the playwright's reputation. For this reason, first options should be specifically defined in an agreement drafted by an attorney experienced in this area.

First options should be distinguished from *rights of first refusal.* This form of arrangment provides that, after an offer has been received by one who is legally able to accept it, that party must then notify the optionee and permit the optionee to meet or beat the offer. Here, too, specificity is important, since time of exercise, as well as other terms, will likely be important to the arrangement.

➤ *See also* Contract, Lawyer, Option, Prior Approval

501(c)(3)

501(c)(3) is actually the sub-section number of the Internal Revenue Code which provides for a certain type of tax-exempt organization. These organizations, which must be organized as public benefit, nonprofit corporations, are charities for purposes of tax-deductible charitable donations and are the organizations which may receive certain government and other grants. The state attorney general is typically charged with policing 501(c)(3) organizations which frequently must file annual reports with the AG's office.

This type of organization should be distinguished from an organization qualifying under section 501(c)(7), which does not entitle donors to write off charitable deductions and which may not be qualified to receive grant monies. 501(c)(7) organizations are traditionally created for the purpose of benefitting the organization's membership, rather than the general public.

501(c)(3) organizations may not legally compete with business organizations and still retain their tax-exempt status. This is because the charity would have an unfair competitive advantage over its commercial competitor and could charge less while still earning more. The Internal Revenue Service realizes that this unfair competitive advantage would undermine commerce and deprive the public of the benefits of legitimate competition. Accordingly, 501(c)(3) organizations which intend to engage in any form of commercial activity should first consult with an experienced attorney and determine whether the earnings will be subject to an unrelated business tax or are so great as to involuntarily convert the organization into a purely commercial venture. A possible method of segregating the profit-making activity from the charitable venture is to have a 501(c)(3) corporation engage in purely charitable ventures while wholly owning a business corporation which may legally conduct business activities and donate some of its profits to its charitable parent while paying taxes on the rest. If there is excess profit, as defined by the Internal Revenue Code, the business corporation could pay its nonprofit parent a dividend.

> ➤ *See also* Charitable Contributions, Corporation, Deferred Giving, Endowment, Nonprofit Organization, Public Service Announcement, Sponsorship, Tax

Fly Man

The term *fly man* (or *flyperson*) refers to the stagehand responsible for the raising and lowering of the set pieces known as flies. The position may or may not be subject to a union contract depending upon whether the production company is a union shop and whether the union in question covers this position.

> ➤ *See also* Rigger, Stagehand, Appendix A

Foreclosure

> ➤ *See* Collateral, Installment, Loans, Mortgage, Uniform Commercial Code

Franchise Tax

➤ *See* Income Tax—Business

Front of House Staff

This term refers to the house manager, box office staff, ushers, and other offstage personnel involved in the public side of a production.

➤ *See also* Appendix A

Government Activities

Dozens upon dozens of performing-arts-related activities are part of the programs of various federal and state government agencies and departments.

FEDERAL

Perhaps the best known of the federal programs are those of the National Endowment for the Arts (NEA). Although the NEA in recent years has received some criticism for some of its funding activities, its peforming-arts-related projects are important. While, generally, the NEA focuses its support on the organizational infrastructure of the arts, there are still some major programs available to individual entertainers. Categories for which fellowships are available are outlined in the NEA catalogs. (*See* National Endowment for the Arts.)

The activities of the Small Business Administration, while not specifically oriented toward the performing arts, have had an impact on their business actvities through the Administration's extensive series of publications on a wide range of business subjects. Regrettably, the loan program is unavailable to performing arts or entertainment businesses. (*See* Small Business Administration.)

Other government agencies involved in entertainment and the performing arts are the Department of Health and Human Services, Department of Education, Commerce Department, Interior Department, Department of Justice (through its Prison Arts Program), the armed forces, Smithsonian Institution, Tennessee Valley Authority, National Park Service, and the State Department (Art in the Embassies and cultural exchange programs).

Many of the programs do not deal with individual artists (the National Endowment for the Arts is the major exception), but are more involved with institutions and organizations.

STATE

All states and provinces and many municipalities have arts and humanities commissions or councils. The state organizations provide funds to entertainers and entertainment-related organizations for a variety of programs. In addition, many states and municipalities have both public and private advocacy programs or groups which, among other things, monitor legislation, assist entertainers and entertainment organizations with projects, and generally attempt to make entertainment more available to the general public. There are awards for significant contributions to the performing arts (for example, the President's Arts Awards, the Governor's Arts Awards in many states, and comparable municipal awards).

➤ *See also* Arts Councils, National Endowment for the Arts, National Endowment for the Humanities, Small Business Administration

Grants

A *grant* is a sum of money given to an individual, organization, or institution for a specific project which has a defined purpose. The major sources for grants are:

1. Government agencies such as the National Endowment for the Arts and Humanities and state arts and humanities councils or committees;
2. Private organizations or institutions, such as foundations;
3. The business community, such as major corporations.

Most grants are given for specific purposes. Some foundations, for example, specify that they will give grants for legal education only; some corporations support symphony orchestras, and so forth.

The largest single source for grants in the arts is the National Endowment for the Arts, which has a separate performing arts department. Its annual *Guide to Programs*, published in August, outlines in detail the eligibility requirements for various grants. A number of federal agencies, notably the Department of Education, also give grants for specific educational purposes.

The other major sources are state arts councils or arts and humanities councils or commissions. They can usually be located in the state capital. Both the size and the nature of grants vary from state to state. Most major cities have their own arts and humanities councils or commissions which generally have grant programs.

A major source of information about private funding is the *Foundation Directory* (see Appendix B). This volume is available in most major libraries.

Scholarships and fellowships for elementary and advanced university study are closely related to the concept of grants. The best approach is to decide which particular university offers the most suitable curriculum, and then inquire what scholarship aid is available at that institution. A good source for information is the *College Blue Book*, a multivolume reference work revised every two years. It includes supplements on fellowships, grants, and loans for study at both the undergraduate and graduate levels, and is cross-referenced by institution and by subject matter. It is available in most libraries.

Various agencies of state and federal government make some money available for scholarships, or underwrite student loans. Such programs are, of course, subject to fluctuations in the economy as well as the direction of the political winds which dictate the size of available budgets for such purposes. A good place to start looking for information is the Office of Student Financial Assistance (see Appendix A).

Every institution of higher learning also has its own student financial aid office. If you've already determined which institution you want to attend, consult with the financial aid office to find out what kind of scholarship, fellowship, grant, or loan assistance is available at that institution.

There are no prescribed general rules about how to apply for a grant, although most grant application forms outline in specific detail what type of information is required. Since a grant always has a purpose, the information the applicant furnishes must stress how the use of the funds will help accomplish the purpose of the grant.

Some granting agencies require the applicant to match the grant funds by a specified ratio. Most granting agencies are impressed by applicants whose match is in the form of real contributions of money or property, rather than so-called in-kind contributions. Applicants who have previously received grants are more likely to be successful in the future. Even previously unsuccessful applicants who continue to apply to the same agency, thereby establishing some familiarity, are also more likely to receive favorable consideration at some point. Some grants are one-time grants; others are so-called continuation grants, *i.e.*, they provide funds for a particular project for a specified number of years, provided that the grantee continues to meet the grantor's criteria. To be eligible for most grants, organizations must be nonprofit and tax-exempt; this restriction does not apply to individual entertainers.

> ➤ *See also* Arts Councils, Education, National Endowment for the Arts, National Endowment for the Humanities, Nonprofit Organization, Appendix A, Appendix B

Green Room

The *green room* is a space located outside the stage area where stage performers can congregate before, during, and after the performance. Most green rooms have an audio monitor and some even have a video monitor, so that actors can be prepared for their entrances. In Europe, it may also serve as a meeting place for performers and audience members. Traditionally painted green, the room may now be any color.

Grip

The term *grip* refers to the stagehand responsible for the placing and removing of set pieces, flats, and the like. This term may be familiar to moviegoers who will see references to *key* and *dolly grips* in the closing credits. These positions are frequently subject to union contracts.

> ➤ *See also* Appendix A

Gross

The word *gross* has at least four common meanings:
1. In poor taste, unrefined, ugly, coarse, garish;
2. 12 dozen, 144 pieces;
3. Big or bulky; excessively fat; and
4. As applied to financial statements, indicating that deductions have not been taken. For example, *gross income* is the total amount of money, property, or anything of value received from any source before any deductions are taken. This is distinguished from *gross profit,* which is the amount of profit left after certain expenses are deducted from gross income and before deducting applicable taxes to arrive at *net profit.*

Gross is distinguished from *net,* which is essentially gross less specific deductions.

When including these terms in a contract, care must taken to define with particularity the items which shall be deducted from gross to arrive at net. The definitional criteria has been the subject of numerous lawsuits, including the battle between Art Buchwald and Eddie Murphy over the extraordinary definition of *net* in determining the compensation due Mr. Buchwald for his contribution to the film *Coming to America*. The definition of *net* in contracts can run for many pages. It is sometimes said that, in the entertainment industry, if it is not specifically defined, the term *net* equals zero.

Although the Buchwald case arose in the context of the film industry, the problem is endemic. It occurs in live theater, music, book publishing, and the like. In fact, virtually every time the word *net* appears in a contract, an experienced attorney should be consulted in order to determine what the actual meaning of the term is in that context.

➤ *See also* Financial Statement, Net, Wages

Group Insurance

Life, accidental death, health and major medical, dental, and disability income insurance policies can be obtained at comparatively lower rates when a single policy is issued to a group which pays one premium to the insurance company on behalf of enrolled members. A group can be formed by a business firm, an organization of entertainers, or any similar organized entity. Most such policies require that the group consists of at least three members, and that a certain percentage of all members participate in the group policy. Premiums can be paid by the employer or organization, or they can be paid by the members through the employer or the organization. Many trade unions, including those in the entertainment industry, have group insurance plans available to their members.

Most major insurance companies offer group health plans. Among the better-known in the hospital and medical field are Blue Cross/Blue Shield and Kaiser Permanente, but there are many local and regional companies which can compete very favorably. Members generally need no physical examination to qualify for life insurance coverage, although medical history is routinely required. As a result of the AIDS crisis, however, more and more companies are now requiring physical examinations.

The federal law known as COBRA requires employers with more than twenty-five employees to permit terminated employees to retain their membership in the company health and medical plans for a period of up to eighteen months, provided the individual personally makes the appropriate premium payments. Many states have similar laws. There is no federal law covering continuation of benefits for other types of insurance, although some employers and insurers may allow former employees to convert from the group plan to an individual plan.

Group life insurance policies are almost always term insurance and, therefore, do not accumulate cash values as do other life insurance policies. Members sometimes cannot select their own amount of coverage. The insurance company cannot cancel an individual member's participation in a group policy other than for failure to make premium payments. Group insurance is used by many companies as an added form of compensation and to induce employees to remain with the business; organizations offer it as a service to members and for the purpose of attracting new members.

There are three types of group medical plans: *indemnity, preferred provider organizations* (PPOs), and *health maintenance organizations* (HMOs). In an indemnity plan, the insurance company receives the premiums from the group and pays for the medical services on either a scheduled or "reasonable and customary" basis. With some exceptions, the participant is able to choose his or her provider. With PPOs, the insurance company contracts with medical providers and organizations to perform services at specific rates. There are economic disadvantages to the participant who obtains services from non-participating providers. In the case of HMOs, the insurance company owns the medical facilities and employs the professionals to provide the medical services. The attempt is to control costs through close supervision of the delivery system.

➤ *See also* Disability Income Insurance, Insurance, Life Insurance

Handicapped Access

➤ *See* Americans With Disabilities Act

Head Shot

➤ *See* Resume

Health Hazards

➤ *See* Safety

Honorarium

➤ *See* Fees

Humanities Councils or Committees

The National Endowment for the Arts has a counterpart devoted to the humanities. The mission of this organization, known as the National Endowment for the Humanities (NEH), is to stimulate humanistic endeavors in the United States and to provide appropriate cultural exchange abroad. The NEH has a wide variety of programs available, including some grants to performing arts organizations and individuals. In addition, the NEH educates state humanities organization members in their appropriate roles and provides the state, as well as local, organizations with financial and other resources. For more information about the NEH you should contact them directly at their Washington, D.C. home office.

State humanities commissions or committees are generally charged with the mission of supporting humanistic activities, including the performing arts, throughout the state. They may publish books of poetry, plays by aspiring playwrights, or even fund certain performances for nonprofit theater groups. The extent of their activity is a function of the amount of money available through federal re-grant funds and the state matching funds.

➤ *See also* Arts Councils, Grants, National Endowment for the Arts, National Endowment for the Humanities, Appendix A

Income Tax—Business

The federal income tax laws require different things from different types of business organizations. Sole proprietors, partnerships, S corporations, as well as limited liability companies (LLCs) and limited liability partnerships (LLPs), do not pay a business income tax on the business's profits; instead, profits and losses are included on the individual's income tax return. In these instances, information returns must be filed by the business so that the Internal Revenue Service can verify that the business owners have properly declared their business income on their personal returns. Form 1065 is filed by partnerships; Form 1120-S is filed by S corps and LLCs. In addition, the business must provide its owners with the appropriate forms, Form 1099-DIV for C corporations if the shareholder receives more than ten dollars in dividends in the tax year, K-1 Form 1065 for partners, and K-1 Form 1120-S for S corporations and LLCs. The business owners will file additional forms with their tax returns, such as Schedule C with Form 1040 for sole proprietors. Limited liability companies use the same forms for tax returns as partnerships.

C corporations are another matter. Corporate taxable income up to $50,000 is taxed at 15 percent. That portion of taxable income over $50,000 but not over $75,000 is taxed at 25 percent. That portion over $75,000 is taxed at 34 percent, but if less than $335,000 the rate is 39 percent. For income exceeding $335,000 but less than $10 million, the rate drops to 34 percent. Between $10 million and $15 million, the rate is 35 percent. From $15 million to $18,000,333, the rate is 38 percent. For all higher earnings the rate is 35 percent. The corporate tax is, in effect, a double tax when paid to shareholders as dividends. First, the corporation's income is taxed, and then, when the income has been distributed to stockholders as dividends, it is taxed again at the individual stockholder's level.

All states, and many cities, impose their own taxes on corporate profits. Some even tax the incomes of unincorporated businesses. That tax is often called a *franchise tax,* though it goes by a variety of names. It is, in effect, a tax on the right to conduct a business. An accountant or the applicable taxing authorities should be consulted to determine the specific tax requirements in your area.

The Internal Revenue Service has published an unusually clear "Tax Guide for Small Business" (Publication 334), which is revised annually and is available without charge from the nearest IRS office (see telephone white pages under "U.S. Government, Internal Revenue Service") or by writing to the IRS (see Appendix B).

➤ *See also* Accounting, Business Tax, Charitable Contributions, Deductions, Estimated Tax, Franchise Tax, Income Tax—Personal, Tax, Tax Preparer, Unrelated Business Income, Withholding Tax

Income Tax—Personal

Income is defined, for federal tax purposes, as money, property, or anything of value which you receive from any source, including but not limited to wages, fees, receipts from sales of work, resale and other royalties, dividends, interest, rent, profits, pensions, annuities, alimony, prizes and awards, jury duty fees, tips, unemployment compensation, profit from the sale of real estate, etc.

If you barter your services, you have received income equal to the fair market value of what you received in exchange for those services. For example, if you perform in a show in exchange for a place to live you will owe tax on the "fair market value" of the rent which you would otherwise have paid for that apartment. There is a presumption that anything you receive will be considered taxable income. The Internal Revenue Code specifies some limited exceptions to this general rule. The exceptions include Veterans Administration benefits and disability payments, some Social Security benefits, proceeds of a life insurance policy when paid to individuals, workers' compensation or other benefits paid for injury or sickness, interest on certain state and municipal bonds, gifts, and inheritances.

WHO MUST FILE?

Federal income tax returns must be filed on or before April 15 of each year by everyone whose income in the preceding calendar year exceeded a specified minimum amount, dependant on the taxpayer's status. Each year, the Internal Revenue Service publishes the minimum amount of gross income figures which require the filing of a tax return. Even if you are not *required* to file an income tax return, it is necessary to file if you were employed during the year and want to get a refund of money which was withheld for income tax purposes. It is also a good idea to file a return so that the Internal Revenue Service will not see a gap in your annual filings and in order to start the statute of limitations for IRS claims or audits running in your favor.

Even though personal income tax returns are due by April 15, an automatic four-month extension may be obtained by filing the appropriate form on or before April 15. Any taxes due are required to be paid on or before April 15, or the taxpayer will be liable for late payment penalties and interest. Delaying the date the return is due does not delay the date the tax payment is due.

LONG FORM OR SHORT FORM?

Taxpayers with taxable income below $50,000 whose income was solely from wages and who have no itemized deductions will generally find it easier to file the short form 1040A as their federal income tax return. All you need to do is to record the amount of income received and tax withheld as shown on the W-2 forms which are required to be provided by employers by January 31. The Internal Revenue Service allows a standard deduction and calculates the tax due or the tax refund based on the number of dependent exemptions claimed. If you also happen to be filing as single, under sixty-five, not blind, and claiming no dependents, you may have it even easier by filing Form 1040EZ. This is available, however, only for income received from wages and tips and not, for example, from unemployment compensation or sales activity.

Persons with larger incomes, self-employed income (such as many successful entertainers), or deductions beyond the standard deduction must complete Form 1040, calculate their tax obligation, and send a check for the payment due or claim a refund.

ESTIMATED TAX DECLARATION

Taxpayers who have income from sources other than wages subject to payroll deduction must file a declaration of *estimated tax* when they file their income tax return. Estimated taxes are required to be paid in equal quarterly installments on April 15, June 15, September 15, and January 15 for the respective preceding calendar quarters. There are several ways to calculate the estimated tax, the most convenient and common being the use of the previous year's self-employed income as the basis for estimating the current year's tax obligations. There are penalties for underpayment of estimated tax as well as for wage earners who claim excess exemptions during the year in order to reduce the amount of money withheld for tax purposes.

➤ *See also* Estimated Tax

ACCURACY AND AUDITS

It is a crime to intentionally falsify tax returns; even carelessness can lead to severe penalties. A tax return may be completed by hand or by computer; in addition, it may be filed either by mailing it to the Internal Revenue Service or "electronically filing" through use of a computer modem. Computer-generated returns tend to have fewer calculation errors—and, in fact, can be advantageous in identifying tax benefits, but the computer adage "garbage in, garbage out" applies to tax information, as well. Some software packages warn of audit traps and guide the user through the deductions. Electronic filing is advisable only if you are expecting a refund.

There are many reasons why the Internal Revenue Service would examine, or *audit,* a tax return. In addition, if a return contains entries which are inconsistent with the IRS statistical averages for those entries or contains internal inconsistencies, the return may be audited. It is impossible to identify the criteria used by the IRS to trigger an audit. Nonetheless, it is believed that taxpayers whose returns have been audited and who have been required to pay additional tax as a result of those audits are more likely to be audited in the future.

An audit can take place in the auditor's office, the taxpayer's place of business, residence, or the office of the taxpayer's professional representative. Audits are stressful, and the best thing you can do is attempt to be calm. Take a deep breath, relax, tell the truth, and merely answer the questions asked—do not volunteer information. Be sure that your records are in order. *Never* merely bring a shoebox full of papers and dump it on the auditor's desk. An audit may result in your return being accepted as written, your receiving a tax refund for overpayment, or your being required to pay additional tax which the auditor calculated is due. In addition, you may be required to pay interest and penalties. The statute of limitations for the government's challenge of tax returns is three years, except in cases of fraud or where the taxpayer failed to report more than 25 percent of gross income.

➤ *See also* Audit

WHERE TO GET HELP

Taxpayers will usually find that the cost of professional help for preparing their income tax return often represents a savings in tax payments, because professional tax preparers are more likely to be familiar with the latest regulations, what may be deducted and what may not be, and the other intricacies of the tax laws. Even they can make mistakes, however. In a survey conducted by *Changing Times,* the Kiplinger newsletter, accountants and professional tax preparers were given hypothetical taxpayer situations and asked to calculate the tax liability. The results were disappointing—very few of these professionals were able to prepare a tax return which would have satisfied a tax auditor. If you deal with a licensed professional who has a good reputation you are more likely to receive accurate, up-to-date information. Taxpayers can also get free help and advice from the nearest office of the Internal Revenue Service. Also, many cities have accountants or tax preparers specializing in the arts, who may provide their services free of charge. Check with the local Chamber of Commerce or telephone yellow pages.

➤ *See also* Tax Preparation

OTHER INCOME TAXES

In addition to the federal income tax, most states require the payment of a state income tax. Many of these states have laws which parallel the Internal Revenue Code, though there are some differences and you should consult with a local tax adviser in order to determine what the state tax laws are in your jurisdiction. Some cities, counties, and other municipalities also impose income tax obligations.

Each taxpayer's situation is unique and it is essential to determine whether you feel comfortable in preparing your own return or whether you prefer that your return be prepared professionally. Certainly, if you are in a higher tax bracket or have a complex financial situation, it is likely to be beneficial for you to work with a tax professional. Entertainers who employ business managers will likely rely on the manager's assistance and expertise in the preparation of tax returns.

➤ *See also* Accounting, Charitable Contributions, Deductions, Estate Planning, Estimated Tax, Income Tax—Business, Tax, Tax Preparer, Wages, Withholding Tax

Independent Contractor

An independent contractor is defined as one who exercises his or her own independent trade, profession, or calling. The *Restatement 2d of the Law of Agency* distinguishes between an *employee,* who works for another and is under the other's control or right of control, from an *independent contractor* who merely provides an independent service or finished product. The *Restatement* contains a list of criteria which may be used to evaluate whether a person is an employee or an independent contractor. These include, among other things, whether the person uses his or her own tools, whether the person is engaged in a traditionally independent calling, where and when the work is performed, whether the person identifies him or herself as being an independent contractor, whether the person performs similar work for others, and whether there is a written agreement characterizing the employee-contractor relationship. The parties' own characterization is the weakest criterion.

Federal and state governments also attempt to characterize working relationships for tax and other reasons. The federal laws cover such issues as taxes, minimum wage, and the like. The federal authorities tend to ignore some of the *Restatement* criteria and, in most cases, characterize individuals as employees wherever possible. State laws evaluate a worker's status for purposes of workers' compensation, unemployment insurance, state income tax, and the like. State authorities tend to follow the federal government's pattern in leaning toward characterization of workers as employees.

Many nonprofit theater groups characterize the performers who participate in their productions as independent contractors. In addition, the organization's accountant, attorney, and insurance broker are all likely to be independent contractors. Theater staff, on the other hand, are more likely to be considered employees. Individuals such as ushers, ticket takers, stagehands, and the like are generally considered to have an ongoing employment relationship.

The most important factor distinguishing an employee from an independent contractor is control. If you have the right to control the conduct of the work—whether or not you exercise that right—the person is your employee. On the other hand, if you have only the right to accept or reject the finished product or service, then the person providing it is an independent contractor.

The distinction is very important for a variety of reasons. First, employers are responsible for obtaining workers' compensation insurance, paying a portion of their employees' Social Security taxes, and withholding all required income and other taxes. Independent contractors pay their own taxes. Employers are liable for all wrongful acts committed by their employees within the scope of their employment and are obligated on all contracts entered into by employees within their actual or apparent authority. Generally speaking, employers are not liable for the wrongful acts of independent contractors or contracts obtained by an independent contractor.

> ➤ *See also* Contracts, Employees, Equipment, Social Security, Tax, Workers'
> Compensation

Industry Practices and Customs

The entertainment industry, including the performing arts, has numerous *common practices* and *customs*. Professionals are familiar with them and assume everyone they encounter will adhere to them. It is essential for aspiring members of the industry to learn them and become familiar with the industry standards before entering into contracts or bargaining for a position.

Some of the most common industry customs include artistic control, which is generally expressly dealt with in contracts and collective bargaining agreements. Despite this fact, it is not unusual for producers to informally extend this right to the director and permit greater flexibility than the contract might allow. Similarly, caricaturing a character in the advertisement of a production, even though a particular entertainer has been cast as that character, is customary and not a violation of that entertainer's rights.

EXPRESS CREDIT PROVISIONS

It is customary in the entertainment industry to have contractual provisions which clearly articulate the credit to be given key individuals in a production. Notwithstanding this norm, there are some customs which may apply when the parties are silent on this subject, or when there is an ambiguity. It is customary for contracts with performers to contain a *record exclusion clause* which reserves the recording rights to the entertainer. It was argued, in *Gold Leaf Group, Ltd. v. Stigwood Group, Ltd.*, that omitting such a clause in a contract meant that the credit which appeared in a film should also be included in virtually identical form on any soundtrack album jacket. This argument was, however, rejected. While this case applied to a motion picture, the same principle should apply to live theater.

It is also industry practice to permit teasers and advertisements to omit contractually required acknowledgements. Unfortunately, the definition of *teasers* is not clear. It was held, for instance, that certain types of adver-tisements for the film *Jaws 2* were not teasers, despite the fact that prominent members of the entertainment industry had considered the format involved to be such for more than thirty years. As a result, these advertisements were not within the teaser exception to the required contractual acknowledgement and, thus, the industry custom was apparently overridden by the director's contract. While there are no cases on this subject outside the film industry, the same principle should apply to live theater, dance, and the like.

IMPLIED CREDIT

In the entertainment industry, it is common to acknowledge the author of a play even if such acknowledgement is not specifically required in the contract. This custom has been claimed to apply to both written and oral entertainment agreements.

REPRESENTATIONS AND WARRANTIES

There is an implied representation that the party selling or licensing property and rights has a legal title and the right to exploit it. Thus, the seller of a lighting sys-tem is implicitly representing that the title is good and that the item can be sold, licensed, or otherwise legally disposed of. Similarly, there is an implied repre-sentation that a tangible item, such as a sound system, is fit for the purpose for which it is being acquired. The Uniform Commercial Code (UCC) provides that any statement related to the goods which is part of the basis of the bargain is considered an express warranty. In addition, the UCC provides for several im-plied warranties, such as merchantability, title, fitness for particular purpose, and the like. Legal commentators and scholars have suggested that similar warran-ties should attach to literary property, such as copyrights in plays and music.

Since the entertainment industry overlaps and encompasses a number of other industries such as music, publishing, motion pictures, and television, it is essential for you to work with experienced professionals who have been involved in comparable arrangements and are familiar with the myriad customs and trade usages which may arise in your transaction. It has been held that specifically identifying a custom or trade usage and expressly rejecting it will effectively override the industry norm. It has also been held that ambiguities in an agreement should be interpreted so as to give effect to the parties' intent, including the understanding that the parties intended all of the aforementioned traditions, customs, and usages to apply. This is particularly true where the individuals involved are professionals in an industry, such as entertainment.

126

➤ *See also* Contracts, Customs, Uniform Commercial Code

Installment

Installment is defined as a part. Thus, in an *installment sale* or an *installment loan,* the whole amount is paid off in parts. Interest charges are customarily added to the face amount, and the total is then divided into equal payments, usually on a monthly basis for one or more years.

The question of title to the property being purchased is separate from the payment method used. The agreement between the parties may state that the title remains with the seller until full payment is made, or that title is immediately transferred to the buyer. The agreement should also cover the seller's remedies if the buyer defaults, which may include, among other things, the right to repossess the item, the right to retain any amounts previously paid, and the right to demand payment of the full amount from the buyer. If there is no written agreement, transfer of possession of the item to the buyer transfers title and the seller merely retains a security interest which must then be perfected, if it is to be predictable.

Mortgages, automobile loans, and other long-term borrowing for major purchases are installment loans. If title passes to the buyer before payment has been made in full and the buyer is given possession of the item being purchased, then the seller retains a security interest in the item (then known as *collateral*), which should be *perfected* in accordance with the appropriate law. Generally, for land and buildings, a security interest is perfected by recording the mortgage document in the same place deeds are filed (usually, with the county clerk or recorder). For all other tangible property, perfection is accomplished by filing a UCC-1 Financing Statement with the appropriate government office (often, the Secretary of State or county clerk).

The method of perfecting a security interest in an intangible item, such as a copyright, patent, trademark, or interest in a business, varies depending upon the asset. For example, a security interest in a copyright may be perfected by recording the appropriate document with the Copyright Office *and also* by complying with the Uniform Commercial Code. The collateral serves as security for the repayment of the loan and may be repossessed if the borrower fails to pay installments when they are due, in accordance with the law under which the security interest was perfected. If the security interest is not perfected, then the seller can sue the buyer for the amount due but may not be able to repossess the property.

Interest on installment purchases is customarily charged on the unpaid balance and the interest rate is generally higher than that charged by banks. State usury and other laws limit the rate of interest which may be charged on loans. Sellers may restrict an installment purchaser's ability to prepay installments, though the contract between the parties may permit the purchaser to prepay all or any portion of the obligation without incurring any prepayment penalty. Laws and regulations covering installment selling and loans vary from state to state. It is always wise to read and understand the entire agreement before signing.

> ➤ *See also* Collateral, Contracts, Foreclosure, Loans, Mortgage, Uniform Commercial Code

Insurance

Life is fraught with risks. *Insurance* has been developed to reduce the consequences of some of those risks. An insurance policy is a contract which transfers some of the risk from the policyholder to the insurance company, in return for which the policyholder pays the insurance carrier a fee known as a *premium.* Some risks cannot be insured, some risks are not worth insuring, and some risks must be insured. To cite three examples: Buying a lottery ticket creates a risk of not winning, which cannot be insured; writing a play which may turn out to be unappreciated is a risk hardly worth insuring against; owning and operating a car is considered by most states a sufficiently high risk to require insurance.

There are some basic things that should be understood about insurance in order to buy wisely. These include the nature of risk, the types of insurance, what to insure, insurable interest, how much to buy, deductibles, telling the truth, and from whom to buy.

THE NATURE OF RISK

Risks fall into two basic categories. One is *pure risk,* where you have no choice in the outcome. If you own a building and a fire breaks out, there is a loss. Pure risks don't allow any other result but a loss. *Speculative risks,* on the other hand, are those in which you have a choice. You have a hand in controlling the risk and can, therefore, make a decision whether you want to take it. Going into business, such as producing a play, is itself a speculative risk. You might make money or you might not. Both types of risk can be insured, though the premiums for insuring against speculative risks are usually quite high.

TYPES OF INSURANCE

There are two general categories into which insurance may be divided: *personal* and *property*. Personal includes life, accident, disability, medical and hospital, public liability, and a few others. Property covers fire, theft, title, and automobile, plus some minor ones of little consequence in an entertainment business. Many of these are discussed in detail in this book under their appropriate alphabetical entries.

INSURABLE INTEREST

In order to obtain insurance, you must have an *insurable interest*; that is, a bona fide interest in the item being insured. This is a means by which the law prevents insurance contracts from being used as gambling contracts and a means of protecting the person or item insured from being exposed to an increased hazard. You can insure a building you own against loss by fire, since you would be economically injured if it were lost. You cannot insure the Empire State Building (unless you happen to own that, too), because you have no insurable interest in it. Permitting insurance without an insurable interest might encourage the insured party to damage the property. Similarly, you can insure the life of your family's breadwinner, but you cannot insure the life of the President of the United States (unless you are the First Lady), again because you have no insurable interest.

The real test of insurable interest is whether the insured or beneficiary of the insurance policy would suffer a loss if the risk covered by the policy came to pass. You need not own a piece of property to have an insurable interest in it. For example, the holder of a mortgage certainly has an interest in a building on which it made the mortgage loan. Nor need you be related to the person on whose life you take out a policy. An employer has an insurable interest in a key employee whose death might seriously damage the earning capability of the business. Similarly, an entertainment organization would have an insurable interest in the lives of individuals with leading roles.

The insurable interest must exist not only at the time the policy goes into effect, but also at the time a claim is made. If you have a fire policy on a building which you subsequently sell, and it then burns to the ground, you no longer have an insurable interest, even if you continued to pay the premiums. The exception is life insurance, where the insurable interest needs to exist only at the time the policy is written. Two examples: If you take out a policy on a key employee who subsequently leaves your business, you can still collect in the event of his or her death, even many years later, as long as you continue to pay the premiums. If you divorce, your former spouse may still collect on your life insurance if you have not instructed the insurance company to change the beneficiary on your policy.

It is sound judgement, therefore, to examine your insurance policies periodically to determine what should remain in effect, what should be added, what can be cancelled, and whether any of the names of the beneficiaries should be changed.

WHAT TO INSURE

While it is theoretically possible to insure virtually anything from a dancer's legs to the success of an opening, the cost of such insurance may be prohibitive. You should, therefore, prioritize your insurance needs. The first and foremost consideration has to be the risk in relation to your capability to afford it. *Fire insurance* is clearly a top priority. A serious fire can put a theater out of business. Even a minor fire can result in a serious loss if your productive activities are interrupted for any length of time. In addition, you may wish to consider *business interruption insurance,* which is intended to provide benefits comparable to earnings lost due to any of several catastrophic events, such as fire, flood, windstorm, etc.

In *automobile insurance,* liability takes precedence over collision. Most states which require vehicle insurance require liability insurance but not collision insurance. Most banks, credit unions, and others who finance vehicle purchases require that the purchaser maintain collision insurance until the loan has been repaid.

If you have a home business office, whether it is in the house or a separate building on your property, be sure you are properly covered. The typical *homeowner policy* expressly excludes business property and activities from its coverage. You may be able to add your home business office to the homeowner policy at a fairly small premium.

If the worst anyone can steal from you is a few hundred dollars worth of books and scripts you may not want to buy *theft insurance.* But if you're a musician with a tempting collection of valuable instruments theft insurance may be essential.

HOW MUCH TO BUY

A big question always is "How much insurance do I need?" In property insurance, that depends to a large extent on the value of the property, how much of a loss you can sustain without insurance, and how much money is available for premium payments. Underinsuring serves little purpose, and can be expensive if trouble develops. For example: The performing arts company owns its own building. The building's current cash value is $250,000. Most fire insurance policies require that you insure at least 80 percent of the fair market value or else you assume some of the risk yourself.

If the company insures the $250,000 building for only $125,000, that's 50 percent of the value. This doesn't mean that the insurance company will pay the losses up to $125,000 and the entertainment company pays the rest. If the particular policy requires 80 percent coverage, and you buy only 50 percent, then the insurance company will pay only 50 percent of a claim. The rest is the entertainment company's responsibility. This is known as *coinsurance,* because the insured is, in effect, sharing the risk of loss with the insurance carrier.

Expensive as fire insurance may be, few entertainment organizations can afford to underinsure or coinsure. In addition, if the building is mortgaged, most lenders require that adequate insurance be maintained on it, often through a carrier acceptable to the mortgage holder, and that the mortgage holder be a named insured, that is, named in the policy as an additional beneficiary.

Overinsuring is wasteful, because property insurance policies do not pay off the face value of the policy, only the actual loss up to the *actual value* of the property. Consider the previous example of a $250,000 building—now insured for $500,000, with the owner paying a higher premium for the higher coverage. Even if the building is totally destroyed, the owner will still collect only $250,000.

There are two methods of defining *actual value* for insurance purposes. It may be defined either as the cost necessary to replace the item or as the current fair market value. Thus, the same twenty-five-year-old building may be worth only $250,000 on the real estate market, but it may cost more than $500,000 to rebuild it. It is generally more expensive to have a replacement value endorsement, though it may be well worth the difference. The principal exception to the rule regarding valuation is life insurance. Since no one can place a precise dollar value on a human life, the purchaser of life insurance is entitled to determine how much insurance is desirable or necessary, and the entire amount is paid to the beneficiaries when the insured dies.

It is essential that all insurance policies be reviewed periodically with an insurance professional familiar with your type of business and situation. Whatever you do, don't buy a particular policy simply because it seems inexpensive. Many factors enter into the determination of premiums, including not only fine-print inclusions and exclusions of coverage, but also the insurance company's cooperation in claims settlements, its financial condition, etc. The mere fact that an insurance company accepts a premium for policy coverage does not prevent it from later repudiating the policy or challenging the values stated as covered. It is a good idea to obtain appraisals which are acceptable to the insurance company when the policy is first written, as a way of reducing the likelihood of having a problem after a loss has occurred. Know exactly what you are buying. It is worth your while to shop around. The Insurance Company Institute provides publications on various types of insurance. In addition, insurance is regulated at the state level, generally by an Insurance Commissioner, whose office may be able to provide you with information about insurance companies, brokers, and agents.

DEDUCTIBLES

Most insurance policies have a *deductible* clause. It means that the policyholder pays part of the claim, say the first $500 or 10 percent of the total, or a waiting period is established, after which benefits go into effect. Insurance companies do this to weed out the numerous small claims which cost more in paperwork than they are worth. In return, the difference in premium costs makes it worthwhile. For example, if it costs you $50 extra in premiums to get full coverage and remove a $100 deductible, you are paying a premium rate of 50 percent on that $100 worth of insurance, which is very high.

TELLING THE TRUTH

A key ingredient of every insurance policy is that the policyholder has accurately completed the application. The statements made by you in connection with your insurance application are known as *representations.* The premise is that the insurance company is relying on your representations when assuming the risk and selling you insurance. If you make any material misrepresentations, one of two serious consequences can result: (1) the policy can be cancelled, or (2) claims will be denied if the false or misleading statements are discovered when a claim is made.

For example, if you apply for fire insurance and tell the insurance company you've had no fires in the past ten years, they will assume that you take proper safety precautions and are a good risk. If you subsequently have a fire and, in the course of the investigation, the insurance company discovers that you have, in fact, had three fires in the last two years, it will refuse to pay the loss and will probably cancel your policy. You will, therefore, have wasted the money you spent on premiums. Had you disclosed your fire history truthfully, the insurance company might never have issued the policy, or might merely have set a much higher premium.

Similarly, life insurance applications must be accurately completed. If the application asks about your hobbies and you are an avid skydiver, you must disclose that fact. It could affect the premiums the insurer will charge, or whether it will write a policy at all. It is better to make full disclosure, even if this will cost you more in premiums, since a policy procured through fraud or misrepresentation may be worthless.

WHERE TO BUY INSURANCE

Insurance is available through three sources: *independent agents, brokers,* and directly from the *insurance carriers' agents.*

The bulk of property insurance is written by independent agents and brokers. Since they can write insurance for a number of insurance companies, they are likely to be less biased and may be in a position to provide you with the best coverage. They are able to issue a binder on your property for a limited period of time from the moment you telephone them, and you are insured for that period of time. Since they are usually local, they can meet with you to analyze your insurance needs, and are on the spot when a claim has to be made.

A great deal of life insurance is written directly by the insurance companies through their own agents. Obviously, they sell only their own product, and are not likely to give you impartial advice on the merits and demerits of the policies issued by other companies. Automobile and medical insurance can often be bought through the mail, without salesmen. This may save some money in premiums (since there are no commissions to pay), but it removes the personal touch and there may be some problems in obtaining payment when a claim is made. Be sure to check with your state's insurance commissioner before purchasing a mail-order policy.

Selecting an insurance broker or independent agent should be done with the same care as choosing a lawyer or an accountant. It should be a professional relationship. The stakes can be very high. Ask around. Consult other business people whose judgment you respect. You may wish to use the same agent or broker for all your insurance needs, since you are likely to have more clout when offering all your premium dollars to one person and that person is likely to be in a better position to integrate your insurance program. It may be that your life insurance agent will not be able to write casualty insurance, although he or she may be able to make some recommendations. Some insurance companies give multipolicy discounts; for example, most automobile insurers have a significant rate reduction for additional vehicles, and many will give better rates on both automobile and homeowner/renter insurance if they handle both policies.

You can send for an excellent, nontechnical booklet published by the Small Business Administration, "Insurance and Risk Management for Small Business." An "Insurance Checklist for Small Business" is available without charge from the Small Business Administration.

> ➤ *See also* Common Carrier, Disability Income Insurance, Fire Insurance, Fire Prevention, Group Insurance, Liability Insurance, Life Insurance, Loans, Partnership, Property Insurance, Security, Underwriting, Unemployment Insurance, Workers' Compensation, Appendix B

Intellectual Property

Intellectual property is the term used to identify the ownership rights in various types of intangible property, including *copyright,* which protects original expression when reduced to a tangible form; *patent,* which protects new, useful, and non-obvious technological innovation (invention and functional design); *trademark,* which protects names, symbols, or logos used to identify particular goods and services; *trade dress,* which protects the "look and feel" of work; and *trade secret,* which protects any formula, pattern, or compilation of information used in one's business to obtain an advantage over one's competitors who do not know or use it. In recent years, the *right of publicity* has developed to enable individuals such as sports figures and entertainers to protect and exploit the economic value of their celebrity status.

> ➤ *See also* Copyright, Customs, License, Patent, Posthumous, Trademark, Trade Dress, Trade Name, Trade Secret

Interest

The word *interest* has both legal and financial meanings.

In legal terms, it means that you have some claim to certain property. For example, if you and a partner each invest $1,000 in a production, you each have a *half-interest* in the business. Similarly, when you sell a van on installment and allow the purchaser to take possession of it, you retain a *security interest* in that van.

In financial terms, *interest* is money earned in exchange for the use of money. If you think of money as a product which you rent, much as you might rent a car, the interest is the price you pay for the use of that product.

Interest rates are usually quoted on an annual basis, even if the period to which they apply is shorter. The interest rate on a retail charge account, for instance, may be quoted at 18 percent per annum; however, if your balance is $100 and you pay it off at the end of the month, you will pay only $1.50 in interest (one-twelfth of the annual amount, which in this case would be $18). Maximum interest rates are often set by state law, in so-called usury statutes, although they vary from state to state. *Legal interest* is also defined by state and federal law; it is customarily 9 percent per annum at the state level, and fluctuates at the federal level. The present trend among states is to deregulate the amount or percentage of interest that can be charged by lenders, relying instead on disclosure requirements contained in the various laws.

The financial world uses a whole host of interest terminology. Two terms are important: *simple interest* and *compound interest.*

Simple interest is calculated on the amount of money involved in the loan, and is either paid to the lender when the principal is repaid at the end of the loan period, or is sometimes deducted from the loan in advance. It does not, itself, earn interest. This form of interest is most common when you borrow money.

Compound interest is paid on the principal plus previously earned interest. The previously earned interest, in effect, keeps increasing the principal amount, or the base upon which interest is calculated. Bank interest traditionally was calculated on a quarterly basis. With the introduction of computers, it is now usually calculated daily, so the amount on deposit grows every day and interest is paid on a higher amount each day. That explains why an annual interest rate of 6 percent will return (yield) not $6 but approximately $6.18 on every $100 deposit.

Manipulating your money to earn the best interest can be rewarding. It is wiser to put your money in a high-yield money market account than a no-interest checking account or low-interest savings account. If you will not need that money for some time, then certificates of deposit, which are customarily restricted for at least six months, would be sensible. There are a host of other options available, and you should consult with your financial adviser and/or banker to determine what specific arrangements will best serve the financial interests of your business.

The interest rate on charge accounts and credit cards can be deceptive because the monthly payment seems small. If you finance a $1,000 piece of equipment at 12 percent for one year, making monthly payments, your total finance charge will be $66.19. If you borrow the money from a bank at 8 percent, pay off the equipment in one lump sum, and repay the bank in twelve monthly installments, the finance charge amounts to only $43.86.

➤ *See also* Banks, Checking Account, Credit Card, Loans, Mortgage

International Alliance of Theatrical Stage Employees and Moving Picture Machine Operators of the U.S. and Canada (IATSE)

The union to which most stage managers, stagehands, etc. belong.

➤ *See also* Theatrical Protective Union in Appendix A

Internet

In the mid-1970s, the Department of Defense began a project which has ultimately emerged as the Internet. This was intended to be an alternative system of communications and it is used today for communications as well as marketing and entertainment purposes. Accessible through a computer modem and subscription to an appropriate connection service, such as America Online, CompuServe, Prodigy, or the like, "net surfers" on the so-called information highway now have access to such information as news updates, stock quotes, book and movie reviews, on-line bulletin boards and interactive chat lines, e-mail, and a variety of other information and entertainment services.

Many theater organizations, as well as entertainment-related businesses, have established sites on the World Wide Web, which is a part of the Internet. The length and breadth of a *web site* is really dependent upon its intended purpose. Thus, if a symphony orchestra wished to use a web site for purposes of marketing future performances, its site might resemble an advertisement and a marquee. There are other applications, as well. Some theater repertory companies put information regarding the artistic director and managing directors of their organizations on their sites. Sites may also contain evaluations of set designs, reviews of performances, and ticketing information which can be e-mailed directly to the box office. One educational site is devoted exclusively to the works of Gilbert & Sullivan. Theater Direct International, a ticket agency, lists on its web site Broadway, Off-Broadway and London theater productions, information about current casting and scheduling changes, and gossip about the theater world in New York City and London, and provides information about obtaining tickets.

Some web sites have e-mail (electronic mail) features built into them and are used for the purpose of generating mailing lists. In this situation, browsers will e-mail their names and addresses directly to the organization and ultimately be placed on the company's mailing list. Some individual owners have even set up their own web sites. Playwrights may put excerpts from their work on the web. Set designers may use the web for purposes of displaying

136

their skill, and entertainers may set up web sites for listing their credits and presenting their head shots or even trying out new material.

The ultimate scope of the Internet and the World Wide Web are unclear. Every day, additional applications and use of the resources are surfacing. The issue of intellectual property protection for material available on the Internet and World Wide Web is just beginning to be litigated.

➤ *See also* Advertising, Computers, E-Mail, Uniform Commercial Code

Investment

In some respects, every purchase or use of your energy is an investment, yet economists, accountants, and business advisers may differ on the precise definition of *investment*. When you attend Julliard, for example, you are investing in your future; if you are successful in your chosen career, you will realize a profit on that investment.

The money you use to acquire some form of property, whether tangible or intangible, with the expectation of a financial return is also an investment and this is the financial context in which the term is most commonly used. The return on investment (ROI) takes various forms: stock dividends, an increase in the value of real estate, profits from the use of equipment, interest on loans, appreciation in value of musical instruments, and others.

Investments have two basic characteristics: They are generally of a long-term nature and they generally provide a reliable return at relatively low risk. It doesn't always work out that way, but that's the expectation when the investment is made. *Speculation* is the antithesis of investment. Speculation can bring a high return, but at greater risk. Buying a horse is an investment; betting on it is speculation.

The quality of an investment is measured by its ROI—how much money you make on every dollar you invest. An ordinary savings account may pay 2 percent interest, or provide a 2 percent ROI. Corporate stock may yield an 8 percent dividend. A larger auditorium may enable you to accommodate a larger audience and increase profit by 10 percent.

A consideration when making an investment is how readily it can be converted into cash if the need arises: *liquidity*. A savings account is easily convertible: just take the money out of the bank. A publicly traded stock is still considered relatively liquid, even though its value may fluctuate and you may not obtain the optimum return if you are forced to sell at a particular time. Used equipment and other assets are even more difficult investments to convert into cash.

All of these factors influence whether or not you should make a particular investment, and also the rate of return. If you want to keep your cash position truly liquid, a savings account may be the best investment, even if it doesn't bring the highest return. Prudent business people will balance liquidity and ROI so that they can achieve reasonable security while fetching an adequate return. If the mortgage on your home or theater bears an interest rate of 8 percent and you can obtain only a return of 2 percent on your savings account, your best investment might be to pay down your mortgage, assuming you have some extra money available. You should determine whether you will be in a position to retrieve some or all of the money prepaid to reduce your mortgage in the event of an emergency.

It is a tradition in the entertainment industry to finance productions through investments. Financial backers, commonly known as *angels,* frequently invest large sums in specific productions. There are a variety of vehicles available for accomplishing these investments, such as limited partnerships, limited liability companies, corporations, and the like. The sale of interests in these business forms is subject to regulation under federal and state securities laws. Complying with these very technical statutes is essential and *must* be undertaken by skilled attorneys who specialize in securities law. While some exemptions from full-blown compliance may be available, they are narrow and their applicability is best determined by a securities lawyer. The film *The Producers* illustrates misuse of the investment process by pointing out how unscrupulous producers can distort the process.

In the past, some tax write-offs were available to investors in entertainment projects. Unfortunately, abuses were rampant and both the Internal Revenue Service and the Securities and Exchange Commmission closed the door on these tax shelters. Today, entertainment-related investments must be profit-motivated, rather than tax-motivated.

Investment decisions are complex, requiring a balancing of liquidity and return, as well as risk. Whenever contemplating an investment, you should consult your accountant, lawyer or other business adviser.

➤ *See also* Accountant, Budget, Lawyer

Investor

➤ *See* Investment

Joint Venture

A *joint venture* is a partnership for a specific or restricted purpose. For example, a playwright and a composer might form a joint venture to produce a collaborative work. Similarly, a ballet company and a symphony orchestra could, for example, undertake a production of *The Nutcracker* as a joint venture. Generally, the rules governing joint ventures are the same as those governing partnerships.

> ➤ *See also* Contract, Copyright, Corporation, Limited Liability Company, Limited Liability Partnership, Limited Partnership, Partnership, Sole Proprietorship

Journals

> ➤ *See* Accounting

Keogh Plan

> *See* Pensions

Labor

> *See* Contract, Employees, Independent Contractor, Wages

Lawyer

Sometimes referred to as an *attorney-at-law,* a *lawyer* is a professional licensed by the state to represent clients in a variety of situations. Lawyers have traditionally represented their clients in court cases, though lawyers should also be used for pre-problem counseling and document drafting; the wording of a long-term contract that you sign may seem plain enough to you, but do you know how a court would interpret it? In fact, proper use of the skills of an attorney as adviser, counselor, and preparer of appropriate documents will minimize your exposure to costly and time-consuming litigation.

Some lawyers are *generalists* and will assist with everything from real estate transactions and family law to criminal representation. With the increased complexity of today's business world, however, lawyers, like other professionals, have begun to specialize. It is probably better to hire a *specialist* in a certain area at a higher fee than a less-expensive generalist who will have to learn the specialty at your expense.

The New York State Bar Association provides this rule of thumb: "Get a

141

lawyer's advice whenever you run into serious problems concerning your freedom, your financial situation, your domestic affairs, or your property."

Legal matters fall into two basic classifications: *civil* and *criminal*. Civil matters concern disputes between parties, such as breach of contract, product liability, personal injury, and the like. Criminal matters concern violations of the criminal law, such as murder, theft, and forgery. Civil matters generally involve money or property, whereas criminal violations could result in the imposition of fines, penalties, and/or imprisonment. You should obtain representation by an attorney experienced in the appropriate area of law whenever you are involved in litigation. The one exception to this rule is small claims court, where attorneys may represent only organizations, and not individuals.

When you discuss a matter with your lawyer, do not hesitate to discuss the fee as well. Fees generally depend upon the amount of time and extent of research required, and the skills of your lawyer. On relatively common matters, such as incorporating a nonprofit organization or drawing up a simple will, the time element is fairly predictable and a fee can easily be estimated. More complicated matters are less predictable. You should request an estimate of the probable cost. Contingent fee arrangements, where the lawyer gets paid a percentage of the recovery when a case has been won, is common in personal injury matters, but almost unheard-of for business and intellectual property litigation and routine legal advice.

Communications between a lawyer and a client are confidential. Except in the case of a crime being planned or committed, where a lawyer is under an affirmative duty of disclosure, a lawyer cannot be compelled—indeed, is not permitted—to reveal what you discuss unless you give your permission. The purpose of this rule is to allow the free exchange between the lawyer and client so that the representation can be effective. Your lawyer can help you only if he or she is aware of all facts. Be sure to tell your lawyer everything, even the sordid details.

WHERE DO YOU FIND A GOOD LAWYER?

Since all lawyers are required to be licensed, it is a matter of finding someone in whom you can have confidence, much as you would find a doctor or any other professional in whom you place your trust. Ask your friends or business acquaintances to recommend someone they have found satisfactory. You may want to talk to several lawyers before you settle on one individual. The state or local bar association will likely be able to provide you with names of attorneys who practice in specific areas, but they will not provide endorsements. In addition, many labor unions provide legal representation for its members or have some form of prepaid legal insurance. If you are a member of an entertainment-related union, you should determine what resources are available to you. If your resources are very limited, the Legal Aid Society (or its local equivalent) may be of help, although they rarely assist with business matters.

For a list of lawyers on a state-by-state basis, see *Martindale-Hubbell®,* at most law libraries. *Martindale-Hubbell* contains—at most—only biographical information, degrees earned, and publications by the attorney, and requires the payment of an advertising fee which some attorneys refuse to pay. For a digest of copyright lawyers, see the *Copyright Directory*, published by Copyright Information Services. For information, and possibly free legal service, with entertainment-related legal matters, contact a Volunteer Lawyers for the Arts organization, if one exists in your state.

> ➤ *See also* Contract, Estate Planning, First Option, Investment, Lease, Letter Agreement, Morals Clause, Option, Sponsorship, Statute of Limitations, Underwriting, Appendix A, Appendix B

Lease

A *lease* is a contract between the owner of property and one who wishes to use it for a specified period. Like any other contract, a lease spells out the rights and responsibilities of both parties during its term. It can be for personal property (office machines, such as computers, photocopiers, etc.), vehicles, and the like, or for real property (buildings, office space, studios, theaters, etc.). Leases are almost always drawn up by the owner's (lessor's) lawyer for the owner's benefit.

Real property leases include the amount of the rent, when it is to be paid, a description of the premises to be rented, the term (length) of the lease, and so forth. There are, however, numerous other clauses. Who is responsible for painting? What restrictions are there on remodeling? (Some leases don't even allow you to put a nail in the wall without the landlord's permission.) Who pays for utilities? What type of sign will you be allowed to use? Who will be responsible for damage to the premises and its contents? Are there common area maintenance charges? Are heat, elevator service, and access to the building provided at night and on weekends? Is the security deposit kept in a separate account for you? Does it earn interest?

It is important that you carefully inspect the premises you are renting *before* you sign a lease. Will the floor sustain the weight of heavy equipment if you need it for your business? Can the electric wiring carry the load of heavy duty equipment such as dimmers? If it can't, whose responsibility is it to install the proper wiring, if such installation is even possible? Are there any zoning, pollution, noise, or other restrictions that would affect your use of the premises?

Such an inspection should also raise other questions. Determine whether everything you see on the premises before you sign the lease will still be there after you sign it; the previous tenant may not have removed all of his or her property. Don't take for granted, for example, that the air conditioners in the windows will stay there after you move in, or that you won't be surprised with an extra charge above the stated rent to keep them. If the lease specifies that you pay for your own utilities such as gas, water, and electricity, determine whether there are separate meters installed for your premises and, if not, how your share is calculated. Inspect carefully to see that everything is in good repair: water supply, radiators, bathrooms, windows, floors, ceilings. The lease should specify who is responsible for maintenance.

If you want to fix up the place by putting in walls and partitions, new wiring, light fixtures and so forth, your right to do that must be spelled out in the lease, providing only that the end result meets all legal standards such as fire and building regulations, and that it doesn't lower the value of the landlord's property or increase his or her insurance rates. The lease should also specify your rights on termination—must you restore the premises to their original condition? May you remove any fixtures which you install? Absent a provision to the contrary, all *leasehold improvements* belong to the landlord and the lessee is not entitled to compensation for them.

If the lease permits you to remodel, be certain that you do not need to obtain the landlord's permission for every dab of paint you put on the wall. If the landlord is unwilling to give carte blanche for painting without prior permission, at least try to get a provision that the landlord's permission will not be unreasonably withheld. One area of landlord responsibility that the tenant should rarely assume is the basic structural condition of the premises, or other conditions required by law. If the roof leaks, the landlord should fix it. If the fire department issues a notice of structural violation, it is the landlord's responsibility to fix, unless the tenant created the violation. The lease should be very specific on this subject. Verbal promises by the landlord mean nothing. Get everything in writing in the lease.

Entertainment organizations have found themselves in trouble when they opened studios or performance space in premises leased for residential purposes. If the lease or the zoning regulations prohibit such activities, you can run into difficulties on several counts. The landlord may want more rent for the commercial use of the space; neighbors may complain if extensive noise, high traffic, refuse, or other objectionable conditions are associated with the improper use of the premises; you may be fined by the municipality for zoning violations and not permitted to use the space for the purpose you desire. Some jurisdictions have enacted special laws permitting artists, including entertainment professionals, to live and work in the same space. You should determine whether such a law exists in your jurisdiction and whether it would be applicable to your situation.

The end of the lease is as important as the beginning. Virtually every lease includes a clause that the tenants leave the premises in the same condition as when they moved in. The deposit required by most landlords is one way in which they make sure that you pay for repairs which have to be made after you move out to restore the place to its original condition.

A *sub-lease* or *assignment clause* is also important. If you find it necessary to move out before the lease expires, do you have the right to find a new tenant to fill the remaining term of your lease? If you have that right, does the landlord have the right of approval of the new tenant? Can the landlord, for example, determine that a certain type of tenant is undesirable?

Finally we come to the *renewal clause.* Suppose you sign a two-year lease with an option to renew. Does it specify at what rent you renew? When do you have to exercise the option? What happens if you don't exercise the option? In some states, the law assumes that you have renewed the lease and all its terms if you have not notified the landlord otherwise in writing by a certain date. In other cases, your lease may have expired, but you remain on a month-to-month basis. In the absence of a lease at that time, the landlord can charge you an increased amount, unless the original lease specifies otherwise.

In *personal property leases,* as for vehicles, office equipment, and the like, the issues are similar and you should be diligent in shopping for the best possible arrangement. Determine monthly payments, the lease period, responsibility for maintenance, early termination penalties, lease-purchase options, and the like. Tax benefits may be available for leasing.

The basic purpose here is to alert you to the necessity of reading all the terms very carefully, taking nothing for granted, assuming nothing that isn't put down in writing, and taking the time to think carefully about the implications of everything you sign. There are no standard terms; everything is negotiable. Be wary of the so-called standard lease, since it will always benefit the lessor. You should also beware of so-called master leases which are common in large real property units, such as shopping centers and malls.

Before you sign a commercial lease, you should consult a lawyer. Tell him or her what your requirements are, what you want to do and don't want to do, and let the lawyer analyze the contract to make sure that your interests are properly protected.

➤ *See also* Contract, Equipment, Lawyer, Tax, Uniform Commercial Code, Zoning

Legality

➤ *See* Lawyer

Letter Agreement

A *letter agreement* is a contract which can cover anything from an arrangement for employing talent to the agreement for purchasing real estate. It is customarily less formal than a traditional contract but is no less binding. It is a letter confirming an agreement. Notwithstanding the letter format, it should be signed by the sender/party and countersigned by all recipient parties. This should be distinguished from a *letter of intent,* which, as its name suggests, is not a binding contract. A letter of intent merely expresses the intent of the parties to ultimately enter into a more formal contract, though the parties may agree on certain fundamental terms and provide that the letter of intent should govern their arrangement until the more formal contract is in place.

➤ *See also* Contract, Lawyer

Letter of Credit

A *letter of credit* is a document in which a bank notifies its agent or correspondent bank that funds are to be paid immediately to the person named in the letter upon proper identification and, if appropriate, evidence that the purpose for which the funds are to be paid has been accomplished; *e.g.*, completion of a theatrical tour. This document replaces the use of a check for payment, and makes money immediately available. In effect, it establishes a credit line for the recipient upon which he or she can draw as soon as the specifications of the letter of credit are carried out. Letters of credit are used primarily for very large transactions, as well as for long-distance and international transactions.

➤ *See also* Banks, Cashier's Check, Certified Check, Uniform Commercial Code

Letter of Intent

➤ *See* Letter Agreement

Liabilities

➤ *See* Financial Statement

Liability Insurance

Any injury for which you or your business may be responsible can be covered by *liability insurance*. There are several forms of liability insurance:

1. *Personal Liability.* This can protect you as an individual; for example, if your dog bites the mailman or someone slips on the ice in front of your house.
2. *Public Liability.* This protects you as a business owner; for example, if a patron suffers an injury while visiting your theater.
3. *Product Liability.* This protects you if you are injured because of a design defect in a product purchased by you, *e.g.*, a short circuit in your lighting or sound system.

Many theater companies buy specific short-term liability insurance to cover themselves for a production conducted in a leased performance space. In fact, most such leases require this type of insurance.

➤ *See also* Insurance

Librettist

The person who writes the *libretto,* typically of an opera or musical play. Libretti may include song lyrics, but the term more typically applies to the sung-through portions of dialogue and exposition which are distinct from song lyrics.

➤ *See also* Composer, Lyricist, Playwright

License

A *license* is the right for one to engage in some regulated activity. For example, states grant drivers' licenses, and municipalities grant business licenses and licenses to pet owners. In these instances, the purpose of the license is, presumably, to protect the public from certain dangerous activities or unscrupulous practices and/or to collect revenue.

A form of license applicable to the entertainment business is the *private license agreement.* As with a license under government authority, a private license grants permission to engage in a certain activity. Here, though, the activity is usually the use for commercial purposes of the owner's (licensor's) rights in some creative work, known as *intellectual property.* Intellectual property includes copyrights, trademarks, and patents, as well as trade secrets and trade dress.

Specifically, any performance right granted either directly by a playwright or, more commonly, through a clearing house such as Samuel French or Music Theater International, is a private license agreement. These agreements typically include such factors as scope of use (dates and location of performances, number of performances, and ticket prices), acknowledgements, publicity, amounts and timing of royalties, and other payments. It is important to keep in mind that even a single performance or workshop production may require a license and royalty payments, regardless of whether or not an admission fee is charged. As with any agreement or transaction involving complex business and legal issues, appropriate legal and financial advice should be obtained before you enter into any licensing agreement.

➤ *See also* Assignability, Contract, Copyright, Intellectual Property, Patent, Royalty, Trade Name, Trademark, Trade Secret, Work for Hire

Lien

A *lien* is a legal device by which one person (or other entity: a bank, the I.R.S., etc.) places a claim or encumbrance on the property of another to secure payment of a debt or obligation. If the debt is not paid, the lien can be foreclosed, or the property sold for the benefit of the creditor. In that respect, it is similar to a mortgage.

Here are two types of lien:

1. *Mechanic's Lien.* If you hire a electrician to install a new lighting system, and then you don't pay them, he or she can file a lien against your property in the appropriate government office if he or she complied with the state lien laws. A landlord may find that a lien has been placed on the property if a tenant contracts for work to be done on the rented premises and doesn't pay for it. A mechanic's lien usually takes precedence over all other encumbrances against the property, including a mortgage but excluding tax liens.

2. *Judgment Lien.* If someone sues you and wins a judgment for damages, they can also place a lien on your property, even though the cause of the lawsuit is totally unrelated to the property (unlike a mortgage or a mechanic's lien). The same procedure and the same results apply as in a mechanic's lien.

Liens fall into two general categories: *possessory* and *nonpossessory.* In the case of a possessory lien, such as a mechanic's lien, an auto mechanic may retain possession of your vehicle until he is paid for the work he performed on it. In the case of a nonpossessory lien, perfection is accomplished by filing a document evidencing the lien with the appropriate government office. Article 9 of the Uniform Commercial Code (UCC) provides the procedure for perfecting a security interest in order to protect a lien.

➤ *See also* Mortgage, Uniform Commercial Code

Life Insurance

Life insurance is actually survivors' insurance. Life insurance is not based on the same kind of risk as property insurance. The risk to the insurance company is in how soon death will occur. Premiums are related to risk. If you are twenty years old and in good health, the probability of your dying anytime soon is substantially less than if you are eighty. Statisticians (called *actuaries* in the insurance world) have figured out those probabilities, and have calculated the premiums so that, on the average, your life insurance is fully paid by the time you die.

Life insurance differs from property insurance in several other important respects:

1. The amount of coverage is not related to the value of the insured item since no dollar value can be placed on a human life. Everyone can choose his or her own dollar value in terms of how much money becomes available to the beneficiaries and what the premium payments are.

2. Most insurance policies have two parties: *the insured* and *the insurance company*. Life insurance has a third one: *the beneficiary*. The insured usually has the right to change beneficiaries at any time through proper notice to the insurance company. There are exceptions, such as a business which carries life insurance on a key employee, with the business as the beneficiary. There, the insured employee cannot change the beneficiary.

3. Most life insurance policies cannot be cancelled by the insurance company after a stated period of time, generally two years, except when the premiums are not paid or misrepresentations were made as to age or other important factors at the time the policy was issued.

4. Whole-life insurance policies have a cash value which increases over the years. This cash value belongs to and is paid to the insured if the policy is canceled or lapses for nonpayment of premiums. The cash

value can also be borrowed by the insured. If a loan is outstanding at the time the insured dies, the loan is subtracted from the benefits and the balance is then paid to the beneficiaries.

5. Most whole-life insurance policies pay annual dividends based on the cash value of the policy and the earnings of the insurance company. They, therefore, represent not only protection, but also investment.

There are literally dozens of varieties of life insurance, but they fall into four major categories: *ordinary (straight), limited payment, endowment, and term.*

Ordinary (Straight) Whole Life is a policy on which the premiums remain constant over the life of the policy (*i.e.*, the life of the insured) or until the insured reaches age 100, and the face value of the policy is paid to the beneficiaries at the death of the insured.

Limited Payment is a whole-life policy under which premium payments are made for a specified period. Thereafter, the premiums stop, but the policy remains in full force and payable to the beneficiaries at the death of the insured. It is more expensive than ordinary life in terms of the individual premium payments, but may be less expensive in terms of total premiums paid, especially if the insured is very young when the policy goes into effect.

Endowment policies are really savings plans with life insurance added (or vice versa). You pay premiums for a stated period of years. At the end of that time, if you are still alive, you are your own beneficiary. The face value of the policy is paid to you. If you have died in the meantime, your beneficiaries collect.

Term insurance is pure life insurance for a specified period of time, generally no more than five or ten years (although some policies provide guaranteed renewal for longer periods). Premiums are commonly constant for a specified period, usually five or ten years. Then coverage ends. Term policies have no cash or loan value, but their premium rates are generally lower than those of other types of life insurance. Term insurance is used primarily to protect unusually heavy responsibilities during a limited period of time. For example, if you have teenagers, a five- or ten-year term policy can make sure the money is available to get them through college in case you're not around to pay the tuition. Mortgage insurance is, in effect, a form of term insurance on the life of the mortgagor (*i.e.*, borrower) for the unexpired portion of the mortgage. If you die before the mortgage is paid off, the insurance policy pays the rest. There are no other benefits. The premiums for this type of insurance are constant throughout the entire term of the coverage, but the benefits decrease as the mortgage is paid off.

Adjustable Universal Life insurance, commonly known as *universal life,* is a *bundled* contract; that is, a term life insurance policy combined (bundled) with an investment fund.

Life insurance policies cannot be bought in the names of other people unless there is an insurable interest. A husband and wife can insure each other, and so can two business partners. A corporation can insure the lives of its executives, and a basketball team can insure the lives of its players. In all these instances there would be a demonstrable loss if the insured died, and, therefore, an insurable interest. Unlike property insurance, where the insurable interest must exist both when the policy is issued and when the claim is made, in life insurance that interest must exist only when the policy is issued. It becomes important, therefore, to examine your life insurance policies periodically to see if the beneficiary should be changed. Such instances occur when the beneficiary dies before you do, when there's a divorce, when a partnership is dissolved, or whenever some other reason for which the beneficiary was named ceases to exist.

➤ *See also* Group Insurance, Insurance

Lighting Designer

The *lighting designer* is the person who designs the lighting plot for a particular production. The design is frequently developed in concert with the stage director and set designer, but this is not universally the case.

➤ *See also* Director, Appendix A

Limitations

➤ *See* Statute of Limitations

Limited Liability Company

Limited liability company (LLC) is a relatively new business form which affords the owners the ability to limit their personal liability for business activities to their investment in the business while enjoying the tax treatment accorded unincorporated businesses; that is, the limited liability company is not a taxable entity. S-corporations afford the same liability limitation, though the tax treatment is not as beneficial as that afforded LLCs, and S-corporations have certain other technical limitations not imposed on LLCs. These include: (1) there may be no more than thirty-five human shareholders in an S-corporation, and they must be American citizens; and (2) there may be only one class of stock in an S-corporation.

Since LLCs appear to be more desirable for many businesses, laws permitting their creation have been adopted in every state but Hawaii and New Hampshire, and it is expected that these states will have also enacted legislation in the near future. You should consult with an experienced business lawyer to determine whether this business form would be advantageous for your business.

> ➤ *See also* Capital Campaign, Corporation, Joint Venture, Limited Liability Partnership, Limited Partnership, Partnership, Securities, Sole Proprietorship

Limited Liability Partnership

An even newer business form is the *limited liability partnership.* This is a partnership which has limited liability. This means that the partners may have their personal liability limited to their investment in the partnership and/or a specific amount set forth in the appropriate state statute. These business forms are intended primarily for use by the licensed professionals usually specified in the appropriate state professional corporation statutes, such as accountants, doctors, lawyers, and the like.

> ➤ *See also* Capital Campaign, Corporation, Joint Venture, Limited Liability Company, Limited Partnership, Partnership, Sole Proprietorship

Limited Partnership

Limited partnerships are customarily used in the entertainment industry for purposes of financing a particular project or series of projects, such as a motion picture or television series, a theatrical production, and the like. A limited partnership is a business form defined by state law as a partnership with one or more general partners, who have full personal liability, and one or more limited partners, whose liability is limited to their investment in the business. The partners may be individuals or corporations. Since the business form is a partnership, partners are taxed on their distributable share of partnership profits and may deduct their distributable share of partnership losses. If the general partner is a corporation, rather than an individual, it must have a substantial net worth. No partner, general or limited, may own more than 80 percent of the limited partnership.

At one time, entertainment limited partnerships were used as tax shelters. They were structured so as to allow the limited partner to deduct a multiple of the amount invested in the project. For example, a company known as Master

Records marketed limited partnership interests which promised investors write-offs of between $4 and $6 for every dollar invested. These so-called abusive tax shelters were challenged by the Internal Revenue Service and many of the investors wound up in securities litigation with the promoters. Few of these shelters ever delivered the promised benefits and, today, they are virtually unheard-of.

Limited partnerships are still in use for funding legitimate entertainment projects and many of the investments have been successful.

➤ *See also* Capital Campaign, Corporation, Joint Venture, Limited Liability Company, Limited Liability Partnership, Partnership, Securities

Limited Run

When a movie house or theater company desires to limit the number of performances for a particular production, it is said to be a *limited run.* A smaller or community theater company is likely to present most of its productions on a limited-run basis, as opposed to Broadway shows, which typically run until audience interest has waned. New theater productions intended for a Broadway run may first open *out of town* for a limited run or *tryout.*

A limited run may be used for purposes of conducting market research. In the film industry, production companies sometimes hold limited runs of new features for purposes of gauging audience reaction. The movie may be re-edited or its advertising reworked after the test audience reaction is evaluated. Limited-run television programs may be used to determine whether the theme, characters, or story have the kind of viewer appeal which will warrant further investment by the network or production company. Limited-run cable programs are common for determining viewer reaction. Even video distributors have been known to use limited run video releases to determine customer interest.

Limited runs for purposes of production market research are becoming more common in the entertainment industry as a means of limiting risk. The information gathered from the experiment is valuable in determining whether a production will have the market appeal that was anticipated when the investment was first made. Fine-tuning before the ultimate release is more likely to produce the desired success for all forms of entertainment production.

Loans

There are a variety of types of *loans.* One is the obtaining of money from another, typically for a price, which must be repaid. Another type involves lending tangible property to another, such as costumes to a theater company.

Monetary loans can come from a variety of sources: friends and relatives who have confidence in you or your entertainment project, your own life insurance policies (if they have loan values), and lending institutions such as banks, credit unions, and the like. Even the credit extended by your suppliers is, in effect, a form of loan. The Small Business Administration is prohibited by its charter from lending money to anyone engaged in the entertainment business, since it is felt by Congress that First Amendment rights of free speech and expression may be affected.

Loans should be distinguished from capital investments. Unlike loans, equity on capital investments is repaid only if and when the business is dissolved. Equity serves as the basis on which the investor is paid a share of the profits, which, in C corporations, are known as *dividends*. While interest on a loan is required to be paid, dividends are customarily granted only at the discretion of a corporation's or limited liability company's governing board. For partnerships or other unincorporated for-profit associations, profit is distributed in accordance with the express agreement of the parties or, if there is no agreement, under the partnership statutes, equally to all partners.

The basic characteristics of a loan are that it must be repaid at some specified time, or in periodic installments, and that interest is charged for the use of the money. Before making a loan, a potential lender will evaluate the likelihood of being repaid. This involves a number of questions. A lender will want to know why you need the money, what you plan to do with it, how and when the loan will be repaid, what your credit rating is, whether you or someone else can guarantee the loan, and so forth. The answers to questions such as these may determine not only whether the loan will be granted, but how much interest will be charged. The greater the risk, the higher the interest may be. A loan guarantor is under obligation to repay the loan if the borrower defaults; it may be very risky to guarantee someone else's loan.

There are at least three basic sources of funds, other than your own:

1. *Equity*: the money which investors provide. As stated above, this does not have to be repaid unless the business is dissolved. Equity is the basis on which investors share in the profits. Equity may also be raised by issuing and selling securities (stock or investment contracts) to family, friends, close associates, and even the public at large. It is imperative that you have an experienced attorney review any of these transactions in order to assist you in complying with the federal or state securities laws.

2. *Trade credit*: the terms on which you can buy supplies without paying

cash at the time of the purchase. You are, in effect, borrowing money for a short term until you pay your bill.

3. *Loans*: the money provided by others with a specific understanding of how and when the loan will be repaid, including the rate of interest.

Loans fall into two basic categories:

1. *Short Term*. These are loans for a period of up to twelve months.
2. *Long Term*. These are loans which you expect to repay over a period of time which exceeds one year, usually in monthly installments. Such loans are made for major expenditures such as the purchase of equipment or real estate.

Short-term loans can often be made as *unsecured loans,* which means that your signature and your credit reputation are sufficient. Long-term loans, on the other hand, usually require some sort of collateral or other guarantee, the pledging of some asset which the lender can foreclose on and sell if the borrower fails to repay the loan, or a personal guarantee. The most common of these is a real estate mortgage in which the real estate itself is the collateral. Other forms of collateral may include stocks and bonds, life insurance policies, accounts receivable, and signatures of co-makers or guarantors, who agree to be personally responsible if the borrower defaults.

What the lender needs to know includes some or all of the following:

1. How solvent is your business?
2. Are your books and records up-to-date and in good order?
3. How much do the owner or owners take out of the business in salaries, dividends, and the like?
4. How many employees do you have?
5. How much insurance coverage do you have?
6. How large are your accounts receivable?
7. How large is your inventory?
8. What are the age and value of your fixed assets such as equipment? How are they depreciated?
9. What are your plans for the future?

For a business loan, the financial statements and tax returns are the principal documents a lender usually requires, especially for long-term loans. They indicate your financial condition and your profit picture. A series of such documents covering several years will identify a pattern and indicate to the lender how much of a risk it is taking by lending the money. It is more difficult for new enterprises to raise funds through borrowing than for established businesses, since the new venture will not have a track record.

The amount of the loan is another important consideration both for the borrower and the lender. Here, again, the borrower's financial statements are a key factor because they reveal the borrower's likely ability to repay the loan. Another factor which lenders take into account is your willingness to invest in your own business. If you make a long-range plan for expansion which will require a loan, it is wise to be able to invest some money of your own. If you approach the potential lender and indicate that you are personally willing to commit a significant portion of the required amount, you'll probably receive much more sympathetic attention. The lender will be more inclined to take the risk if it knows that you are sharing that risk.

The limitations a lender sets on the borrower, the rate of interest it charges, and the other terms of repayment are all related to the lender's interpretation of how great a risk it is taking. That does not mean, however, that every lender interprets the same set of facts the same way. Banks are more restricted in their flexibility than unregulated lenders. Some lenders are more conservative than others. Some have had good experience with small business loans or may have a policy of encouraging small local businesses to develop. Some may consider a particular type of collateral very secure, while others may not. All of this influences the borrower's experience with a particular lender, and if the first approach does not succeed, or if the limitations and interest rates are not acceptable, it is sensible to approach another lender.

In addition to the financial documents which most lenders want to see, a carefully thought-out business plan also contributes a great deal to a successful application. The business plan should, among other things, set forth the amount of money desired and the use of those proceeds, what the conditions in your own business and in the field in general are, how you foresee your own business growth proceeding, any sales plans, how your business is managed, and so forth. Here, again, the business plan not only provides the lender with a picture of how safe the loan might be, but how thoroughly you have considered the need for the money and how competent your own understanding of your business situation is.

Borrowing money can be quite complex. Discussion of your financial needs with your accountant or your banker often provides much valuable information on the most practical ways to solve those needs through a wide range of borrowing opportunities. Two excellent booklets on the subject are available without charge from the Small Business Administration: "ABCs of Borrowing" and "Sound Cash Management and Borrowing." Though neither deals expressly with the entertainment business or the performing arts, they are informative for small business in general.

LOANS OF TANGIBLE PROPERTY
Loans of tangible property, such as costumes, sets, props, and the like should be memorialized in writing. Many cultural organizations are remiss in documenting loans; some institutions have virtually no record of the ownership of items in their possession. A loan document should contain, at a minimum, a detailed description of the work, name and address of the lender, duration, and terms and conditions of the loan.

➤ *See also* Amortization, Banks, Bridge Financing, Business Plan, Capital, Collateral, Contract, Credit, Financial Statement, Foreclosure, Installment, Insurance, Interest, Mortgage, Year-End, Appendix B

Lyricist
The *lyricist* is the person who writes the words of a song. Some lyricists work independently, writing only lyrics, while others may collaborate with a composer, with each party writing some portion of both the music and the lyrics. There is no standard regarding which comes first, the lyrics or the music. Most writing teams develop their own style in this regard, however, even established writing styles may change. For example, in the later years of their collaboration, Gilbert & Sullivan worked very independently from each other.

A lyricist may also be a librettist and/or a composer.

➤ *See also* Collaboration, Composer, Copyright, Librettist, Playwright

Magazines

➤ *See* Periodicals

Mailing Lists

Whether you use the mails to make announcements that will bring patrons to your theater, or whether you use the mails to generate mail-order purchases of season tickets, the *mailing list* can be very important. Mailing lists come from two primary sources: your own lists which you compile over the years, and lists which you can buy from list brokers or other organizations.

Your own list should be the most effective. Since the quality of a list is measured by how many names on it can be expected to respond favorably, a list of patrons or others who have indicated an interest in your company can be one of your most valuable assets. Keep your list up-to-date. A card file maintained in alphabetical order is convenient. Also available are a variety of software programs for use on your personal computer, and specialized mailing list programs, which print mailing labels, phone lists, and so forth. Whenever you have a new patron, whenever you come across a prospect, add it to the list. Depending on your needs, that list may be sufficient for your purposes. An invitation to an opening, for example, may produce enough attendance from just such a list.

There may, however, be occasions when you want to reach a larger audience. There are literally hundreds of specialized lists available. The usual procedure is to buy the one-time use of such a list. There are lists of doctors, society matrons, plumbers, and business executives. Lists of business executives may be further broken down by title or size of business. You can buy lists of theater patrons, members of particular organizations, and many others. The cost depends on the nature of the list, and almost always includes a complete set of mailing labels. Costs generally run between $35 and $50 per thousand names, though some lists cost more.

Discuss your list needs with a reliable list broker, who should be able to give good advice and obtain special lists for you. If you can't find a satisfactory list broker locally, an inquiry to any of the brokers given in Appendix A may be helpful. If you want to do a mailing to the members of a specific organization or the subscribers of a specific publication, a direct inquiry may be appropriate. For a fee, some of them make their member or subscriber lists available. You can also pool your list with others in compatible businesses. For example, the Portland [Oregon] Area Theater Alliance publishes and mails a newsletter which includes its members' openings.

The size and nature of a list is not the only consideration, however. How *clean* a list is must also be considered. *Clean* means how current the list is. During the course of a year, people move away, change jobs, and die. On a list which has not been used and cleaned in a year, you can expect as much as 20 percent undeliverable mail. That's an expensive proposition when you consider that even a simple mailing piece will cost fifty cents or more. Ask a list broker how recently a particular list has been used and updated. If it wasn't very recently, ask for a credit on any undeliverable returns in excess of 5 percent. Most reputable brokers will stand behind their promises of clean lists.

Before you make a commitment to rent a large list, you may wish to test it. Suppose a broker has four lists, each of which has 10,000 names. All four look good to you, but you can never be sure. Instead of buying 40,000 names and discovering that some of the lists were not suited to your purpose, buy only a representative sample of each list at first—say 1,000 names. Now you have a mailing of 4,000 pieces which will cost much less than taking a chance on 40,000.

Careful recordkeeping is necessary when you test or when you do any sort of mail promotion. You may accomplish this by coding the responses from a particular mailing. There's too much money tied up in using the mails to skimp on tracking down the results.

What kind of response can you expect from a list? That depends on the quality of the list and the nature of the promotion. Under normal circumstances, a list user considers 2 percent a satisfactory response. In other words, if you send out 10,000 pieces announcing an opening, 200 attendees could be considered acceptable. A response of 10 percent or higher could be expected from an unusually good list, such as your own patron list.

All of that has to be related to costs. To send out 10,000 pieces requesting charitable donations to your nonprofit organization, at a total cost of $5,000, for example, and wind up with only a 2 percent response may not even pay for the cost of the mailing. On the other hand, if you take in $10,000 on a 2 percent response, that may yield a nice return.

You may never see the names on a purchased list, since some list owners will make labels available only directly to your printer or mail house for mailing purposes, but you do obtain the names of people who respond. Add them to your own list for future mailings.

➤ *See also* Advertising, Direct Mail, Prospect List, Recordkeeping

Manager

There are several kinds of managers involved in the entertainment industry. Two of the most common are *personal managers* and *business managers,* both of which are distinguishable from agents, who play a different role in an entertainer's career, and the British usage, which refers to the individual known in America as a producer. Many entertainers have a management team which includes, among others, an agent, a personal manager, a business manager, and an attorney. This group of advisers may cost as much as 30-40 percent of the entertainer's gross receipts.

Personal managers are usually involved with an entertainer in a one-on-one arrangement. They assist with career development and are involved with the entertainer on a day-to-day basis. They typically advise and counsel their clients on such matters as selection of artistic material, publicity, public relations and advertising, selecting the format for and artistic talent to assist in presentation of the entertainer's talents and, overall, in regard to general practices in the industry, including selection of an agent. The personal manager provides liaison services between the entertainer and those with whom he or she deals on a business and professional basis. A personal manager is the confidante and primary adviser of the entertainer, frequently becomes the entertainer's "best friend," and often even lives in the entertainer's home.

Business managers, who are often accountants or lawyers, are involved with the entertainer's economic activities. They can assist with collection of monies due and payment of bills or can be much more involved in the entertainer's financial matters and act as investment advisers, as well.

New York and California laws specifically prohibit managers from engaging in activities which amount to "seeking employment" for their clients; that is the function and province of the agent. Both personal and business managers owe their clients a fiduciary duty; since business managers are frequently privy to the entertainer's most intimate financial dealings, they have an even higher responsibility. There are numerous instances where entertainers have been "fleeced" by unscrupulous business managers, and the resulting litigation often resembles an acrimonious divorce more than a business dispute.

Entertainment organizations also have managers, who may have titles such as *general manager* or *managing director* and run the day-to-day operations of the organization, or *stage manager* and assume responsibility for production activities. There are no precise job descriptions for most types of manager, and the title is somewhat flexible so that the parties can accommodate the specific tasks to fit the needs of the organization or individual. It is recommended that both the manager and the party hiring him or her be represented by attorneys skilled in entertainment and business law so that the resulting arrangement will more likely not be vulnerable to a later challenge of "overreaching," "unfairness," or "unconscionability." The terms of the agreement should always be set down in writing.

➤ *See* Agent, Contract, Director, Morals Clause, Producer, Appendix A

Managing Director
➤ *See* Manager

Marketability

Marketability is simply whether a given work can be sold to its intended audience. One of the key factors in marketability is price, but price is by no means the only factor. Indeed, price is rarely the patron's first concern. Before a patron asks how much, a tentative decision has already been made that it might be nice to attend the particular production. Price follows the determination of need or desire.

Before a ticket can be sold, the production must fill a need. The need may be emotional, such as a spectacular musical; it may be prestige, such as a world premiere; it may even be financial or philanthropic, such as a benefit. The next question is how the work meets that need. This is where such intangible elements as reputations of the company and production staff, author and composer, as well as current fads or trends, become important. Tastes differ among people and change from one year to the next and one generation to the next.

Entertainment companies need not compromise their artistic integrity for the sake of popular appeal but, to survive economically, it is essential to create marketable work; that is, you should be sensitive to what theatergoers are seeing and what they're not seeing (and why). If theater attendance is down, is it a problem of show selection or price, or being behind or ahead of the times? Don't merely imitate what successful companies are doing. For most companies, there are always a few shows that have broader appeal than others. What is it that draws audiences to those shows? What are the prices? Listen carefully to what's happening during your own intermissions. What are patrons particularly interested in seeing next? What are they seeing and not seeing? What are they asking for? Is price an issue?

The effect of critics' reviews varies greatly from market to market. New York theater critics have effectively been able to close a show; a small town critic, by contrast, is not likely to have the same clout. You should, nonetheless, be attentive to reviewers' comments and incorporate helpful suggestions where appropriate.

➤ *See also* Marketing, Ticket

Marketing

Marketing may be characterized as the method of promoting a production or project. Note the word *method.* Marketing is not a single activity. *Marketing, advertising,* and *selling* are often used interchangeably, but advertising and selling are only parts of the marketing process. Other elements of the total marketing operation include publicity, timing, pricing, the image of the production company and the shows it presents. A well-directed musical, for example, may receive critical acclaim but not be marketable. Marketing, then, refers to all the things that happen to a work between the time it is selected for production and the time the patron buys a ticket to it.

➤ *See also* Advertising, Marketability, Nonprofit Organization, Publicity, Public Relations, Subscription Sales

Master Class

An advanced-level seminar conducted by a master of a specific discipline is known as a *master class.* Common master classes include acting, vocal, and dance techniques. They may be unique presentations or part of an ongoing program. Some masters conduct their programs in a series of locales. Class size is typically limited to a small number of students.

Materials

➤ *See* Suppliers

Media

➤ *See* Advertising

Mediation

➤ *See* Alternative Dispute Resolution

Minimum Wage

The *federal minimum wage law,* known as the Fair Labor Standards Act, was established in the 1930s. It covers the entire country and was last amended in 1990. Many states also have their own minimum wage laws which apply in some areas of work not included in the federal law, such as working papers for minors. In states where both state and federal minimum wage laws exist, the higher rates and standards apply. In 1992, the minimum hourly wage became $5.75. With some exceptions specifically stated in the law, no one can lawfully be paid less than that.

Overtime must be paid at a rate of 1.5 times the employee's regular hourly rate for all hours beyond forty hours per work week. Overtime cannot be averaged over more than one work week; in other words, if an employee works thirty-eight hours one week and forty-four hours the next, he is entitled to four hours of overtime pay for the second week. Furthermore, the work week cannot be capriciously changed from week to week (to avoid overtime obligations). A change can be made only if it is intended to be permanent.

There are several important exceptions to the minimum wage law which could affect an entertainment business:

1. The spouse, or children under age twenty-one, of an individual owner of an entertainment business need not be paid the minimum wage or overtime.

2. Executive, administrative, and professional personnel are customarily exempt from being paid a minimum wage or overtime. The law specifically includes in the category of professional employees those in the entertainment field whose work is original and creative. The important thing is not by what title the employee is known, but what

the employee actually does. When there is a question of qualifying for exemptions in this category, the basis on which the Labor Department determines eligibility is outlined in the Secretary of Labor's Regulations, 29 C.F.R. Part 541.

3. Salespeople who work away from the employer's premises on a commission basis are also exempt from both the minimum wage and overtime provisions. This exemption applies only to people who sell, however, not those who do other work off the employer's premises.

4. Under certain circumstances and with special certificates from the Department of Labor, students may be employed at wage rates below the minimum on a part-time basis or during school vacations. This also applies to learners in vocational education programs.

The federal law also requires that no differentials in wages are allowed if they are based on the employee's sex, color, or any other discriminatory reason. Wage differentials are permitted only when they are based on seniority, merit, or any other bona fide job-related factor. The Labor Department is quite strict in the enforcement of this law. Failure to pay minimum wages or overtime is a federal offense. Not only can the Secretary of Labor or the employees themselves go to court to recover unpaid wages, but serious violations may also be subject to civil or criminal prosecution. The law requires employers to keep accurate records of wages, hours, and other information. Such records must be kept for at least three years (two years for time cards, piecework tickets, etc.).

Questions on wages, overtime, hours, discrimination, and other subjects covered by the Fair Labor Standards Act can be directed by both employers and employees to any of the offices maintained throughout the country by the Wage and Hour Division of the U.S. Labor Department. The telephone book white and blue pages list them under "U.S. Government, Department of Labor, Employment Standards Administration." In the entertainment industry, members of trade unions are typically subject to collective bargaining agreements which establish wages and working conditions. Labor union agreements are administered by the National Labor Relations Board.

➤ *See also* Employees, Union, Wages

Model Release

➤ *See* Contract, Photographs

Money Order

If you have a checking account, you can write your own checks. If you have a savings account, you may use cashier's checks. Regardless of whether you have a bank connection, you can obtain *money orders*. Money orders are available from a variety of sources, including banks, the U.S. Post Office, American Express, and others. They are written in specific amounts and are sold to anyone with the cash to buy them. A fee may be charged, which may be based on the amount of the money order. Money orders can be cashed, with proper identification, at any office of the agency which issued them (*e.g.*, any post office in the case of postal money orders), or they can be deposited like checks in a bank account. A potential drawback to paying expenses by money order is that the payor does not receive the cancelled checks.

➤ *See also* Banks, Cashier's Check, Checking Account, Certified Check, Credit Unions, Savings Bank

Moral Rights

➤ *See Droit Morale*

Morals Clause

Many entertainment contracts contain so-called *morals clauses*. This is because the reputation of the entertainer is said to affect the reputation of the hiring entity. These clauses can be as specific as requiring the entertainer to be depicted "in a decent and virtuous manner, and as champion of right and the enemy of wrong" or as general as prohibiting the commission of illegal acts.

Care should be taken to avoid entering into an agreement which will inhibit the entertainer's free expression unless there is a bona fide reason for the inhibition. Some entertainers, such as Marilyn Monroe and Madonna, have actually enhanced their box office appeal by engaging in what was considered to be questionable behavior—in Monroe's case, posing nude for calendars, in Madonna's case, her controversial demeanor and *Sex* book. Other entertainers, such as Michael Jackson and Pee Wee Herman, have suffered a backlash of negative publicity as a result of their alleged improprieties. A skilled entertainment lawyer should be consulted when negotiating a contract.

➤ *See* Contract, Lawyer, Manager, Obscenity, Pornography

Mortgage

A *mortgage* is a conveyance by a borrower to the lender of a conditional title as security for the repayment of a loan, usually made for the purchase or refinancing of land and/or buildings (real property). This could include an entertainer's home as well as a production company's commercial building. In effect, the borrower (mortgagor) grants to the lender (mortgagee) a conditional transfer of title (ownership) to the property, even though the borrower is in possession of it and is the legal owner of it. The borrower can do anything with the property, including selling it. In the case of a sale, the loan obligation secured by the mortgage must either be paid off or transferred to the new owner. When the loan is paid off, the mortgage, by its terms, is terminated. That is, the fee (legal title) in the property automatically revests in (returns to) the borrower (owner).

Mortgages are usually paid off in monthly installments over a period of years. If the borrower defaults on the mortgage, there are a variety of options available to the lender, including accelerating the loan or foreclosure. If the loan is *accelerated,* the entire balance of principal, interest, and other charges is immediately due and payable. In the event of *foreclosure,* the lender may sell the property. If the property is sold for more than the amount due on the mortgage, plus costs related to the foreclosure, the excess must be paid to the borrower.

Mortgage transactions, like most financial transactions, require careful consideration and examination of all the details. Important among these are the rate of interest and term of the loan. While fractional differences between interest rates may seem insignificant, the amount of money involved can be significant. Interest rates can be *fixed* or *variable.* This means that the interest may fluctuate as the economy changes. The fluctuation may be based on a variety of factors, though the most common is the Consumer Price Index as determined by an identified bank. Variable rates generally have a floor, or minimum rate, and may or may not have a ceiling.

A few other questions: Does the lender allow the mortgage to be assumed by a subsequent buyer if the property is sold before the mortgage is paid off? That may be important, because an assumable mortgage may make it easier to sell a property. What (if any) are the penalties if you are late with a payment or want to prepay the balance of the mortgage before it is due? Are you required to pay into an escrow account at the bank from which the bank pays your annual or semiannual real estate taxes, insurance premiums, etc. (but on which it pays you no interest), or can you put the money in your own savings account, earn interest, and pay the taxes and other bills yourself? Are you prohibited from giving a second mortgage?

A *second mortgage* (or third, fourth, etc.) is given to secure any additional loans on the property. For example: Suppose the total price of the property you want to buy is $90,000. You make a down payment of $10,000 and obtain a first mortgage loan of $80,000. You may want to remodel the property, which will cost $10,000. You may be able to obtain this sum by granting a second mortgage on the property. A second mortgage can also be used to raise cash on a piece of property you already own if you have a first mortgage at a low rate of interest which you don't want to disturb by refinancing that first mortgage at a higher interest rate. Second mortgages may also be used to generate additional cash for other purposes, such as purchasing a vehicle or financing a vacation. In this case, the amount lent may be a percentage of the amount of equity the borrower has in the property; this is commonly known as a *home equity loan.*

First mortgages are generally granted to a bank or other large institution for the basic financing of a property. Second mortgages are also granted to banks but there is an increasing number of nonbank lenders engaging in the second mortgage business. In the event of a foreclosure (and in most, if not all, other cases), the first mortgage has a claim ahead of the second mortgage if there are not sufficient funds to pay off both. Since the risk is greater to a second mortgagee, the interest rate on a second mortgage is generally higher than on a first, and the term is generally shorter, usually not more than fifteen years. Banks and other lenders normally require that the property be insured against loss from fire and the like.

A loan on a piece of personal property (*i.e.,* other than real estate), such as an automobile, is usually protected by a security interest, which is perfected by filing a UCC Financing Statement in the appropriate governmental office and otherwise complying with Article 9 of the Uniform Commercial Code. The basic principles of payment, interest, insurance, and foreclosure apply in such mortgages, as well.

➤ *See also* Banks, Collateral, Foreclosure, Installment, Interest, Lien, Loans, Uniform Commercial Code

Music Director

A *music director* is typically the person who is resident with a particular production company, as distinguished from a guest conductor. A music director may also be a conductor, or may be responsible for vocal or orchestral rehearsal and direction. The music director may also be involved in the selection of musical talent.

➤ *See also* Conductor, Director

National Association of Campus Activities

➤ *See* Appendix A

National Association of Performing Arts Managers and Agents

➤ *See* Appendix A

National Endowment for the Arts

The *National Endowment for the Arts* (NEA) is an independent agency of the federal government created by Congress to encourage and support American art and artists, including those in the entertainment industry. It pursues its mission by awarding grants to individuals and organizations concerned with the arts throughout the United States. The NEA's mission is "to foster the excellence, diversity and vitality of the arts in the United States; and to help broaden the availability and appreciation of such excellence, diversity and vitality." There is a specific program for performing arts. Grants are available in numerous categories. Some grants are made to nonprofit organizations on a matching fund basis, some are made directly to individual artists. Deadlines for grant applications occur on different dates for different grants. Specific details about each grant are spelled out in the Endowment's "Guide to the NEA."

> ➤ *See also* Arts Councils, Government Activities, Grants, Humanities Councils or Committees, National Endowment for the Humanities, Performance Art, Appendix A, Appendix B

National Endowment for the Humanities

A federal agency created at the same time as the National Endowment for the Arts, *The National Endowment for the Humanities'* (NEH) mission is to aid and encourage humanistic endeavors throughout the United States and to encourage international cultural exchange. Many of its programs are aimed specifically at theater arts. Like the NEA, it awards grants to nonprofit organizations and individuals involved in humanistic endeavors, including writers, entertainers, directors, and the like. The NEH also works with state and local counterparts by providing regrant money and educating the boards of the state and local affiliates on methods by which they can prime the humanistic pump in their locales.

> ➤ *See also* Government Activities, Grants, Humanities Councils or Committees, National Endowment for the Arts, Appendix A

National Labor Relations Board

> ➤ *See* Minimum Wage, Union

Net

When *net* precedes another word, such as *price, profit, income, worth,* or *weight,* it means that deductions have been taken and that the described subject is free and clear. When used as a verb, it usually indicates the means of achieving a final, true income or profit, after all expenses and taxes have been deducted from the selling price, as in "We should net $10,000 on this production." The opposite of net is *gross.*

There is a great danger in not precisely defining this term. In a leading case, screenwriter Art Buchwald charged that the words *net profit,* as used in his movie arrangement for the film *Coming to America,* inappropriately entitled the production company to deduct from its gross receipts such items as payments on future movie deals, overhead, meals, entertainment expenses, and a vast array of what he characterized as frivolous charges. The court agreed with Mr. Buchwald and criticized the practice. Despite the fact that this case arose in a film industry context, its precepts are applicable to virtually every facet of the entertainment industry, and underscore the importance of meticulously defining the items which may be deducted from *gross* to arrive at *net*. In addition, *net income* should be distinguished from *net profit*.

➤ *See also* Accounting, Financial Statement, Gross

Nonprofit Organization

A *nonprofit,* or *not-for-profit,* organization is created for the purpose of serving the public. The organization may be incorporated under the state nonprofit corporation code or it may be an unincorporated association. It may or may not be tax-exempt. For a nonprofit organization to achieve tax-exempt status, it must apply to and receive from the Internal Revenue Service (IRS) a letter ruling on its eligibility. The IRS evaluation can take some time. The organization may also have to qualify for tax exemption under the state tax laws.

Only organizations which are characterized by the IRS as tax-exempt under Section 501(c)(3) of the Internal Revenue Code may avail donors of a charitable deduction for donations. These organizations must be engaged in performing educational, scientific or related public benefit, and may not be privately owned by anyone or created for the purpose of merely serving a particular constituency. Many state taxing authorities do not automatically extend tax-exempt status to federally recognized organizations; the organization may have to apply directly to the state for such status. Many performing arts production companies and schools are qualified as tax-exempt under both federal and state tax laws.

Qualified charities may supplement their income through *benefits*; *i.e.,* a performance or other function the profits from which accrue to the benefit of the organization. The organization may itself sponsor the event, or the sponsor may be an auxiliary support group or even philanthropic citizens. A ticket buyer may claim as a charitable contribution any amount paid for the ticket which is in excess of the actual value of the ticket; for example, the purchaser of a $100 benefit ticket to a theatrical performance the regular ticket price for which is $25 would be entitled to a $75 charitable contribution for tax purposes.

Labor unions and other *mutual benefit* organizations may also be structured as nonprofit corporations, but they will not be considered tax-exempt under Section 501(c)(3); rather, they may be permitted to qualify under Section 501(c)(7); in this event, donations are not tax-deductible. In addition, 501(c)(7) organizations are not entitled to the other privileges available to public charities, *i.e.,* reduced postage rates, the right to receive certain grants, and the like.

➤ *See also* Capital Campaign, Charitable Contribution, Community Theater, Corporation, Endowment, Grant, Marketing, Pubic Service Announcement, Tax, Ticket, Unrelated Business Income

Obscenity

The United States Supreme Court has defined *obscenity* as relating to "works which depict or describe sexual conduct" and developed a test for determining whether a work is legally obscene. The test, known as the *Miller test,* requires a determination of:

(a) Whether the average person applying contemporary community standards would find that the work, taken as a whole, appeals to the prurient interest . . . , (b) whether the works depict or describe, in a patently offensive way, sexual conduct specifically defined by the applicable state law, and (c) whether the work, taken as a whole, lacks serious literary, artistic, political, or scientific value.

The court also stated "that sex and obscenity are not synonymous, and a reviewing court must, of necessity, look at the context of the materials, as well as its content."

A work of art, even erotic art, is not necessarily *obscene.* The determination of the work's character will depend on a host of other factors, and will be on a case-by-case basis. Unfortunately, the characterization is quite complex and will, of necessity, occur after the work has been completed. Anyone choosing to present an erotic production should seek the advice of an experienced entertainment lawyer before beginning the project. Exposing the work to the public could result in criminal liability if it is ultimately determined that the work is obscene. Obscenity may also refer to lewd or disgusting language or behavior, which may not result in criminal liability yet may subject the perpetrator to ostracism or social censure.

➤ *See also* Morals Clause, Performance Art, Pornography

Off-Broadway

Off-Broadway has traditionally been considered the more avant-garde live theater forum in New York City. It began shortly after World War I and gained prominence in the 1950s. The Off-Broadway theaters are typically smaller than Broadway houses and provide an opportunity for unknown talent to make a mark. Initially, Off-Broadway productions were considered to be experimental; later, everything from Greenwich Village firehouses to old coffeehouses were converted into theater spaces and the most cutting-edge live theater is now available in *Off-Off-Broadway* houses.

While Off-Broadway theaters customarily present more radical and controversial productions, the companies are almost uniformly subject to union agreements. Off-Off-Broadway theaters, on the other hand, rarely have union arrangements and are considered the counterculture of the New York theater scene.

➤ *See also* Broadway, Regional Theater

One-Night Stand

Although this term is well-known in its interpersonal context, in the entertainment industry *one night stand* specifically refers to a performance conducted once only. An common example of this usage would be a benefit performance.

Open Call

An *open call* is a casting process whereby anyone interested in being considered for the production has the opportunity to audition. This is distinguishable from a *closed* procedure where the only candidates for casting are those individuals who have been invited to audition (usually through their agents) or where auditions are not held but roles are precast.

➤ *See also* Agent, Audition, Callback, Director, Producer

Opera America

See Appendix A

Option

An *option* is a form of contract in which a person or entity is granted the right to acquire a property, extend a contract, hire a person, or the like. An option or option contract can be formal or informal and may be a part of another arrangement. For example, an author-publisher contract may grant the publisher the option to convert the book into a play. A playwright may option the production of a work to a theater company. While options may be informal, it is in the parties' best interests to have them spelled out in writing with some particularity, since ambiguities are likely to result. Thus, the option agreement should determine the period, scope, and terms of the arrangement. A skilled entertainment attorney should be consulted when preparing an option in order to ensure that the arrangement accurately reflects the parties' understanding.

➤ *See also* Contract, First Option, Lawyer, Prior Approval, Regional Theater

Organizations

➤ *See* Appendix A

Outstanding Check

Any check which you have written but which has not yet been paid by your bank is an *outstanding check*. Outstanding checks have to be calculated in the monthly reconciliation of the bank statement, and should be closely monitored. If a check is outstanding for an unusually long time, it is wise to find out why it has not been cashed. Perhaps it was lost or stolen, in which case it may be prudent to issue a stop payment order and write a new check.

➤ *See also* Bank Statement

Parity

Parity is a term used to define equivalency. In the entertainment industry, it is commonly used in union contracts and provides, among other things, that comparable work in different contexts should be entitled to the same rate of compensation. In general, compensating men and women who perform the same tasks with the same payment and other benefits is an example of parity.

➤ *See also* Contract, Union

Partnership

When two or more people engage in a creative project or entertainment business, it may be organized as a *partnership*. This could be a long-term collaboration between a composer and lyricist, such as Gilbert & Sullivan or Comden & Green, or a public relations team, such as Rogers & Cowan. This requires an agreement between the parties. It should be written, but can be oral or even implied by their dealings.

A big danger in a partnership is that each partner has full power to contract debts for the partnership. In addition, the wrongful acts of each partner will expose the partnership to liability. Each partner is personally liable for those debts, regardless of which partner incurred them or is responsible for them. If the business goes under, the creditors can collect not only from the assets of the business but also from each partner's personal income and assets such as checking and savings accounts, homes, cars, etc.

It is important to avoid becoming partners by accident. The laws of many states interpret a close business relationship in which two or more people agree to work together as equivalent to a partnership. The absence of a written agreement doesn't make the relationship any less binding. Any relationship of this nature should be set forth in writing and all creditors should be made aware of the arrangement so that an unintentional partnership is not created.

The Uniform Partnership Act has been adopted in some form by almost every state. This law establishes certain presumptions which will apply to a partnership unless the parties agree otherwise. There is only one area in which the parties cannot affect their own arrangements; that is, with respect to the rights of creditors. Some of the presumptions may present the partners with shocking results; for example, the statute provides that, unless the parties agree otherwise, there is a presumption that they will share equally in profits and losses. This is true even if one partner's contribution of capital and ongoing participation is much greater than that of the other partner(s). There is also a presumption that no partner is to be compensated for work performed unless there is a specific agreement to the contrary. The only compensation to which a partner is entitled without a specific arrangement is the annual share of profits.

When a partnership is established, it is best to have an agreement describing each partner's participation—for example, how much of a share each partner has, whether they are active or inactive (silent) partners, and what happens if one partner leaves. If one partner dies, for example, the law provides that the partnership is dissolved and the business may have to be liquidated, unless provisions are made in the contract for the remaining partner(s) to carry on by buying the deceased partner's share from his or her heirs. Since that may involve a sizable sum of money which often is not readily available, partners often take out insurance on each others' lives, specifying that the proceeds are to be used to pay the heirs for the deceased partner's share.

There is no formality required for the establishment of a general partnership, though, if it is using a partnership name, that name must be registered as an assumed business name. If you are forming a limited partnership, however, then you must file documents evidencing the partnership with the appropriate state or local office (the Secretary of State or other state office and, in addition, in some states, the County Clerk or other county officer). Whichever form of partnership you desire, it should be formed with the assistance of a skilled business lawyer after you have carefully thought through your business plan.

> ➤ *See also* Capital Campaign, Contract, Corporation, Insurance, Joint Venture, Limited Liability Company, Limited Liability Partnership, Limited Partnership, Sole Proprietorship, Tax

Patent

A *patent* is a document issued by the federal government which certifies an inventor's claim to his or her invention and protects the rights in his or her discovery. Patents cover inventions of a mechanical or utilitarian nature, as distinguished from copyright, which protects artistic creativity, or trademarks, which protect brand names. But what exactly is an invention?

Raymond Lee, a former U.S. Patent Examiner and one of the nation's foremost authorities on patents, puts it this way: "Suppose that while preparing a batch of dye, you accidentally dropped part of your breakfast into the vat and discovered, much to your surprise, that it improved the color coverage considerably. Would that make you an inventor? Absolutely—provided you remember what it was you dropped in."

A wide variety of inventions may be eligible for patent protection. The four which are probably of most concern to those involved in the entertainment industry are: *mechanical, process* or *method, composition of materials,* and *design. Letters patent* are issued for the first three, which are valid for twenty years from the date of application and may not be renewed. Design inventions are eligible for *design patent protection,* which lasts for fourteen years.

A *mechanical patent* is granted for an object the mechanical construction of which is new and different. A totally new device for lighting, for example, would be eligible for a mechanical patent.

A *process* or *method patent* is granted for new ways of producing an object. A new method of varnishing parts of scenery, for example, could be eligible for a process or method patent.

A *composition of materials patent* is granted for a method by which existing materials are mixed or compounded to create new and different materials. This generally applies to such products as medicines, plastics, and other chemical formulations. It could also apply to a totally new mixture for makeup or hair dye.

A *design patent* protects new and original designs or ornamentations for functional objects, not the way those objects are constructed. The design patent covers how an object looks, while the mechanical patent covers what the object does. If the object has no function at all but is purely decorative, then copyright laws apply.

For an imaginative example, we again quote Mr. Lee: "If you invented a new kind of radio, you would apply for a mechanical patent. If that radio, in addition to being new inside, also looked like a grapefruit, you would need both a mechanical patent *and* a design patent. If you made a conventional radio look like a grapefruit, just a design patent would suffice. If you created a grapefruit sculpture with no radio inside, it would fall under copyright."

Unlike copyright, which is quite simple to perfect, achieving patent protection is much more difficult. It requires careful documentation of your invention. Specific sketches and notes at the earliest stages of discovery, dated and witnessed, help to document your priority.

A preliminary patent search will usually determine whether someone else already holds a patent on a discovery which is the same as or similar to yours. This generally costs between $400 and $600, depending on the complexity of the search.

Once your patent application has been filed, you are entitled to claim *patent pending* on the product of your invention. This affords a certain amount of protection and establishes a claim in case someone else comes up with a similar idea later on. If you desire international protection for your invention, you must apply for a patent in every country within which you desire protection. This must be done promptly after your application for a U.S. patent is filed and, in no event, after the U.S. patent has been issued. Once letters patent have been issued, you should use "Patent No. _____" on the product.

It is important to apply for a patent properly and speedily because someone else may file first. In addition, there is a one-year bar in patent law; that is, if you do not file for your patent within one year of the date you first disclosed the invention to the public, you can never obtain a patent on that invention.

The legal work required in *prosecuting* a patent is best done through a patent agent or patent attorney. The applicant is permitted to do it, but the complexities are monumental. If you seek legal assistance, it must be from a lawyer who is registered to practice before the patent bar. At this point, extensive patent searches should be conducted, drawings and specifications have to be prepared, forms have to be filled out, and filing fees have to be paid. The costs for such legal services are rarely below $1,500 for design patents, $2,500 for mechanical patents, and can be much higher. It's worth the effort and expense if you intend to exploit your invention. Before you retain a patent attorney or patent agent, ask about fees and what he or she will do for you.

If your invention cannot be discovered by someone else after the product employing it is on the market, so-called reverse engineering, then trade secret

177

protection may be even more beneficial than patent protection, since trade secrets may last forever or until they are independently discovered. For example, if you desire to patent a new formula for makeup, which contains one or more catalysts not discoverable after the makeup is opened, trade secret protection will likely be appropriate.

The address of the U.S. Patent Office is Washington, D.C. 20231. A detailed booklet, "General Information Concerning Patents," is available.

> ➤ *See also* Copyright, Intellectual Property, License, Public Domain, Trademark, Trade Dress, Trade Secret, Appendix B

Payroll Tax

> ➤ *See* Withholding Tax

Pensions

Self-employed entertainers and those who are employed by businesses without *pension plans* can set up their own retirement funds and gain considerable tax advantages, as well as financial security for their retirement years.

1. If your business is a sole proprietorship, limited liability company, limited liability partnership, or partnership, you may each year deposit up to 15 percent (but no more than $7,500) of your self-employed income in a Keogh Plan.

2. If you are employed by a business which does not have a pension plan, you may establish your own Individual Retirement Account (IRA) with up to 15 percent (maximum $2,000) of your annual salary.

3. Dividends, rents, interest, etc. are not eligible for inclusion under either the Keogh or IRA plans.

4. The money you put into your Keogh or IRA plan is not taxable in the year in which it was earned. The deposits, as well as the interest they earn, are taxable when you withdraw them. The assumption is that you will be in a lower tax bracket when you retire and can also take advantage of special retirement tax benefits then. For example, if your self-employed income this year is $20,000 and you put $3,000 into your Keogh Plan, you pay taxes on only $17,000. You are, in effect, deferring your tax obligation on the other $3,000 until you retire and presumably are in a lower tax bracket. If you are in the 28 percent bracket now, you save $840 this year.

5. You must leave the money in your Keogh Plan until you are at least 59½ years old. If you withdraw it earlier, you not only have to pay back taxes

based on your tax rate in the year that you earned that money, but you'll also face stiff penalties.

6. If you die before age 59½, your beneficiaries receive immediate payment. If you are permanently disabled before 59½, you may receive your full amount at once, with no penalties.

7. If you have employees who work for you at least twenty hours a week and five months per year for three years, you *must* include them in your Keogh Plan and contribute the same percentage of their earnings as you contribute for yourself. Employees have full vested rights to all contributions made in their behalf.

HOW TO INVEST

There are a variety of ways to invest your Keogh Plan: mutual funds, annuities, bank accounts, certificates of deposit, etc. Whatever plan you choose, it must be one that is approved by the Internal Revenue Service. If the amount each year is not substantial, you may wish to put the funds into certificates of deposit. They bear a higher rate of interest than regular savings accounts and the deposits are protected. The savings institution acts as a trustee and generally charges no fee. Talk to your lawyer, accountant, financial advisor, or banker. They can give you the best advice on whether to start a pension plan at all, or on one that suits your particular circumstances.

➤ *See also* Financial Planning, Social Security, Tax

Per Diem

Per diem literally means "per day" and has come to be used in union agreements to refer to an amount of money which must be paid in a particular context. For example, a per diem payment may be mandated for a travel day even if the entire day is not spent in travel. Similarly, a per diem payment may be mandated if an individual works only a portion of a day on a given task. Per diem payments are used as a means of controlling expenses and the policy governing them frequently states, for example, that a production company will reimburse an individual for their actual costs of travel, meals and lodging up to the stated per diem amount.

➤ *See also* Contract, Union

Performance Art

Performance art is a relatively new art form in which an individual or group of individuals attempt to make a statement through their activity and the props they might use. Performance art has included such creations as nude cavorting on stage by a former porn queen, political statements such a museum presentation of lovemaking by two lesbian lovers with video accompaniment, flag-burning, and vomit art by political activists who swallow colored material and regurgitate it at certain events. Most performance art is controversial and the artists are usually activists. Many have unsuccessfully applied to art agencies, such as the National Endowment for the Arts (NEA), for grants and their rejection has been the subject of litigation.

Performance art is protected by the First Amendment, though many performance artists intentionally attempt to expand the boundaries of protection by developing new and more exotic presentations. For example, the ex-porn star has used a speculum on stage, inviting audience inspection. One performer challenged members of the audience to shoot him with a loaded revolver. Another invited observers to sit on the tops of ladders in a room which was later partially filled with water and electrically charged. Some performance art has been accused of going beyond controversy and, in fact, being illegal. For example, violating the obscenity laws or subjecting the observers to false imprisonment.

➤ *See also* National Endowment for the Arts, Obscenity, Pornography

Performing Rights

One of the exclusive rights granted to a copyright owner, to perform a musical work for the public, *performing rights* include *small performing rights* and *grand performing rights*.

Small performing rights refer to performance of the work without sets or costumes, or as part of a story. Small performing rights may be exercised when, for example, the work is performed by an orchestra, on the radio, on television as part of background music, or in a nightclub by a band or singing group.

Grand performing rights refer to performance of the work with sets, costumes, and generally in a dramatic context.

➤ *See also* Contract, Copyright

Periodicals

Since entertainment is a creative process, an artist's education never really stops. New ideas, new techniques, and new opportunities continue to emerge. A great deal of information can be found in the *entertainment periodicals* which are published throughout the world. Some of these are elaborate magazines with full-color illustrations, others are newspapers, some are simple but informative organizational newsletters. Some, such as *Variety,* deal with the entertainment industry as a whole, while others may be devoted to only a particular audience or area, such as labor union newsletters and the *Sondheim Review.* Some are published monthly, many every other month, quite a few only four times a year.

➤ *See also* Appendix B

Petty Cash

Proper bookkeeping and accounting methods require that all expenses be paid by check and entered on the books under the proper category. There are always small expenses, such as local carfare or delivery tips, which are impractical or too small to warrant writing a check. A *petty cash fund* is established for this purpose. The petty cash fund is usually rather small, typically $50 to $100.

To establish the petty cash fund, a check is drawn and cashed. The cash is kept separate from all other monies, usually in a cash box for this purpose. Whenever a payment is made from the petty cash fund (for example, if a make-up artist runs out to buy several jars of much-needed cold cream during a dress rehearsal), a *petty cash voucher,* showing the date, the amount withdrawn, its purpose, and the person receiving the funds, should be placed in the petty cash container along with the remaining petty cash money. The combination of cash on hand and vouchers must always total the original amount of the fund.

When the fund reaches a certain point, generally around $20, all the vouchers are added up, and a new check is written in the amount of the vouchers. That reconciles the petty cash account and replenishes the cash back up to the original amount.

When preparing the business's financial statements, the accountant will apportion the petty cash payments into the proper expense categories.

The petty cash fund should be used only for business expenses. It should not be a substitute for a bank. It is typically recommended that petty cash not be used as a vehicle for cashing employees' personal checks. Even the owner of the business must be rigorous in following the procedure established for petty cash use.

➤ *See also* Accounting, Financial Statement

Photographs

Photographs record events, serve as sales tools, or may themselves be art. The technical aspects of photography could fill a library. Almost everyone has handled a camera at one time or another, but there is a big difference between snapshots and professional photography. Portrait photographers can arrange all sorts of lights, backgrounds, reflectors, positions, and the like, and they often shoot the same subject over and over again with various exposures, shutter speeds, lighting arrangements, etc., until they feel fairly confident that they have the shot they want.

Photography, especially for the professional, requires certain equipment: a fairly good camera and a tripod, at the very least. Most professional photographers use several cameras and, for interior and portrait work, specialized lighting equipment. Skilled portrait photographers are professionals who command a great deal of respect and who charge a respectable amount for their work. Many, such as Richard Avedon and Annie Liebowitz, have been recognized as superstars and their work is acknowledged as photographic art.

Photographers, like other artists, specialize. Some devote their talent to taking publicity shots. It is important to work with a photographer in whom you have confidence and whom you feel can capture your image or the publicity shot you desire. There are numerous professional associations which provide their membership with forms of recognition in order to acknowledge skill levels.

PUBLICITY PHOTOS

The rules change a little bit with publicity pictures which you hope to have printed as news (without charge) in newspapers or magazines. A little human interest becomes important. A photo of an important scene in a play may add drama, as well as personality. Having a noted figure attending your opening may add credibility and prestige. Other publicity photographs which may be appealing include you receiving an award, performing charity functions, or attending someone else's opening. You'd be surprised what magazine and newspaper editors consider newsworthy. If the photograph shows someone doing something visually interesting, it has a better chance of appearing in print.

If you hope to have your photographs published in a newspaper or other two-color periodical, don't submit Polaroid snapshots. Avoid color slides or prints, too; they typically lose a lot when they are converted to black and white. Editors almost universally prefer eight-by-ten-inch black-and-white glossies, and it is wise to give editors what they want. These glossies are also relatively inexpensive to reproduce in quantity.

IDENTIFICATION

Be certain that all photographs are properly identified. Write your name and address on the back of every print. Use a soft pencil; ballpoint and roller-ball pens press through and spoil the image. Alternatives are rubber stamps or adhesive labels.

Publicity photographs *must* have a caption securely attached. The best way to do this is to type the caption on a piece of paper with two or three inches of blank space at the top. Then tape or glue the top of the sheet to the back of the photograph so that the caption sticks out below the photo. For mailing purposes, you fold the part that sticks out over the front of the picture. When the editor opens it, he or she doesn't have to turn the picture over to see what it's all about. Be sure the caption also includes your name, address and phone number, so that it can be easily identified with the accompanying press release.

MAILING

Prints should always be sent in a envelopes large enough to hold them without folding, and backed with a piece of cardboard or chipboard. Mark the front of the envelope "Do Not Bend." Address the envelope before you insert the photos to avoid possible damage from the pressure of a ballpoint pen.

If you want your prints returned, be sure to enclose a self-addressed, stamped envelope of the proper size and with the proper postage.

MODEL RELEASE

If an individual is recognizable in any photograph that may be used for commercial purposes, it is necessary to obtain a *model release,* even if it's your best friend or someone who works for you. If the model is under age, the release must be signed by the parent or legal guardian. The best time to have a release signed is at the time the picture is taken. This may seem awkward, but you can always say that your lawyer or your printer told you to get a release. If someone refuses to sign a release, don't use the picture under any circumstances. You'll only be inviting trouble.

The model release (a form available at major photographic supply stores or in a number of the books listed in Appendix B) is the legal means by which an individual whose likeness appears in a photograph gives permission for the photographer (or anyone claiming through the photographer) to use that photograph for advertising or other commercial purposes. Such releases are not necessary for noncommercial use such as publicity photos, but most photographers consider it advisable to obtain model releases for all purposes.

You never know when you might want to use the picture for advertising or other commercial purposes.

> ➤ *See also* Contract, Model Release, Portfolio, Press Release, Public Relations, Publicity, Resume, Appendix B

Playwright

A *playwright* is an individual who writes plays. Playwrights are typically entitled to program credit and royalty payments. Most playwrights are self-employed and write on their own schedule; however, a playwright may be commissioned to create a new work or to assist in converting a book into a play. A playwright may also be a lyricist or librettist or may collaborate with a lyricist, librettist, or composer in the creation of musical works.

> ➤ *See also* Adaptation, Collaboration, Commission, Composer, Copyright, Librettist, Lyricist, Appendix A

Pornography

Pornography is frequently defined as including obscene work, though pornography appears be a narrower term related only to that which is obscene in the legal sense.

> ➤ *See also* Morals Clause, Performance Art, Obscenity

Portfolio

A professional *portfolio* contains a presentation of your work. The portfolio consists of your resume, clippings or reviews, and photos or headshots.

To show clippings to best advantage, cut them carefully out of the newspaper or magazine and mount them flat under two-sided acetate sheets. Do the same thing with programs or other documents. You may even wish to have them laminated.

Photographs can also be mounted under two-sided acetate or other protective sheets. For eight-by-ten-inch prints, ten-by-twelve-inch sheets are most suitable since they allow you to show prints either vertically or horizontally without turning the portfolio binder around.

Arrange the contents of your portfolio in some logical sequence, so that the person who reviews it doesn't have to jump from one idea to another.

The portfolio itself can be one or more ordinary loose-leaf binders or a more professional zippered case which has the three-ring binder feature built in. Don't skimp on this. It's the first impression a person gets of you, your attitude, and your work.

You should keep your portfolio in a clean, safe, cool place. You should not leave it on a kitchen table or some potentially disastrous location. Slides and prints get dirty and warp easily.

➤ *See also* Photographs, Publicity, Resume

Posthumous

In the entertainment business, *posthumous* refers to work which is reproduced or completed after the death of the artist, writer, or composer. Many reproductions involve creativity in their execution and completion, so the fact that a work is posthumous is important, since the creator cannot have been involved in this aspect of the work. Many creators' wills contain provisions covering control of posthumous work and establish an artistic executor who is charged with the specific responsibility of dealing with post-death exploitation or other disposition of the decedent's intellectual property.

➤ *See also* Estate Planning, Intellectual Property

Press Release

A *press release* is a document issued for the purpose of disseminating information to the media. The format is traditional and should be used.

1. A press release should always be typed, double-spaced, on one side of the sheet only. If the release runs to more than one page, type *more* at the bottom of each page except the last, where you type *###* or *end.*
2. The press release should be typed on 8½" × 11" letter-size white paper, with plenty of margin space on all sides so that the editor can make notations, corrections, or changes.
3. If the press release is not typed on stationery, the name and address of the sender should be typed at the top, centered on the page. Skip a few spaces and, at the left, type the date the release is sent, and immediately below it type the earliest date it is to be used. If it can be used any time, type *For Immediate Release.* Otherwise, type: *For release on* _____. Lined up with the date lines, but far to the right, type the name of the individual who can be contacted for further information, and immediately below it that person's telephone number (include area code).

When you write the press release, remember a few basic rules of newspaper writing. First of all, get all of the important information into the first paragraph. Those are the five Ws of journalism: who, what, when, where, and why, plus how. Not all six apply to every story but, where they do, they should lead off the first paragraph of the release. The subsequent paragraphs should be written in descending order of importance, so that the least important information comes at the end. When a story must be reduced because of space constraints, it is cut from the end.

What will appeal to a particular newspaper is unpredictable, but one type of press release is almost sure to be ignored: a release which sounds like nothing more than an ill-disguised sales pitch. Editors are interested in news and features; sales messages belong in the advertising columns. Study newspaper-writing style by reading the papers from that point of view. Sentences are short. So are paragraphs. Good stories are written to appeal to readers, not to the egos of writers. Using fancy words with obscure meanings will reduce the odds of a press release being used. The simpler and more direct the press release, the better its chance of being printed.

If the editor thinks there may be a feature story in the activity announced in the press release, a reporter may be assigned to contact you. If the reporter has never heard of your company or the production you are mounting, he may want to know more about it for a possible feature. Anything in your release that might intrigue an editor is a bonus.

Timing is an extremely important factor. A daily newspaper can process a release for print overnight if it wishes. A weekly newspaper often has deadlines a week ahead of publication date. Monthly magazines usually require information two and even three months ahead of time to get it into print.

Most newspapers and magazines, even small weeklies, have special editors for special departments. A general news release can go to the city editor. A release on an opening could also go to the arts editor. Since editors are busy people, sending a release to the wrong department could be counterproductive. A phone call to determine the name of the appropriate editors is worthwhile. Finally: photos. Don't submit color slides or poor-quality photos. Most editors want five-by-seven- or eight-by-ten-inch black-and-white glossies, with the picture caption and your name and address securely taped to the back. Some papers will take photos of any size, but the bigger size stands a better chance. Getting a picture into the papers is worth the investment to have a good one taken. If appropriate, be sure to indicate which side is up.

Two tips on mailing photos:

1. Never fold the picture. Get a large enough envelope and use a piece of cardboard for protection.
2. Address the envelope before you enclose the picture. Addressing the

envelope later may find the pen tip pressing through and defacing the photograph. For that same reason, never write on the back of a photo, except very lightly with soft pencil or crayon.

➤ *See also* Advertising, Photographs, Publicist, Publicity, Public Relations, Public Service Announcement

Price Fixing

➤ *See* Robinson-Patman Act

Prior Approval

Prior approval is a contract term which imposes an obligation on a party to obtain approval from the appropriate person before proceeding with a specific activity. This could relate, for example, to the obligation imposed on one party to a contract to obtain the other party's approval before assigning the contract or any rights contained in it to another party. It is common for individuals in the entertainment industry to require prior approval of certain forms of publicity, assignments, conveyances of particular rights, and the like.

➤ *See also* Contract, First Option, Option

Producer

While the functions of a *producer* typically include: (1) identifying the various creative elements of a given production and bringing them together; (2) locating viable venues; (3) developing a suitable budget; (4) monitoring script development and implementation; (5) arranging for and supervising advertising and publicity; (6) casting; and (7) engaging a director, producers are perhaps best-kown as the financiers or fundraisers for productions.

Although the working producer will typically be an individual, the actual financing for a production may come from his or her own funds or from a consortium of people and organizations who wish to underwrite all or a portion of the production. Individuals who are not themselves producers but merely investors in productions are often known as "angels." Occasionally, a performance of a given production may be performed solely for the angels and their invitees.

In the film and television industries, there are numerous categories of producers, including producer, executive producer, and the like. The music industry also has its own separate designations.

➤ *See also* Audition, Advertising, Box Office, Director, Manager

Producers Guild of America

➤ *See* Appendix A

Professional Name

Writers, entertainers, and others in the public eye frequently adopt names other than the one they were given at birth as their *professional name.* These names are customarily intended to attract public attention and, in some cases, to describe the individual's professional attributes. For some time, traditional American names had been preferred, though ethnic names have become more popular. Some names are adopted for the purpose of attracting comment because they are so unusual, such as Whoopi Goldberg or Slash, or may be a variation on the given name, such as Cher (from Cherilyn) or Madonna (who only dropped her surname). The individual may legally adopt the professional name or may use it only for professional purposes while retaining his or her given name for legal purposes.

The professional name may be protectible as a service mark and, if so, may be registered as such. It may also be protected under the right of publicity which has been adopted in many states. Since celebrity endorsement is an important form of commercially exploiting one's reputation it is important to prevent the improper use of a celebrity's name or likeness without his or her permission. Legal doctrines such as unfair competition, right of privacy, right of publicity, trademark law, and the like assist the celebrity with that protection.

Copyright law also recognizes the fact that many individuals who are involved in the creative process use professional names. It, therefore, provides copyright protection for works which are published under a pseudonym.

If contracts are to be signed in a professional name, it is important that the user register it as an assumed business name, have a legal name change, or be known in the industry under the professional name. If the individual does not legally change his or her name, then it is probably best to sign a contract using both the given name and the professional name, indicating that the person is "also known as (aka)."

➤ *See also* Contract, Copyright, Publicity, Trade Name, Trademark

Promotion

➤ *See* Advertising, Direct Mail, Printed Materials, Publicity, Public Relations

Properties Master/Mistress

The *properties master* or *mistress* is the person responsible for the acquisition or creation of *props* to be used in a production, and for their care and maintenance during the production.

Property

> *See* Mortgage, Property Insurance, Property Tax

Property Insurance

A wide range of insurance coverage is available to protect you against loss by theft, fire, flood, storm, or the like. The most common of these is known as *comprehensive insurance,* which covers a number of related risks at a premium rate lower than that for covering those risks separately. Typical of such policies is a homeowner's or renter's insurance policy, which is available in most states and includes protection against loss from fire, wind damage, vandalism, theft, personal liability, and so forth. Similar types of policies are available for businesses.

Premiums for property insurance policies vary widely, depending on the potential risk. A frame building, for example, generally costs more to insure than a brick building. Hurricane insurance is quite expensive to obtain in areas frequently subject to hurricanes; this is also true of earthquake insurance.

Separate policies to protect against theft or burglary can also be obtained. Theft and burglary insurance varies in cost, depending on the crime rate in the insured's area, and the nature of the coverage.

Each policyholder's property insurance coverage should be tailored by the insurance agent or broker to suit the specific needs for coverage, the potential size of the loss, and the cost of the premiums. Typically, musicians will insure their instruments, writers may insure their computers, and some entertainers may insure their libraries or collections of memorabilia. Entertainment companies should insure their property against fire, flood, and the like, although many skimp on coverage due to budgetary constraints.

> *See also* Fire Insurance, Insurance, Property

Property Tax

Property tax is a common form of municipal taxation. Most cities, counties, and states use property taxes as the primary source of their revenue.

Property taxes fall into two categories: *real estate* and *personal property.* Real estate (with some exceptions, such as religious buildings and some farmland) is taxed locally. A specific tax rate per dollar of value, known as the *millage rate,* is established, and each piece of taxable property is then assessed according to its value. The assessed value is not necessarily the same as the market value of the property. Thus, taxes can be increased in two ways: either by raising the millage rate or by reassessing the property at a higher value.

Another form of property tax in some states is the *automobile registration fee,* which is a state property tax. This may be a flat fee or based on a schedule or formula.

An *inventory tax,* which exists in some states, is also a property tax. Entertainment businesses maintaining inventories in states where inventory taxes exist should be careful to control their inventories, particularly near the assessment date.

➤ *See also* Property, Tax

Prospect List

➤ *See also* Mailing Lists

Pseudonym

➤ *See* Professional Name

Public Domain

Music, scripts, and scenery may be protected from reproduction and other exploitation by copyright or other intellectual property laws, such as trade dress. If a work is not protected, then it is in the *public domain* and it may be copied by anyone without restriction. Work may enter the public domain when the period of copyright protection has elapsed, when formalities previously required for copyright creation were not adhered to, or if there is no other form of intellectual property protection. Once a work has entered the public domain, it cannot be protected. If, for example, a public domain play such as Shakespeare's *Romeo and Juliet* is modified and modernized into *West Side Story,* the new production is copyrightable, though anyone else can go back to the source and develop his or her own modern adaptation of the original Shakespearean work.

The federal government cannot, itself, copyright work, although it may own copyrights created by others and assigned to it.

➤ *See also* Copyright, Patent, Trade Dress

Public Relations

Public relations means exactly that: relations with the public. Public relations covers every aspect of your contact with the outside world: publicity, advertising, community involvement, performance, even an individual's own appearance and conduct when encountering the public, or when seeing a casting agent.

How do you, as a performer, create your image? Generally, in much the same way you have created an image of yourself as a person. People have certain impressions of you: stingy or generous, soft-spoken or blunt, calm or excitable, talkative or quiet. There is no one trait and no one time when images take hold. They are the cumulative experience people have of you. Talent counts. So does reliability. If you get a reputation for always missing promised dates, or for great variations in the quality of your performances, your reputation will suffer. These criteria also apply to the image of an organization.

There are at least two aspects of public relations: The first is how you conduct yourself as an artist, as a professional, and as a businessperson. The second involves the many things you can do to obtain notoriety. This need not always be related directly to performance, although you would hope that your public relations ultimately produces more work.

For many entertainers or entertainment organizations, hiring the services of a publicist or public relations agency is important. These professionals have the knowledge and experience to assist in obtaining maximum visibility. The cost of hiring professionals may be worth it, since the results they achieve should ultimately produce work or other favorable attention.

➤ *See also* Advance Man, Advertising, Marketing, Photograph, Press Release, Promotion, Publicist, Publicity

Public Service Announcement (PSA)

The Federal Communications Commission requires radio and television stations to dedicate a certain percentage of each broadcast day to free *public service announcements* for the benefit of nonprofit organizations. These PSAs may include, for example, promotion of homeless shelters, the Red Cross, and other relief agencies, as well as announcements for nonprofit entertainment organizations. PSAs may promote the organization in general or spotlight a particular event. It is an excellent form of publicity and, since it is free, advance notification is essential. Some stations, however, require such a long lead time that it is impractical or even impossible for last-minute production publicity. The person in charge of publicity for a nonprofit entertainment organization should prepare the appropriate information release which must include identification of the organization as a 501(c)(3) entity and other standard information comparable to that included in a commercial press release. Some organizations actually prepare their own PSAs, which may be aired by the media for the organization. Frequently, talent will donate their time for this purpose.

➤ *See also* 501(c)(3), Nonprofit Organization, Press Release, Publicity

Publicist

A *publicist* is an individual who, as the name suggests, is responsible for obtaining publicity. The publicist may have several clients or work for only one entertainer or entertainment group. He or she can be an employee of an agency, an employee of the entertainer or group, or an independent contractor engaged in his or her own business. Skilled publicists are worth their weight in gold. The visibility and publicity they can obtain for their clients can make the difference between success or failure. An experienced publicist will have contacts in the media and may, by use of creative projects, thrust his or her clients into the limelight. They may also be able to regain public acceptance after a particular nasty event has occurred to mar the reputation or integrity of the talent involved. When, for example, Michael Jackson was charged with child molestation, his publicists worked hard to dispel that image and place the entertainer in a more favorable light. The damage control was quite effective and attention was diverted from Jackson's alleged improprieties to his relationship with Lisa-Marie Presley.

Creativity is an important attribute of a successful publicist. Some have developed programs for the purpose of exposing their clients to the media and the public. One publicist, for example, developed a program of celebrity sports events in which individuals donated money to charity in order to have an opportunity to team up with entertainers and play golf or tennis.

The media loved the event and the exposure obtained by the entertainers was extremely beneficial.

In order to obtain the services of a publicist who will enhance your career, you should look for someone whose values are similar to yours. Your agent should be able to identify a person who has the skill you desire and, after you have had an opportunity to interview the publicist, you will likely be able to determine whether he or she is compatible with your objectives. It is probably best for you to conduct your interview with your attorney, agent, and financial adviser all involved, since the publicist will be part of your management team. Be sure that you can work with your publicist and that you are willing to cooperate with him or her. If the publicist feels that you can obtain publicity by engaging in risky or distasteful ventures and you are unwilling to participate in this program, then you have wasted your time and money in working with this individual. Personality is important and you should remember that the publicist is helping you to develop, enhance or perpetuate your public image. Be sure that the image is one you are willing to live with.

➤ *See also* Advance Man, Advertising, Press Release, Public Relations, Publicity

Publicity

There are several ways to gain visibility in the media: One is to pay for advertising; another is to be the focus of a story. Any mention you get in the media is *publicity,* and good publicity is often the result of an effort on the part of the person being publicized. Many entertainers and entertainment organizations hire publicists expressly for this purpose.

For an individual, the first step toward getting publicity is to overcome modesty or shyness. For anyone, the next step is to realize that editors are always on the lookout for interesting stories.

Publicity has at least two values. One is ego gratification. It feels good to see your photograph or a favorable mention about you or your company in the news. The other value, even more important to your career, is that publicity is a marketing tool. To get the most out of publicity, a few basic principles should be observed:

1. *Timing.* If possible, you may wish to have the publicity coincide with a opening or event in which you are involved.

2. *Directness.* Make your presentation as simple and as straightforward as possible. Editors can (and often do) rewrite and cut to suit their own styles. If the editor thinks there's more to the story than your announcement, a reporter may be assigned to interview you. Accommodate the reporter's needs and deadlines.

3. *Angle.* Provide the editor with a news peg if possible. An opening, a charity function, an award, moving into a new theater location, the attendance by a notable figure at one of your performances—these are all news pegs.

4. *Press List.* Your publicity will typically be with newspapers and radio or television stations in your area, and with regional and national magazines. Occasionally, your local emphasis may expand if, for example, you are featured in a location outside your regular market.

   It is a good idea to maintain a list of press contacts; this can be done as simply as maintaining three-by-five-inch index cards or a computerized record. If there is more than one contact at a given newspaper

193

(city editor, entertainment editor, features editor, etc.), make up a separate entry for each. Keep a record for each entry of the contacts you've made, the date, and the results. If you don't succeed on the first contact, it is good to know when to make another, and you can time it according to the dates shown for that entry. Make a note of the reaction: Were they favorably impressed, polite or curt, enthusiastic or disinterested? Did they tell you to call again at a specific later date? Do they want photos? All of this is useful because the more you can tailor your publicity to the particular editor's needs, the better your chance of getting it into his or her publication.

Note: Particularly in small towns, unless the subject is a general news announcement, such as an opening, it is best not to give the same story to more than one editor at a time. Give the editor a few days or a week to make a decision on a feature story. If the first one isn't interested, then take it to the next. Your credibility with editors will be jeopardized if they unknowingly run the same feature story.

5. *Approach.* Most members of the media are approachable. In some instances, a phone call will generate enough interest for a reporter to be assigned to the story. In other instances, it is better to issue a press release.

Aside from the print and electronic media, there are numerous other publicity opportunities for entertainers and their work. You may persuade a restaurant, hotel, bank, or other place of public accommodation to sponsor a performance. If you are fortunate enough to be selected for a grant, the recognition itself will advertise you as a credible entertainer. A guest appearance on a radio or television talk show is another good opportunity to reach large numbers of people. Some entertainers have donated their time to charities or causes in which they have a special interest. In addition to benefiting the charity, the entertainer also gets some well-deserved media visibility.

You should collect as much as possible of the publicity about you and your work and use it as part of your own promotional materials. Reprint some of the articles that have appeared about you in newspapers or magazines. Make a list of the radio or television stations on which you've been mentioned or have appeared; you can videotape these appearances yourself or, often, arrange to obtain a copy from the station. What others say about you and your work is often more compelling than what you say yourself.

➤ *See also* Advance Man, Advertising, Marketing, Photograph, Portfolio, Press Release, Professional Name, Promotion, Publicist, Public Relations, Public Service Announcement

Quantity Discount

➤ *See* Robinson-Patman Act

Recordkeeping

Business records should be retained for at least three years, the statute of limitations for tax audits covering items other than fraud or non-disclosure of income. The statute of limitations for tax fraud is six years, and there is no limit for concealment.

Some records should be kept longer. For example, if you remodel a building, adding value, the costs of remodeling will be added to your *basis* in this building and that information should be available to you when you sell the building so you can reconcile any tax gain or loss on the sale. Information regarding the purchase price of assets, including costumes, lighting and sound equipment, a library or scripts or scores, and other items on which you may be required to pay income or personal property tax, should also be retained. It is also critical that employers maintain records relating to employees for the period prescribed by state law, which in many states is three years.

➤ *See also* Accounting, Audit, Mailing Lists, Statute of Limitations, Tax

Regional Theater

Regional theater is the term applied to a nonprofit resident theater presenting performances for audiences in its region. These theaters and their productions may or may not be subject to union contracts. Typically, the amount individuals earn when working at regional theaters is less than that paid for Broadway or Off-Broadway productions. Many regional theaters are considered "staging grounds" for new works and new talent. Some theater agreements provide that actors who originate a role shall be offered the same role if the production moves to another theater or the New York stage and, while League of Regional Theaters member companies honor these agreements, they typically do not offer this type of contract except in special circumstances, such as certain types of co-production.

> ➤ *See also* Broadway, Off-Broadway, Option

Release

> ➤ *See* Contract, Extras, Photographs

Renting

> ➤ *See* Lease

Repertory

The term *repertory* typically refers to the practice of presenting productions in a staggered sequence so that a broader variety is available to the audience over a shorter period of time. For example, a company specializing in Shakespearean productions may present *Romeo and Juliet* one night, *Macbeth* on the successive night, and *The Merry Wives of Windsor* on the next night, repeating this sequence numerous times within a comparatively short period of time, such as a month or two. Although many organizations have incorporated this term in their name, for example The Seattle Repertory Theatre, that does not necessarily mean they have adopted repertory as their method of operation.

Repossess

> ➤ *See* Collateral, Foreclosure, Installment, Mortgage

Residency

The term *residency* is used to define an arrangement whereby an individual, whether a performer or a production person, is engaged by a company for a fixed period of time, frequently a production season. Many educational institutions have adopted this arrangement and funded the position often known as *artist-in-residence* for purposes of exposing students to experts in the various aspects of the performing arts. Production companies who utilize this arrangement often will present seminars, workshops, or other educational opportunities for interested members of the local performing arts community. The arrangement is governed by contract and typically requires the individual in residence to present a minimum number of workshops, performances, and the like in addition to being available for one-on-one counseling. In exchange for these services, the resident is typically given a stipend and may, in some cases, be provided with living accommodations.

➤ *See also* Contract

Resume

A *resume* is a brief summary of your professional training and experience. A resume is used as a way of introducing yourself for a wide variety of purposes: when you approach an agent or a casting director, when you seek a job or teaching position, when you want to furnish background material for a newspaper interview.

Performers typically utilize *head shots* rather than traditional resumes. The head shot consists of an eight-by-ten-inch photo (usually black-and-white) with the performer's name, address, and telephone number; height, weight, hair and eye color; a summary of professional experience; and union affiliation given on the reverse.

The traditional resume consists of several clearly defined sections, each of which should be identified and separated from the others:

1. *Personal statistics.* Name, address, telephone number, media in which you work.
2. *Work experience, including teaching positions.* Start with the most recent one and work backwards. Indicate what your job function was and include dates of employment and references.
3. *Professional experience.* Productions in which you've participated, awards, honors, workshops you've conducted, lectures you've given, articles you've had published, membership in professional organizations, etc.
4. *Educational background related to your work.* Complete educational background is usually needed if you're applying for a teaching position.
5. *References.* Two personal references and two professional references from people not related to you are normally sufficient. The references are customarily stated to be available upon request and are not actually included with the resume.

A resume (as distinguished from a *curriculum vitae*), should not exceed two pages and should ideally be one page. If you have extensive professional and work experience, education, honors, publications, and the like, you may wish to prepare a *curriculum vitae* in addition to your resume. A *curriculum vitae* is frequently several pages long and includes much more detailed entries than a resume.

Resume services are quite common and may assist you in preparing a quality document.

➤ *See also* Agent, Computers, Photographs, Portfolio

Rigger

The term *rigger* comes from the nautical use describing the person who was responsible for *rigging* a sailing ship; that is, tying and weaving all of the appropriate lines, pulleys, hooks, sail gear, and the like. In the entertainment industry, it refers to the individual responsible for "rigging" scenery, curtains, and other overhead fixtures, including light bars, audio equipment, etc. Even though the context is different, rigging gear in entertainment resembles a ship's rigging, in that the lines are fastened to pinrails. These individuals typically will belong to a union.

➤ *See also* Fly Man, Stagehand, Appendix A

Right to Work Laws

Right to work laws have been enacted in some jurisdictions for the purpose of allowing individuals who do not wish to join a union to work even in companies which are subject to labor union agreements. The nonunion workers may be required to make a *fair share payment* (typically an amount equal to or somewhat less the amount that would otherwise be paid as union dues) in order to economically equalize the arrangement, since these workers receive the same wages and employer-provided benefits as union members.

➤ *See also* Union

Robinson-Patman Act

The *Robinson-Patman Act* is a federal law enacted by Congress in 1936 to prohibit any practice which would tend to stifle free competition in the marketplace. Among the law's major prohibitions are price discrimination between customers and other special concessions which are not justified by cost or other business reasons. Thus, it is unlawful to sell tickets through one outlet at a lower price than a comparable ticket is sold at another outlet.

Differences in price based on quantity are legal; a price based on an order for one hundred tickets can be lower than a price based on a single ticket. Special concessions which affect the price and are not otherwise justified are also illegal; thus, senior citizen discounts are permissible, yet charging a patron for reserving tickets while not charging a comparable patron for a similar service would be unlawful.

The essential thrust of the Robinson-Patman Act is to protect competition by making it illegal for one patron to have an unreasonable advantage over another. The law also protects arts organizations when they buy raw materials and supplies. It is illegal for your supplier to charge you one price for a bolt of cloth and charge another company in your area a lower price for the same quantity. None of this prohibits special sales or other price reductions, as long as all customers buying the product under the special conditions are treated equally.

➤ *See also* Box Office, Ticket

Royalty

A *royalty* is a per-unit payment for the use of a particular piece of property. The term originally described the payment a king would receive for granting rights to the use of his lands. It is still used to determine payment for such land uses as oil drilling, whereby the owner of the land is paid a specific amount per barrel of oil extracted from the land. The term is also used to describe payment for the use of intellectual property, including copyrights, patents, and trademarks.

For writers and composers, a royalty is generally a specified price for a specific use of the artist's protected creative work.

A common royalty in the entertainment industry is the fee charged by a clearing house, such as Samuel French or Music Theater International, for the performance of a protected play. The fee is non-negotiable and is based on a formula which includes such factors as ticket price, number of seats, number of performances, and the professional, amateur, or collegiate status of the producing company. It is wise to consult an experienced entertainment lawyer before signing any royalty agreement.

➤ *See also* Community Theater, License, Season

Safety

Performing arts groups should observe industrial hygiene and *safety* principles. Hazardous materials and processes must be recognized, evaluated, and controlled.

Stage or film crews should learn to identify materials, to read labels and material safety data sheets, and to keep records of materials and processes used. If it is not clear whether the materials or processes can be harmful to health, advice can be sought from numerous sources such as government agencies, arts organizations, and publications, as well as from industrial hygiene and safety professionals. This latter group can provide help in controlling safety and health hazards in any workplace. They can recommend appropriate ventilation, machine guarding, and protective equipment advice, and the cost of their services is tax-deductible to a business and may be tax-deductible for certain individuals, as well.

Following are some safety guidelines which should be adhered to and a list of agencies and individuals you can contact for additional information.

1. Public Law 10-695, passed by Congress in 1988 and effective as of November 1990, requires manufacturers to label art products that contain ingredients that may be chronic health hazards; for example,

inks or paints that contain solvents which might not cause problems with occasional, short duration use, but which might cause nerve damage over a prolonged period of concentrated use. Of course, the law has some limitation, in that it applies only to art materials, and many artists use materials or processes which are not specifically identified as art materials and processes. Artists, therefore, have an increased responsibility to learn about the materials they use. If you work with metals, you must know what happens when a metal is heated. If you work with resins, you must know the health effects of the resin components, and how and when adverse effects are likely to be caused. If you work with fibers, you must know about the health effects of dyes and dusts. Problems continue to surface; for example, it is now recognized that many glazes contain harmful lead and that lead crystal should not be used for prolonged storage of consumable liquids. The State of California has even passed legislation to monitor those who are involved in creating any pottery vessel which may be used in connection with food.

2. Follow safety rules, use guarding devices, and wear appropriate protective equipment when using machine tools of any kind. Do not wear jewelry or loose-fitting garments such as scarves, ties, necklaces, or the like.

3. Read instructions thoroughly and follow them.

4. Have electrical wiring and tools checked periodically by a professional electrician to be sure connections are in good condition and that tools are properly grounded.

5. Have an emergency response plan and post it in near a phone. It should describe what to do in case of a spill, a splash in the eyes, a bad cut or puncture, and who to contact, such as 911, etc.

6. Ventilate properly. Remember that, for any system to work, whatever amount of air is exhausted from a space, an equal amount of air must be brought in to replace it. Be sure that your exhaust system does not interfere with the existing furnace or other exhausts.

AGENCIES THAT PROVIDE INFORMATION

Occupational Safety and Health Administration, (OSHA); National Institute of Occupational Safety and Health (NIOSH).

ORGANIZATIONS AND INDIVIDUALS
Center for Safety in the Arts; Arts, Crafts, and Theater Safety (ACTS); Gail Barazani, researcher and writer on occupational health in the arts (see Appendix A).

BOOKS
Ventilation: A Practical Guide, Artist Beware, Stage Fright, The Artist's Complete Health and Safety Guide (see Appendix B).
➤ *See also* Fire Prevention, Workers' Compensation

Sales Tax

Most states and many municipalities impose a *tax* on retail sales to consumers. The tax is collected at the point at which the sale is made, and is based on a percentage of the price. The amount of the tax varies from place to place, as does the type of product or service on which it is collected. In some areas, for example, restaurant meals or services are taxable, in others they are not. Food bought at retail is almost never subject to sales tax, although nonfood items may be taxed.

Theater companies selling tickets in areas where sales taxes apply must obtain a certificate from the local taxing authorities which authorizes them to collect the sales tax. How, when, and where the sales taxes are then forwarded by the company to the taxing authorities varies, but it is always illegal to retain the collected sales tax as personal or business income. Records must be kept to relate total sales to sales tax collections. Sales receipts and invoices are usually sufficient for this purpose. The sales tax must always be shown as a separate item from the price.

A sales tax situation peculiar to the entertainment business involves selling tickets for shows in areas where there are sales taxes, for example, in the case of a touring show. It may be possible to obtain a temporary sales tax certificate for the period of the show.
➤ *See also* Tax

Savings Bank

A bank whose main function is to handle savings accounts on which it pays interest, although it also performs numerous other banking functions, most notably in mortgage lending. In many states, savings banks are not permitted to handle checking accounts.
➤ *See also* Banks, Commercial Bank, Credit, Money Order

Scale

This term, frequently known as *union scale,* refers to the minimum amount which must be paid for a defined task. It is established in the union contract for the particular type of job. Name talent will generally command higher compensation, though an individual may elect to "work for scale" in certain instances. For example, talk shows customarily pay scale, regardless of the celebrity of the guest. Similarly, high-priced performers may agree to accept scale as a special accomodation to worthy lower-budget production or company.

> *See also* Tour, Union, Wages

Scholarships

> *See* Grants

Schools

> *See* Education, Grants

Screen Credit

> *See* Credit

Season

The term *season* refers to the period during which a company's productions are presented, typically fall through spring, and parallels the academic calendar. Summer stock, however, would have only a summer season. The season is important for individuals in the entertainment industry since awards are presented based on a season's activities. For example, for a Broadway production to be eligible for a given season's Tony Awards, it must have opened during that season. Similarly, Grammy Awards will be presented in the fall for achievements which occurred during the last preceding season, as the term is defined by the music industry.

A season will also have relevance for financial purposes. Thus, a company will prepare its budget for the next season. Income will be generated from ticket sales during the season and may be enhanced by the advance sale of *season tickets.* In order for a company to announce a season, it must have secured the performance rights to each protected work (play, musical, ballet, etc.) by prepaying the estimated royalties for the planned use of that work during the scheduled season. It is for this reason that many small production companies do not offer a season but present productions one at a time as the company is able to afford the royalties and other production costs.

➤ *See also* Agent, Budget, Contract, Royalty, Union

Securities

The term *securities* refers to investment instruments, such as stocks, bonds, limited partnership interests, or any arrangement whereby one party pledges money or something else of value and another party performs the required work. Securities are strictly regulated at both the federal and state levels within the United States and by most countries.

In order to sell or offer to sell any security in the United States, the offerer must have the security approved by the Securities and Exchange Commission unless the offering is exempt from S.E.C. review. In addition, every securities transaction must also comply with the laws of every state in which the transaction occurs or is planned.

The federal securities laws include the Securities Act of 1933 (for original issues) and the Securities and Exchange Act of 1934 (for resales of securities). Other federal laws have been enacted for the purpose of governing other aspects of the securities market, such as the Trust Indenture Act, which regulates a portion of the bond market. Every state has a "blue sky" law, which regulates securities transactions within the boundaries of that state.

Securities are used in the entertainment industry for the purpose of raising capital in a variety of contexts. Thus, a single production may be funded by creating a limited partnership and obtaining capital by selling limited partnership interests. Similarly, a production company may obtain its funding by selling stock in the business corporation or selling interests in the limited liability company. A classic example of this type of arrangement is presented in the movie *The Producers*.

In the 1970s and '80s, entertainment ventures were popular vehicles for the creation of tax shelters, many of which were declared by the Internal Revenue Service to be "abusive." These so-called tax-motivated investments were structured in such a way as to theoretically provide the purchaser with several dollars' worth of tax deductions for each dollar invested during the first or second year and a fair return on the investment during the latter years. If, for example, an individual in a 50 percent tax bracket, invested $10,000 and received a tax deduction of $40,000 within the first year, then the individual would be ahead since merely paying the tax on the $10,000 would net $5,000 in spendable cash, whereas investing $10,000 would enable the individual to shelter $20,000 worth of income. Regrettably, most of the arrangements were flawed and aggressively attacked by the IRS. While some of these "shelters" did work as originally planned, the vast majority were struck down and the investors not only lost their investments but wound up paying taxes, interest, and penalties for the amounts the intented to have sheltered.

Record companies, too, became involved in the tax-motivated arrangements by selling investments in *master recordings* which were intended to provide multiple write-offs during the early stages as well as ultimate profit. Many of the so-called master recordings were by unknowns who never became successful and the alleged value of the master recordings was unjustified.

➤ *See also* Capital, Capital Campaign, Contract, Corporation, Limited Liability Company, Limited Partnership, Sponsorship, Subscription Sales, Tax, Underwriting

Security

The image of a celebrity being accosted by papparazzi or zealous fans has become commonplace. It is for this reason that *security* guards are frequently hired as bodyguards and for crowd control. Stage doors frequently have security guards who restrict entry and who are available to assist performers in exiting the building. While some entertainers include bodyguards in their retinues, most rely on the producer to provide this service.

Security also has application to computers, which may be protected from hackers who may attempt to gain access to confidential or proprietary information through a modem connection. The vehicles for this purpose range from simple passwords to physical keys and include, among other things, complex software programs. As the skills of the would-be intruders increase, the methods used for security also must gain sophistication.

➤ *See also* Computers, Insurance

Seminars

➤ *See* Education

Service Mark

➤ *See* Trade Name, Trademark

Services

➤ *See* Contract, Union

Set Designer

A *set designer* is the person who designs sets for any production. The individual may be a member of the company or may be an independent contractor. He or she may also be involved in the set construction, though this is by no means universal. Many set designers have another career as a visual artist and independently work in that profession. For example, Maurice Sendak, who is best known for his illustration of children's books, has gained acclaim for his innovative set design for *The Nutcracker*. Similarly, Jerry Williams, a successful West Coast set designer, has been recognized as a sculptor and created a monumental work which is on display in Springfield, Oregon.

➤ *See also* Contract, Independent Contractor, Technical Director, Union, Appendix A

Slides

➤ *See* Photographs

Small Business Administration

The *Small Business Administration* (SBA) is a government agency which was created for the purpose of assisting small businesses. Although its charter prohibits financial assistance to entertainment-related businesses (since it was felt by Congress that this might interfere with First Amendment free expression), another significant service rendered by the SBA to small businesses—including entertainment businesses—is an extensive and expanding list of publications on a wide range of business subjects, discussed in clear and easy terms. These include such topics as cost control, business life insurance, cash flow, sales agents, budgeting, accounting procedures, and many more. Many of these publications are free; the cost for others is very modest. A complete list is available at any SBA office or from Washington, D.C. Ask for *The Small Business Directory*.

➤ *See also* Government Activities, Appendix A

Small Claims Court

Small claims courts exist in every state to help people resolve small claims. *Small* means different things in different places. The range is generally $500 to $2,500 for the maximum amount for which suit may be brought.

The concept of small claims court is that most small claims are not complex enough to require the expertise of an attorney. That's why many states don't even permit lawyers in small claims court unless they are representing themselves or a corporation. If you face a lawyer in small claims court, it is the judge's responsibility to make sure that your interests are properly represented. Most complex legal procedures and many technical rules of evidence don't apply. The proceedings are informal, quick, and inexpensive.

Staff members are often available to help people fill out the forms. Filing fees average around $50. More and more states are requiring alternative dispute resolution—mediation or arbitration—for small claims cases. Small claims courts have one drawback: most states do not allow for an appeal except in very limited circumstances. The judge's decision is usually binding.

➤ *See also* Alternative Dispute Resolution, Collection Problems, Statute of Limitations

Social Security

Social Security is a federal program enacted in 1935 which has become the basic method of providing income to people after they retire or become severely disabled, and to their survivors. People over age sixty-five and the disabled, regardless of age, have health protection under Medicare, which is administered by the Social Security Administration.

Ninety percent of working people, including the self-employed (such as artists), pay into the Social Security fund. Employees, employers, and self-employed people make Social Security contributions during their working years. When the person retires, becomes disabled, or dies, monthly cash benefits are paid to replace part of the earnings that are lost. Employers and employees pay an equal share of Social Security contributions. If you are self-employed, you pay contributions at a somewhat lower rate than the combined rate for an employee and an employer, but that does not reduce the ultimate benefits. As long as a person has earnings from employment or self-employment, the contributions must be paid, regardless of the person's age and even if they are already receiving Social Security benefits.

Social Security contributions are calculated on a combination of two factors: a tax rate and an annual income base. These are established by Congress and change periodically. The tax rate is applied to all income up to a certain maximum which also changes periodically. In other words, even if the *rate* were to remain the same or go up only slightly, an individual's total Social Security obligation can increase substantially if the annual base is increased. An employee's Social Security contributions are deducted by the employer from wages every payday. The employer matches the employee's payment and sends the combined amount to the Internal Revenue Service, which is the collection agency for the Social Security Administration.

Self-employed people whose annual earnings exceed a specified minimum must include their Social Security contributions when they calculate their estimated tax payments and pay any difference when they file their individual income tax. This is required even if no income tax is owed. Wages and self-employed income are entered on each individual's Social Security record during the working years. This record is used to determine retirement benefits or cash benefits. A fairly complicated formula is used to determine the average annual income earned. The monthly checks are reduced proportionately for workers who retire anytime between age sixty-two and age sixty-five. Delaying retirement beyond age sixty-five earns extra credits and increased monthly check amounts. There is also a minimum for people who have worked under Social Security at least twenty years but whose earnings were unusually low.

Social Security benefit amounts are increased automatically each July if the cost of living in the previous year has risen by more than 3 percent over the year before. Future benefits will also increase because they are based on the higher payments made into the fund. People who work for more than one employer in the same year and pay Social Security taxes on both incomes can get a refund on any payments in excess of the required maximum. The employers do not receive a rebate of the excess payments. For retirees between ages sixty-five and seventy who continue to have employment income, Social Security benefits are reduced by a ratio of benefits to earnings. Anyone over age seventy can earn any amount without reduction in benefits.

Social Security records are identified by the wage earner's Social Security Number. All U.S. citizens—including newborns—and noncitizens who work in the U.S. must obtain a Social Security Number. It is also used for identification on income tax returns and on many other official documents. A Social Security card can be obtained at any Social Security office (there are about 1300 throughout the country), and must be shown to an employer at the commencement of employment. The amount withheld from wages for Social Security purposes is also reported to every employee on the W-2 form, which is furnished to all employees once a year for income tax purposes.

Social Security benefits do not start automatically; you must apply for them. The Social Security Administration lists the following conditions under which you may apply for benefits:

1. If you are unable to work because of an illness or injury that is expected to last a year or longer, no matter what your age.
2. If you are sixty-two or older and plan to retire.
3. When you are within two or three months of sixty-five, even if you don't plan to retire. You will still be eligible for Medicare, even if you continue to work.
4. Qualified beneficiaries of a decedent.

All the information in your Social Security file is confidential.

An excellent booklet, "Your Social Security," is available without charge from any Social Security office. The Social Security Administration is listed in the telephone book white or blue pages under "U.S. Government, Health, Education and Welfare, Social Security Administration."

➤ *See also* Estimated Tax, Pensions, Wage Tax

Sole Proprietorship

Sole Proprietorship is the simplest method for organizing a business. Few formalities are needed. Most municipalities require even sole proprietors to obtain a business license. Most states require filing a certificate if you conduct the business under an assumed name instead of your own. The Secretary of State's office in most states can tell you what and where to file. Even a sole proprietorship is well-advised, especially for tax purposes, to have a business checking account and a federal taxpayer identification number. Talk to your banker or business adviser about this.

If the business has employees other than the proprietor, it has to maintain and pay for workers' compensation insurance, Social Security taxes, and the like. Avoiding these fringe costs on the owner's earnings is often regarded as a benefit of the sole proprietorship form. On the other hand, the absence of such benefits to the owner when the need for them arises can be one of the disadvantages of this form of organization.

Finally, and importantly, the sole proprietor is personally and fully liable for the debts of the business. If the business fails, its creditors can go after the owner's nonbusiness income and assets such as car, home, and savings.

➤ *See also* Corporation, Joint Venture, Limited Liability Company, Limited Liability Partnership, Partnership

George Spelvin

George Spelvin is the "Kilroy" of the theatre. He does not exist, yet his name has appeared time and time again in virtually every type of performance and serving in most capacities. This insider's joke is at least a half-century old and universal among theater professionals. Who do you blame for something going wrong? George Spelvin. Who fills out a cast when someone gets sick? George Spelvin. And, when nobody wants to play the corpse, George will. Gladly. He'll do almost anything to get his name in the program. Indeed, he co-authored this volume and is solely responsible for all errors.

Sponsorship

Sponsorship is an arrangement whereby an individual, group or organization will take financial responsibility for a particular production, performance, performer, or company. These arrangements are customarily established by contract and will typically include a variety of conditions and may require acknowledgement for publicity purposes or anonymity in some cases. Sponsorships may be gifts, such as the charitable donations made to a company which is structured as a (501)(c)(3) charity, or they may be structured as loans, which must be repaid. They can also take the form of investments, providing the sponsor with some form of ownership and future rights. These arrangements are quite complex and generally require the aid of skilled business attorneys.

➤ *See also* Contract, Endowment, (501)(c)(3), Lawyer, Nonprofit Organization, Securities, Tax

Stage Manager

The *stage manager* is the person who, as the term suggests, is in charge of the stage. That is, the individual responsible for all backstage operations of a production. In a small company, the stage manager may also function as an assistant director. Typically, the stage manager's job takes off when the stage director's job winds down.

The stage manager is responsible during the run of a show for ensuring that all personnel are present and accounted for, that all backstage details are in order, and that the company is prepared for the curtain to rise. The stage manager calls a show; that is, directs each scheduled change during the presentation, from the house lights being dimmed, to the curtain call. He or she will ensure that all performers are ready at the top of the show, that set pieces and props are properly placed and ready for changes, and that lighting changes occur on time. More and more production companies utilize headsets for backstage personnel, which facilitates this process by allowing the stage manager to speak directly with the lighting and sound technicians during the show. It is the stage manager's responsibility to fix any backstage problems which occur during a show. Depending on the complexity of a particular production, assistant stage managers may also be employed. Stage managers may or may not be union members.

➤ *See also* Call Board, Director, Union, Appendix A

Stage Name

➤ *See* Professional Name

Stagehand

A *stagehand* is an individual who handles the stage pieces, including scenery and set pieces, most notably in the context of scene changes. These individuals may be union members. Virtually every live production uses the services of one or more stagehands for set-up, scene changes, strike, and the like. In community theaters, these positions are typically unpaid and may incorporate the functions of riggers, fly men, and other positions which would be discrete in a larger, unionized company.

➤ *See also* Fly Man, Rigger, Union, Appendix A

Statement

A *statement* is a recapitulation of a set of financial transactions or conditions, such as bank statements, financial statements, income statements, and others. When the word *statement* is used alone, it generally refers to a statement of account. This is a recapitulation sent by a seller to a buyer, usually on a monthly basis, to indicate all purchases and payments made during the period and any unpaid invoices from prior periods. The statement lists each purchase according to the invoice number and lists each payment received, either by date or by invoice number against which it is credited. The final balance is what is owed by the buyer to the seller on the date the statement is prepared. The difference between an invoice and a statement is twofold: (1) A statement is primarily a recapitulation of what is owed and what's been paid; and (2) does not generally indicate why or for what the money is owed. That's why invoice numbers are used for reference.

➤ *See also* Accounting, Bank Statement, Checking Account, Financial Statement

Statute of Frauds

This is a law which was passed to prevent fraud and perjury by requiring certain important transactions to be evidenced in writing. These include transactions in real property, disposition of money or other property after death, transactions for personal property in excess of a specified value, and personal service transactions which may not be completed within one year.

The law is quite complex and there are numerous technical exceptions; for example, if the service has been provided, the *Statute of Frauds* would not apply. A frequent application of this doctrine in the entertainment industry is performance contracts. Since an actor's participation in an open-ended run could extend longer than one year, the Statute of Frauds would apply, and a writing (contract) would be required or the arrangement would be subject to a Statute of Frauds defense if either party breached the agreement. Note: This is true even if the play closes after only one week, since it *could* have run for more than a year. Another common application in the entertainment industry is contracts for the purchase of merchandise or equipment costing more than $500.

➤ *See also* Contracts, Uniform Commercial Code

Statute of Limitations

The legal system provides remedies for nearly all injuries, yet there comes a time when the potential claimant should be prevented from asserting those rights if they have not been pursued. It is for this reason that *statutes of repose* have been enacted as defenses to otherwise valid claims. Some of these are known as *statutes of limitation.*

In some situations, the law fixes the period for the statute of limitations, such as three years for copyright infringement. In other cases, the law is intentionally silent and the court must determine whether, in fairness, a reasonable period has elapsed so as to bar the claim. These statutes of repose, known as *laches,* apply in, for example, trademark cases and other situations where it is felt that the complainant, knowing of the wrong, has allowed it to continue, misleading the perpetrator into believing that its actions were acceptable. As a matter of public policy, in some cases, there is no statute of limitations, such as murder or concealment of income for income tax purposes.

➤ *See also* Audit, Lawyer, Recordkeeping, Small Claims Court

Stop Payment

If you tell your bank not to pay a check which you have already issued, it's known as a *stop payment order.* There is usually a charge for this service. Proceed with caution. In most states, it is against the law to stop payment on a check except for a very good reason. Such reasons include a check that was lost in the mail, or where a contract has been cancelled but the check has already been issued as a down payment and not been returned. To stop payment on a check for an otherwise valid transaction may be illegal or a breach of contract. A valid stop payment order must, of course, be given before the check has cleared your bank. In commercial transactions, this must be done before midnight of the day following the day the check was issued. The stop payment order may be telephoned to the bank, but must be confirmed in writing as soon thereafter as possible. Be sure to make a checkbook entry to indicate that a check has been stopped.

➤ *See also* Checking Account

Strike

In the entertainment industry, the term *strike* refers to the dismantling of a set. Striking a set may occur immediately following the last performance of a production or a company may schedule the strike for another time. Touring companies will not only strike the set but must make it road-ready. In a unionized company, the strike will typically be handled by the appropriate backstage personnel; in a community theater, by contrast, the entire cast and crew will typically be involved.

➤ *See also* Union

Subscription Sales

The term *subscription sales* has application in at least two contexts in the entertaiment industry. It applies to the arrangement between an investor and an promoter when selling securities for the purpose of financing a performance, production, season, or company. Before a security may be sold in the United States or any state, a *subscription agreement* is customarily prepared and deposited with an independent party known as an *escrow agent* until the amount of sales which was established as a *trigger* has been reached and funds may by released.

In the context of ticket sales, this term refers to the arrangement whereby tickets are ordered either singly, in blocks, or for a season. This may occur through telemarketing, direct mail, or box office sales. Subscription sales may be to the general public but are more commonly offered to preferred purchasers, such as giving season ticket holders the first opportunity to purchase tickets to a special production.

➤ *See also* Marketing, Securities, Ticket

Taft-Hartley Law

The *Taft-Hartley Law* is a federal statute enacted for the purpose of regulating certain labor-related activities. Among other things, this statute provides the President of the United States the ability to apply for a court order delaying a strike for a prescribed period in order to encourage labor negotiations and provide for a "cooling-off" period. Taft-Hartley injunctions are rarely applied for, since their use does, to some extent, interfere with free and open labor-management relations. Although these injunctions are typically used for the purpose of protecting national security, such as the Taft-Hartley injunction which was obtained during the Korean War for purposes of delaying a threatened steel workers strike, they have been threatened during entertainment industry labor disputes such as the 1995 baseball strike.

➤ *See also* Union

Talent Agent

➤ *See* Agent

Tax

A *tax* is the compulsory payment of money, established and enforced by law, to a governmental body for purposes of meeting the general expenses of government. Taxes are normally based on a percentage of the value of the taxable subject, *e.g.,* income, property, or sales. Taxes are not based on the use of a specific benefit. Compulsory payments which relate to a specific benefit or service are not generally called taxes, even though they are also established and enforced by law and paid to a governmental body. These costs, including license fees, highway tolls, and sewer assessments, are usually fixed amounts instead of percentages.

In the case of full-time entertainers, all reasonable and customary business expenses are deductible, even if they exceed the year's income from entertainment employment. In the case of people who have full-time jobs not in the entertainment industry but who work in the industry in their spare time with the intent to profit, business expenses related to their entertainment activity may be deductible up to the amount of income realized from their entertainment income in any given tax year. In the latter category, it is very important to observe the Internal Revenue Service guideline which establishes a presumption that an activity is a business rather than a hobby if it makes a profit in three out of five consecutive years. People who pursue entertainment activities purely as a hobby probably cannot deduct their expenses.

A critical factor, if the IRS questions your business deductions, is your intent. In other words, did you really intend to make a profit? Did you really intend to conduct a business, even if only part-time? Your business intentions will be much easier to substantiate if you have kept a good set of financial records, if you can show that you have invested in materials and equipment, have a separate business bank account, have advertising literature with your business name, and similar evidence; in other words, conducted your entertainment activities as a business. For example, purchasing this book, as distinguished from merely borrowing a copy, will go far in establishing your credibility as a businessperson.

Under the three-out-of-five-year rule, you are more likely to be able to substantiate your position that you are a professional entertainer and not an amateur if you show a profit early in the five-year period. There are legal methods by which you might be able to manipulate some deductions. For example, you may legally prepay certain expense items, such as insurance premiums or rent, thus "bunching" your deductions in one year and reducing them in the next year. Similarly, you may postpone buying certain items until after year-end. There may come a time, especially in a year when income and expenses are very close, when you may find it worthwhile to defer some expense items in order to show a profit that year. That will, in turn, allow you to take all the deductions in the next year.

No matter what tax category you're in, the most essential point to remember is that a sound and consistent method of recording every expense item is critical in case your return should be audited.

> ➤ *See also* Accountant, Accounting, Amortization, Audit, Business Tax, Business Trips, Capital Gains, Charitable Contributions, Computers, Deferred Giving, Depreciation, Entertainment Tax, Estimated Tax, Expenses, 501(c)(3), Income Tax, Independent Contractor, Lease, Nonprofit Organization, Property Tax, Record-keeping, Sales Tax, Securities, Social Security, Sponsorship, Tax Preparer, Travel, Unemployment Insurance, Unrelated Business Income, Wages, Withholding Tax, Workers' Compensation, Year-End

Tax-Exempt

> ➤ *See* (501)(c)(3), Nonprofit Organization

Tax Preparer

A *tax preparer* is an individual who assists a person or business with preparation of tax returns. To represent a taxpayer in the tax courts and before the Internal Revenue Service, however, the preparer must be a Certified Public Accountant (CPA), an attorney, or an Enrolled Agent. An Enrolled Agent must have passed a stringent four-part test. There is no licensing or state regulation of tax preparers except in the state of Oregon, where tax preparers must be state-licensed. To become a Licensed Tax Preparer in Oregon, for example, an individual must pass a state-administered test. A Licensed Tax Preparer may sign tax returns on behalf of another but only under the direction of a CPA, attorney, or Licensed Tax Consultant who has satisfied even more demanding requirements.

> ➤ *See also* Accountant, Audit, Computers, Income Tax—Business, Income Tax—Personal

Technical Director

A *technical director* is responsible for coordinating the technical details of a production, including set design and construction, lighting and sound design, costumes and properties. Many technical directors are also set designers and they frequently directly oversee set construction. A technical director may be responsible for contracting with backstage personnel. A technical director may or may not be a union member.

217

> *See also* Contract, Set Designer, Union, Appendix A

Telemarketing

> *See* Tickets

Telephone

The *telephone* has become not only the major mode of modern communication, but also one of the items in the monthly overhead. As a result of deregulation, telephone services are quite competitive.

SHOP AROUND FOR THE BEST BUY

Services: There may be only one telephone company in town, but that company will likely offer many different services. These are the four most common basic line services, depending on your location and your needs:

1. Individual-line message-rate service, with a monthly allowance of message units.
2. Individual-line message-rate service with no message unit allowance. This is most economical for telephones which are used primarily to receive incoming calls rather than to make outgoing calls.
3. Individual-line flat-rate service which allows an unlimited number of calls within a specified calling area.
4. Party-line flat-rate service. This is the least expensive but, if another party on your line is using the phone, you cannot use the line.

Equipment: You should also shop around for the best buy in telephone equipment. You may wish to rent a phone from your local phone company. Telephones today are integrated with all kinds of equipment, such as clock-radios and fax machines, and other technologies. Phones can be cordless, video, or cellular. While cordless phones provide some convenience, they also have some drawbacks. Some models do not have the sound quality of traditional phones, and there may be some privacy issues in using them.

MESSAGE UNITS

In many parts of the country, especially in metropolitan areas, the *message unit* is the way telephone usage is measured and billed. One call is not necessarily one message unit. Distance and time both determine how many message units the call will cost. The time of day when the call is made can also determine the cost of each message unit.

LONG DISTANCE

Place as many calls as you can by direct dialing. Once you use the operator for such services as person-to-person, collect, and credit card calls, the cost goes up substantially. Charges differ according to the time of day you place your call. The highest rate is charged during weekday business hours. The charge for a *long distance* call is determined by the time at the place where the call originates. Placing a call from Los Angeles to New York before 8:00 A.M. gets the call to New York before 11:00 A.M. since there's a three-hour time difference. Conversely, placing a call in New York at 6:00 P.M. can still reach a business office in Los Angeles at 3:00 P.M. It does not pay, therefore, to make a call at 4:55 P.M. when a five-minute wait can cut the cost of that call by a third or more.

It is often more worthwhile to dial direct and take a chance on reaching an answering machine or someone other than the person you want, rather than placing an expensive person-to-person call. The operator-assistance charges do not apply if you need help because there's trouble on the line when you try to dial the call directly. But be sure to tell the operator about it.

WRONG NUMBERS

If you reach a *wrong number,* call the operator, tell him or her you reached a wrong number, and ask for credit. That applies for local calls where message units are counted as well as long distance calls.

KEEPING TRACK

If your business phone and your home phone are one and the same, the business calls are a tax-deductible business expense. Long distance calls are easy enough to identify—the telephone bill shows the number you called and the date and time you called it. For local business calls, keep a log of telephone calls. Every time you make a local call, note it in the log. If you're in a message-rate area, estimate how many message units you used, based on the length of time and distance you talked, and make a check mark for each message unit. At the end of the month it's easy enough to add up the business calls by counting the check marks.

CELLULAR (MOBILE) TELEPHONES

Cell phones have become a popular tool. They provide people with the opportunity to make or receive calls nearly everywhere. There is considerable competition between both cellular phone manufacturers and the cellular network companies. It is, therefore, worthwhile to shop around before purchasing a cellular phone or subscribing to a cellular network. These phones are extremely convenient, yet there are medical, environmental, and privacy issues which have not yet been resolved.

FACSIMILE (FAX) MACHINES

Fax machines have made the phone even more valuable. By connection to a standard phone line in your home or business, a fax allows instant transmission and receipt of copies (facsimiles) of documents via the telecommunications network, such as confirming memoranda, shipping instructions, even photographs, sketches, and diagrams. Faxing makes it possible for two individuals a few miles or several states apart to negotiate the terms of a contract, usually within the time it takes to make a phone call or two. It may be more efficient to have a phone line dedicated to use by your fax machine. It is possible, however, to get by with a single line, connecting the fax only when you are actually going to send or receive a document. Many fax machines are designed to distinguish between a voice call and a fax call.

MODEM

Another device which has enhanced telecommunication facilities in recent years is the *modem.* A modem (modulator/demodulator) is a device which converts the *serial* or *asynchronous communications* output of a computer into sound (and vice versa) so that it can be transmitted via the telecommunications network between distant computers. Modems give their users access to an ever-increasing number of database services, including electronic mail; hotel, travel and airline reservations; home shopping; news wire services; periodicals; legal, medical, and general information databases; and many others.

BEEP TONE

If you hear a *beep tone* every fifteen seconds while you're talking, it means that your conversation is being recorded by a third party. In most states, it is legal to record your own telephone conversations, even if it may be illegal to record a in-person conversation.

DEBT COLLECTION

The law prohibits making harassing or threatening telephone calls to obtain money that is owed. If you should receive such a call, report it to your telephone company business office.

FRAUD
It is illegal for anyone to use a credit card or charge calls to another number without authorization. If you lose your telephone credit card, or if you find calls on your bill that you did not make, contact your telephone company business office. Be careful when using your own telephone credit card to protect the number.

DISPLAYING YOUR PHONE NUMBER
While it's good for a business to have its phone number (including area code) listed on its letterhead, business cards, invoices, promotional literature, and wherever else it puts its name in print, individual entertainers often opt for unlisted numbers, instead utilizing their agents for professional contacts.

Most major phone companies now offers a service known as *Caller ID*. This allows subscribers to the service to identify all callers through a computerized readout on authorized equipment. Calls from unlisted phones are identified as *anonymous* or *unlisted*; other callers may block display of their number by entering a code before dialing out. The other side of this issue is another new service, which allows a phone customer to prevent further incoming calls from certain phone numbers by entering a code when a call is received from that caller.

INFORMATION PLEASE
The charge for directory assistance varies (and, for local numbers, must be waived for the legally blind). It pays to look up numbers yourself. Where such information charges are in effect, the telephone company normally makes directories for areas other than your own available upon request; there is sometimes a charge for these directories. Area codes for the entire country are printed in the front section of all telephone directories. Many phone companies now offer an additional "service" of directly connecting the caller to the number sought for a nominal charge (typically fifty to seventy-five cents).
> *See also* E-Mail

Theatrical Protective Union (IATSE)
The union to which most stagehands and the like belong.
> *See* Appendix A

Theft Insurance
> *See* Property Insurance

Ticket

Tickets are used to identify a person who is permitted to enter a theater and view a movie or stage show. They may be purchased directly at the box office or through a ticket outlet such as Ticketmaster or Fastixx. Many companies sell season tickets, often at a discount, in order to obtain operating capital early in their season. Telemarketing has become common in the entertainment industry, usually in connection with season ticket sales. With the advent of the computer age, many companies are using computer software to track ticket sales, attendance, and related accounting. "Paperless" transactions are being discussed, yet they have not caught on in the entertainment industry.

> ➤ *See also* Box Office, Computers, Discounts, Marketability, Nonprofit Organization, Robinson-Patman Act, Subscription Sales

Title

> ➤ *See* Installment, Lien, Loans, Mortgage, Uniform Commercial Code

Tour

This term *tour* refers to taking a show "on the road" and describes the scope of the performances. It will, for example, be said that a production is *on tour* when the company presents performances anywhere other than its principal house. Union members involved in a tour will typically receive a differential in their scale. The amount of work involved in arranging a tour is a function of the size of the company and the extent of the performance. If, for example, a single entertainer is touring and relying on local talent for the majority of production details, the arrangement may be less complex, though more time will likely be involved in setting up the production, than if a self-contained Broadway musical is to go on the road.

> ➤ *See also* Scale, Union

Tour Manager

A *tour manager* is the person responsible for overseeing all aspects of a tour. This is the individual who performs the tasks of a company manager for a tour. He or she will be responsible for coordinating with all of the local individuals and organizations in the communities where the show tours.

> ➤ *See also* Manager, Tour

Trade Dress

Trade dress is a relatively new form of intellectual property protection which is available without registration on the non-functional "aspects" of certain items. Packaging is functional and, thus, not copyrightable, yet products are frequently identified by their distinctive packaging—for example, *Playbill*'s yellow and black title. The distinctive "look and feel" of an item is known as its *trade dress,* which is protectible.

> ➤ *See also* Copyright, Intellectual Property, Patent, Public Domain, Trademark, Trade Secret

Trade Libel

> ➤ *See* Disparagement

Trademark

A *trademark* is described in the Trademark Act of 1946, as amended in 1989, as "any word, name, symbol, or device, or any combination thereof adopted and used by a manufacturer or merchant to identify its goods and distinguish them from those manufactured or sold by others." A trademark serves not only to indicate who made the product, but often suggests a certain level of quality based on the manufacturer's past performance. Typical trademarks known far and wide are the oval Ford symbol, the distinctive lettering of Coca-Cola as well as the familiar bottle shape, the Nike swoosh, and many others. When a movie company uses a unique symbol in connection with its productions, for example, the M-G-M lion, that symbol is a trademark. While trademarks need not be registered, registration helps to protect the owner's exclusive right to use the trademark.

The difference between trademarks and *trade names* is that a trademark identifies a product, while a trade name identifies the producer of the product. When a trade name is designed in a unique fashion and is used on the product, it can become a trademark and be registered as such.

Trademarks must appear on the merchandise or its container, or be associated with the goods or services at the point of sale, and must be used regularly in interstate commerce to remain valid. Certain material may not be used in trademarks, such as the United States flag, the likeness of a living person without his or her permission, and several others.

Generic marks, *i.e.,* words which are the noun describing a product or service, such as "chair" for a chair, are not protectible. If a mark is "merely descriptive," such as *TV Guide* for a publication listing television offerings, then it may be protectible if it has acquired a "secondary meaning" by notice of use, promotion, and visibility. Before a mark is actually used in commerce, an "intent to use" application covering the proposed mark may be filed with the Patent and Trademark Office. Once the mark is actually used, this filing will mature into a registration.

Trademarks which are already in use may be federally registered with the U.S. Patent and Trademark Office, Washington, DC 20231, by furnishing a written application, a drawing of the mark, three specimens or facsimiles of the mark as it is actually used, and a fee of $245. The registration is valid for ten years and can be renewed for further ten-year terms. When a trademark is not used regularly on a product or its container, the registration lapses, even if the ten-year term isn't up. After a mark has been federally registered, notice of the registration should accompany the mark wherever it is used. Various means are available to do this, the most common being ® which is placed right next to the mark. Note that ® may be used only in connection with federally-registered marks.

Variations of a trademark are *service marks,* to identify a service rather than a product; *certification marks,* which are not related to a specific product or manufacturer, but might indicate regional origin, method of manufacture, or union label; and *collective marks,* used by members of an association, cooperative, or other organization. All these can be registered in the same fashion as a trademark.

The Patent Office does not give legal advice regarding trademarks, nor can it respond to inquiries about whether certain trademarks have been registered. The Patent Office does maintain a file of registered marks which are arranged alphabetically where words are included, or otherwise by symbols according to the classification of the goods or services in which they are used. These files are open to the public in the Search Room of Trademark Operations in Washington, D.C., and it is advisable to have the files searched to determine whether the same or a similar trademark has already been registered.

During the period when the application for federal registration is pending, it is common to use the designation ™ for trademarks, and ˢᴹ for service marks. These designations have no official status but merely give notice of a claimed property right in the mark.

There is also a state trademark registry in every state in the Union. State registration is beneficial only within the registering state and does *not* permit the use of ®. The remedies for infringement laws are often different from those available under the federal statute.

A detailed booklet, "General Information Concerning Trademarks," is available for fifty cents from the Superintendent of Documents, U.S. Government Printing Office, Washington, D.C. 20402.

➤ *See also* Copyright, *Droit Morale*, Intellectual Property, License, Patent, Professional Name, Trade Dress, Trade Name, Trade Secret

Trade Name

Many businesses use a name for public identification which differs from the name of the owner. You may be Sam Jones, but the sign on your door reads Performing Arts Management. That's a *trade name*. Since trade names can't be held legally responsible for anything, it is almost universally required that a trade name be registered with some governmental authority, often the Secretary of State or the county clerk. The initials *d/b/a* or *dba* (doing business as) appears on such documents as legal papers and credit reports to tie the trade name to the owner, as in: "Sam Jones *d/b/a* Performing Arts Management." Trade names may also be known as *assumed business names* (*abns*) or *fictitious business names*.

To protect a trade name from unauthorized use by others, it may be registered with the federal government as a trademark if certain conditions are met.

➤ *See also* Intellectual Property, License, Professional Name, Trademark

Trade Secret

A *trade secret* is any information which is non-public and which provides a commercial advantage, for example, patron lists. Trade secrets are protectable only so long as they remain secret, and one who improperly discloses a trade secret may be liable for damages. Since trade secret law and trade secret protection are quite complex, you should consult with an experienced intellectual property lawyer in order to establish a trade secret program if you feel your business has trade secrets.

➤ *See also* Intellectual Property, Copyright, License, Patent, Trademark, Trade Dress

Travel

➤ *See* Business Trips, Tax

Traveler's Checks

Traveler's checks are extremely popular because they are very safe to carry, and are recognized almost everywhere in the world. The safety factor exists because purchasers sign their checks once when they buy them, and then again when they use them.

Two precautions: (1) Do not accept a traveler's check unless the person who offers it signs it in your presence. Compare the signatures and accept the check only if they match; and (2) a traveler's check with *both* signatures but no endorsement is as good as cash if it is lost or stolen. Immediately upon receiving a traveler's check as payment, endorse it with your name, the words *for deposit only,* and your checking account number. Then handle it like any other check on your bank deposit slip. A new feature in traveler's checks is a check which may be used by either of two designated parties.

➤ *See also* Banks

U.S. Department of Commerce

➤ *See* Government Activities

U.S. Department of Labor

➤ *See* Employees, Government Activities, Wages

Underwriting

The term *underwriting* is used in the insurance and securities industries to define the arrangement for establishing the contract. An insurance underwriter is customarily responsible for establishing the rate to be charged for the insurance and determining whether to assume the risk and enter into an insurance contract. This is also the person who will reevaluate the actual loss experience when a policy is up for renewal, in order to determine whether a new premium rate is appropriate.

In the securities industry, the underwriter helps structure the securities offering in order to be assured that the investment interests are both lawfully and practicably salable. The underwriter typically takes responsibility for arranging to have the investment securites sold and may appoint other securities dealers for purposes of expanding the sales team. In this situation, the principal underwriter, who interacts with the issuer and arranges for salespeople, is known as the *lead underwriter* and coordinates the sales activity. There are several standard methods of underwriting securities. The most common method in the United States is the *best efforts* arrangement, in which the underwriter merely guarantees to use his or her best efforts in selling the security, without guaranteeing that the securities will actually be sold. Typically, the underwriter will be paid a percentage of the amount actually raised only if the offering is successful.

Firm underwriting is an arrangement in which the underwriter actually purchases the securities up front, and attempts to resell them to investors. This type of arrangement is very unusual in smaller offerings, such as those used in the entertainment industry, and is prohibited by Regulation D of the federal securities law, under which the vast majority of securities in the entertainment industry are sold. This type of underwriting should be distinguished from *standby underwriting,* in which the underwriter agrees to purchase all securities which have not been sold to investors by a particular date for a specified price. The standby commitment is typically not used for small offerings, such as those which are common in the entertainment industry, and is also prohibited by Regulation D. Arrangements involving securities underwriting are very technical and must be undertaken with the assistance of an experienced securities lawyer.

➤ *See also* Insurance, Lawyer, Securities

Unemployment Insurance

Unemployment insurance is a government program which provides cash benefits to qualified unemployed people who are seeking work but have not yet found a job. Eligibility requirements and the size of weekly checks vary from state to state. Benefits are funded by mandatory payments made by employers in the form of a payroll tax. The weekly check received by the unemployed is based on the amount of money the individual earned during the qualification period.

Unemployment insurance is exactly what the name implies: insurance which provides benefits as a matter of right, as long as the unemployed applicant meets the conditions of the law. The specific rules and regulations which apply in the different states are available through each state's Department of Labor. Unemployment compensation is usually unavailable to independent contractors and other self-employed persons.

In the entertainment industry, frequent unemployment is common. It has been said that 5 percent of the eligible performers earn 95 percent of the available income. Unemployment compensation is critical to performers who are "between engagements." In fact, some entertainment employers have actually factored unemployment payments into the performer's compensation schedule.

➤ *See also* Employees, Independent Contractor, Insurance, Wages, Workers' Compensation, Tax

Uniform Commercial Code (UCC)

The Uniform Commercial Code (UCC) is the evolutionary embodiment and codification of the law of commercial transactions. Begun in the 1940s as a joint project of the American Law Institute and the National Conference of Commissioners on Uniform State Laws, the Code brought together in a single document many of the common law principles and a number of earlier uniform laws governing such transactions. Some of these laws are: Uniform Negotiable Instruments, Uniform Sales Act, Uniform Bills of Lading Act, Uniform Stock Transfer Act, Uniform Conditional Sales, Uniform Trust Receipts Act.

Since its first enactment, effective July 1, 1954, the UCC has undergone a number of revisions with reissues of Official Text and Comments in 1958, 1962, 1966, 1972, 1977, and 1987. All states except Louisiana have adopted one or another version of the UCC, either in whole or in part, and many have adopted later amendments as they appeared. Some states have incorporated their own language and modifications while maintaining the basic UCC matrix.

The purpose of the UCC has been to simplify, clarify, and modernize the law governing commercial transactions. Its underlying policy is to permit the continued expansion of commercial practices through custom, usage, and agreement of the parties. Both of these goals have been very successfully achieved by making the law fairly uniform throughout the various jurisdictions that have adopted the Code. Today, the UCC continues to deal comprehensively with the various statutes relating to commercial transactions.

Its articles cover broadly and specifically many aspects of personal property and the contracts and other documents concerning them, including: Article 1—General Provisions (and definitions); Article 2—Sales; Article 3—Commercial Paper; Article 4—Bank Deposits and Collections; Article 5—Letters of Credit; Article 6—Bulk Transfers; Article 7—Warehouse Receipts, Bills of Lading, and Other Documents of Title; Article 8—Investment Securities; and Article 9—Secured Transactions, Sales of Accounts, and Chattel Paper. A new section, Article 2A—Leases, was added in 1987. Many states have adopted Article 2A into their commercial codes. The drafters are currently considering another article, dealing with the Internet and computer networks in general.

All of these articles have application to the entertainment industry. For example, when a theater company purchases a sound system on credit, Article 2 would apply, since a sound system is within the definition of "goods" covered by that article, and if the seller wished to perfect its security interest in the system until the debt was fully retired, Article 9 would apply.

➤ *See also* Cancelled Check, Checking Account, Collateral, Contract, Creditor, Foreclosure, Industry Practices and Customs, Installment, Internet, Lease, Letter of Credit, Lien, Mortgage, Statute of Frauds

Union

A *labor union* is an organization established for the purpose of representing its members in their dealings with employers. Initially, many employers were hostile toward the union movement and forced individuals who worked for them to sign contracts in which the individual agreed not to join a union. These *yellow dog* contracts were outlawed by federal law and, today, the union movement has achieved acceptability.

The dynamics of union arrangements, as between the employers, workers and different unions, is quite complex. Many union disputes involve battles between unions over jurisdictional issues, such as which union will represent a particular group of individuals. Other labor disputes involve attempts by unions to force a particular employer to enter into a collective bargaining agreement. Today, most of these issues have been resolved.

The National Labor Relations Board regulates the interactions between unions, their members, and employers. It is involved in the definition of *collective bargaining units* (the individuals to be covered under a given collective bargaining agreement) and conducts elections to determine which union will represent the members of a specific bargaining unit. Thus, any one employer may have contracts with several different unions. The vast majority of the entertainment industry is governed by some form of union agreement. Union contracts customarily cover wages, benefits, and working conditions.

Unlike most industries, where the collective bargaining unit is a segment of employees of a single employer, in the entertainment industry, the collective bargaining unit is a category of worker, who may by an employee or an independent contractor performing services for several different companies. Thus, a member of the American Guild of Musical Artists, who will likely be an independent contractor, will receive the same contract benefits whenever the member performs for a company which is a signatory to the AGMA master contract. Similarly, United Scenic Artists represents set designers, costume designers, and lighting designers, regardless of whether they are employees or independent contractors.

Jurisdictional disputes have arisen over a producer's intended use of foreign nationals to serve in positions that could be filled by American union members. For example, when the Broadway production of *Miss Saigon* was being cast, the union threatened a labor action if certain principals from the original London cast were hired for the Broadway production.

➤ *See also* Contract, Employees, Independent Contractor, Minimum Wage, Parity, Per Diem, Right-to-Work Laws, Scale, Season, Set Designer, Stagehand, Stage Manager, Strike, Taft-Hartley Law, Technical Director, Tour, Voice-Over, Visa, Wardrobe, Appendix A

Universal Copyright Convention (UCC)

The Universal Copyright Convention is a treaty that was open for signature in the mid-1950s and which provides international protection for copyright owners in the nations which have become parties to it. The protection must be at least as good as the protection available for nationals of the country where the enforcement occurs.

In order to obtain international protection under the UCC, a copyright owner must obtain a copyright in a signatory nation, comply with that nation's copyright laws, be a citizen or domiciliary of a nation which is a party to the UCC, and use the international copyright symbol © in the copyright notice, along with the full name of the copyright owner and the year of first publication.

Eighty-three countries are parties to the UCC. While this treaty is quite beneficial for international protection, it is not as popular as the Berne Copyright Convention, which has 88 signatory nations. The UCC is administered and periodically revised by UNESCO. This means that the administering entity considers and recommends modifications to the treaty which must be agreed to by a signatory nation in order for the change to be binding on it.

➤ *See also* Berne Copyright Convention, Buenos Aires Convention, Copyright

Unrelated Business Income

Qualified nonprofit corporations, such as theater and other performing arts companies, often engage in commercial activities, for example, sales of souvenir programs, novelties, and the like. If the primary function of the

231

organization is commercial, however, then it should not be entitled to tax-exempt status. The Internal Revenue Service periodically reviews the extent of a company's commercial activities, in order to make this determination.

When in doubt about the extent of its commercial activities, a nonprofit organization should apply to the IRS for an advisory opinion known as a *Revenue Ruling.* These rulings customarily state the facts as presented by the requesting organization and, based on those facts, the determination by the IRS whether the organization should be permitted to retain its tax-

exempt status. If a ruling is requested before engaging in the commercial activity—which is very common—and a negative response is received, the organization should not engage in the activity and jeopardize its tax-exempt status.

According to the Internal Revenue Code, a nonprofit tax-exempt organization such as a theater company may engage in *some* commercial activity, provided the commercial activity is for the purpose of assisting the organization in fulfilling its mission and provided that the commercial activity is closely related to the nonprofit function of the organization. If a theater is located in close proximity to a number of restaurants, operating its own restaurant (as opposed to merely a concession stand) is unnecessary and could jeopardize the organization's tax-exempt status. Sellers of souvenirs must be careful to handle only items which are related to theater or movie exhibitions.

The extent of commercial activity can also be a problem. For example, when the Metropolitan Museum was asked to license reproduction of certain patterns in its fabric collection, it applied to the IRS for a Ruling, since it was anticipated that the royalties from this project would be several hundred thousand dollars. The IRS ruled that the unrelated business income would not jeopardize the Museum's tax-exempt status, though the unrelated business income would be taxable. Some organizations actually set up wholly-owned business corporations as subsidiaries to handle their commercial activities.

➤ *See also* Business Tax, Nonprofit Organization, Income Tax—Business, Tax

Vehicle

The term *vehicle* is used to describe a work, usually a play or musical, written for the express of showcasing a particular artist. For example, the musical *Funny Girl* was written with Barbara Streisand in mind.

➤ *See also* Commission

Visa

A *visa* is a permit to travel in a country other than that of the traveler's citizenship and residence. The visa is issued by the country in which the travel is to occur, and is customarily attached to the traveler's passport. The visa must be obtained prior to the traveler's departure and must be presented upon arrival in the issuing country.

While some countries are so informal that nothing but proof of citizenship is necessary for foreigners' travel within its borders, such as the arrangements between the United States and Canada or the arrangement within the European Economic Community, other countries are more formal, requiring an official passport issued by the traveler's government, establishing the right to leave their country. Still other countries will not permit entry unless official permission is sought by the traveler and granted by the host country through the visa. More commonly, Third World and communist countries require visas from American travelers.

The mere fact that one has obtained a visa means that the traveler may work in the country granting the visa. Special arrangements must be made to perform services for compensation and many countries have protective legislation prohibiting the performances of services for compensation unless the individual or hiring entity can establish that a national of that country could not perform a comparable service. In addition, it must be established that the service is necessary or desirable.

The United States requires foreign nationals performing services in this country to obtain work visas, which are known as *green cards* because they are green. It is illegal for a foreign national to be compensated for work performed in the United States unless a green card has been obtained. Both the employer and the employee are subject to fines for violating these laws. It is for this reason that employers in the entertainment industry must require every employee to complete a form I-9 which establishes the employee's right to work in this country.

➤ *See also* Employees, Independent Contractor, Union

Voice-Over

A *voice-over,* or VO, is the recording of a narrative to accompany a filmed production which may be aired on television or in the theater, or in a commercial. Voice-overs may also be used to replace the voice of a person depicted on screen; for example, during the filming of the last Inspector Clouseau film, David Niven was so weak that it was determined to use Rich Little's voice instead of Niven's.

Voice-overs have also long been used in the dubbing of foreign films. Today, VOs are being used as a means of enabling visually-disabled individuals to "see" the non-audio portions of a production. The process, known as *audio narration,* has become popular for video productions and is in the process of being developed for television and live theater. It has been common for VOs to be used for purposes of adding professional singing to films when the celebrity depicted is unable to present the desired quality. For example, Marni Nixon sang for Deborah Kerr in *The King and I,* as well as for Audrey Hepburn in *My Fair Lady.* Voice-over talent is typically union-affiliated.

➤ *See also* Contract, Union, Appendix A

Volunteer Lawyers for the Arts

Volunteer Lawyers for the Arts (VLA) began in the late 1960s when three New York lawyers recognized the need for legal specialists to assist the art community. The concept caught on and spread throughout the country. Today, more than half the states have some form of VLA organization providing entertainment-related legal services. The organizations initially provided *pro bono* (free) legal services to artists and arts-related organizations with arts-related legal problems. Today, many of the organizations charge fees based on a sliding scale for the services provided. Most of the organizations have an educational component and present seminars for their constituents. Some of the organizations also publish books and newsletters. Most VLA groups have arts law libraries and make publications available either for free or at a nominal charge.

➤ *See* Lawyer, Appendix A

Wages

Wages must be differentiated from *income*. Wages are given to employees who are paid either on an hourly basis or receive a fixed salary. Most full-time or regular employees of theatrical production companies are paid wages; most talent and crew members hired on a per-production basis are paid as independent contractors. Employers are responsible for withholding from their employees' wages federal and state income tax, Social Security, Medicare, workers' compensation insurance, and other employment-related charges. Independent contractors are not paid wages; rather, they receive contractual payments from which they must pay their own tax obligations.

Most entertainers and stagehands are independent contractors, rather than employees. Entertainment companies which hire members of entertainment unions such as Artists Equity, American Guild of Musical Artists, or a craft union, whether as employees or as independent contractors, may have little or no control over the amount of money paid for a particular job. These rates are fixed by the union contract, as are other benefits to be paid.

> ➤ *See also* Accounting, Apprentice, Business Expense, Employees, Fees, Gross, Income Tax—Business, Income Tax—Personal, Independent Contractor, Labor, Minimum Wage, Scale, Social Security, Unemployment Insurance, Withholding Tax

Wardrobe

The term *wardrobe* describes the collection of costumes belonging to a company or those used in a particular production. It is administered and conserved by a wardrobe master or mistress, who is responsible for construction, cleaning, care, and storage. Wardrobe professionals are typically union members. Many costumes have become extremely valuable because of their association with a particular production or artist; in fact, many have been donated to museums. Others have been offered for sale at either auction or other public sale. Many private collectors specialize in film and theatrical costumes, and some businesses have been built on a foundation of costume- and memorabilia-collecting; for example, the Hard Rock Cafe is famous for its collection of costumes and musical instruments.

➤ *See also* Union, Appendix A

Will

➤ *See* Estate Planning

Withholding Tax

Regardless of how much you earn, some portion of an employee's wages or salary must be *withheld* by the employer from each paycheck for the payment of the employee's income taxes. The employer acts as the collection agent for the Internal Revenue Service and for state and local governments which impose income taxes. If you are an employer, there are several specific procedures to follow:

1. You must obtain an Employer Identification Number by filing form SS-4 with the Internal Revenue Service.
2. The I.R.S. then provides you with a number of copies of Form 501, which has to accompany the remittance of the tax money you withhold from your employees (including yourself, if you are incorporated and draw a salary).
3. The employer deposits the tax money in its bank with Form 501, according to the following schedule:
   a. If the total Social Security taxes (both employer and employee contributions) and federal withholding taxes is less than $200 at the end of a quarter then no monthly deposit is required and you must only pay the tax due with your quarterly 941 report.
   b. Generally, if at the end of a month, the tax due is greater than $500, you must make the deposit within fifteen days after the end of the

month. However, certain large employers may be required to make semi-weekly payments.

The bank gives you a receipt for the deposit and, in turn, deposits all the money and all the Forms 501 with the Internal Revenue Service. Every calendar quarter, every employer is required to file Form 941 directly with the Internal Revenue Service. This form is a summary of all the withholding tax payments that were made on behalf of the business's employees during that quarter.

4. Between January 1 and January 31 of each year, every employer is required to furnish a W-2 form to all employees, showing wages for the prior calendar year. This is a summary of all the wages paid during the previous year, and all income taxes and Social Security taxes withheld during that period. Employees must file the W-2 form with their income tax returns. The form must be furnished to all employees who were on the payroll at any time during the previous year, even if they worked for only a day and even if they are no longer employed by the company. If a terminating employee requests that his or her Form W-2 be provided at the time of termination, the employer is required to do so.

One important observation: When cash supply is short, some employers are tempted to use for other purposes the funds they withheld to pay taxes. That's a temptation which should be resisted. Failure to deposit the withholding taxes is a very serious federal crime and may subject the owners of a business to personal liability even if the business is insolvent.

Any individual who is not an employee of another (*i.e.,* self-employed) is required to pay his or her own estimated tax on a quarterly basis. This is one of the areas where individuals who are independent contractors can get into trouble. Since they are not employees of another business, they are required to make quarterly estimated payments; failure to do so will subject the independent contractor to penalties and interest payments.

➤ *See also* Employees, Estimated Tax, Income Tax, Tax, Wages

Workers' Compensation

The law has always held an employer liable for injuries or death suffered by its employees if the condition arose from the employer's negligence in not providing safe working conditions. *Workers' compensation* laws in every state allow employees or their heirs to recover damages from the employer's workers' compensation insurance carrier for injuries or death suffered by employees while on the job, regardless of whose fault it was, unless it was self-inflicted or caused by intoxication. The laws vary from state to state, and so does the extent of the insurer's liability, but, in most states, an employer is required to carry workers' compensation insurance. Premiums are generally based on a percentage of the payroll as related to two factors: the hazard of the job and the claims history of the employer. Premiums may be reduced, therefore, by increasing safety precautions and decreasing the likelihood of injuries.

Entertainers need not carry workers' compensation insurance if they work alone. The moment you hire an employee, however, even a part-timer, the workers' compensation law of your state will likely apply. Before you put anyone on the payroll, talk to your insurance broker or contact your state labor department to find out what's required of you under your state workers' compensation law. Even if you are not required to obtain workers' compensation insurance for yourself or a single employee, you may voluntarily do so and the cost of such insurance may be worthwhile. The premiums are a deductible business expense and one work-related injury is sufficient to put you out of business if you're not insured.

If a theater company owns its equipment, then the individuals who operate it will likely be employees. It is, however, quite common for theater companies to rent equipment and have the individuals who operate the rented equipment characterized as independent contractors. This is for the purpose of avoiding the necessity of purchasing workers' compensation insurance. When dealing with an independent contractor, you should have a written agreement specifying the individual's employment characterization as an independent contractor, making it clear that the worker is responsible for his or her own insurance, including workers' compensation insurance covering his or her activities for the theatercompany.

➤ *See also* Employees, Equipment, Independent Contractor, Insurance, Safety, Tax, Unemployment Insurance

Work-for-Hire

The term *work-for-hire* is defined in Section 101 of the Copyright Right Revision Act of 1976 as a work created by an employee within the scope of his or her employment or a work which is a contribution to a collective work, a part of a motion picture or other audiovisual work, a translation, a supplementary work, a compilation, an instructional text, a test or answer material for a test, a derivative work, or an atlas, and the parties have agreed in writing that the work to be created is a *work-for-hire.* If the work is defined as a work-for-hire, then the period of copyright protection is one hundred years from the date of creation, or seventy-five years from the date of publication, whichever period expires first, and the work may not be subject to protection under the Visual Artists Rights Act of 1990.

The copyright in a work-for-hire is actually owned by the employer or commissioning party, rather than the individual creating the work. This should be distinguished from an *assignment of copyright,* in which the assignee merely holds the right for the period set forth in the assignment and the creator of the work may rescind the transaction after the end of the thirty-fifth year and before the end of the fortieth year from the date of assignment, regardless of the period set forth in the assignment agreement. Assignments of copyright are valid only if they are in writing.

A work-for-hire should also be distinguished from a *license,* which is merely a specified right to use the copyrighted work of another. A license may be oral or written, though oral licenses may not be exclusive and are revocable at the will of the licensor/owner. A license, too, may be revoked by the copyright owner after the thirty-fifth year and before the end of the fortieth year regardless of any agreement to the contrary. Both assignments of copyright and copyright licenses may be recorded with the U.S. Copyright Office. In fact, the only method by which the assignee or licensee can be assured of being protected from another person claiming superior rights during the assignment or license period is through registration of the appropriate instrument.

Some jurisdictions have enacted laws which complement the work-for-hire provision of the federal copyright law by providing that the specification of a work-for-hire arrangement requires the alleged employer to pay all employment-related fees. Thus, in California, for example, the state labor law provides that a work-for-hire contract may not be enforced unless all employment-related obligations have been fulfilled by the alleged employer.

➤ *See also* Commission, Contract, Copyright, License

Workshops

➤ *See* Education

Xerography

Xerography is a photomechanical process for reproducing a printed image. Some theater companies lawfully use this process for inexpensively producing programs and advertising literature. Others illegally reproduce copyrighted scripts and other performance materials. The term *xerox* derives from the specific process developed by the Xerox Corporation employing its machines. Since XEROX is a registered trademark and in danger of become generic by the common misuse of it both as a noun and a verb, the corporation has been extremely aggressive in reminding the public that "You can't xerox a xerox on a xerox." You should properly be photocopying on a Xerox, Canon, Mita, or the like.

➤ *See also* Copyright

Year-End

The term *year-end* is used by accountants, tax preparers, and others involved with financial information, to describe the close of a year for a variety of business and tax purposes. Most often, the business year is the same as the calendar year, but it may be a *fiscal year,* which is any prescribed twelve consecutive months. For tax purposes, individuals and S corporations must operate on a calendar year; their year-end will, therefore, be December 31. The Internal Revenue Service has taken the position that a business which does not properly designate another fiscal year will be on a calendar year.

Many entertainment businesses have elected a fiscal year which begins July 1 and ends June 30. This is because summer months are generally less active and tax preparation is less likely to interfere with routine entertainment business activities. It is also convenient for an entertainment business to have its full-year financials available for inclusion in grant applications which are due in the fall months. Similarly, the skewed year allows entertainment tax preparers to manipulate income and expenses in order to benefit from the calendar year tax period used by others. When applying for a loan, the lending institution may demand a copy of the most recent year-end financial statement as a means of evaluating the credit-worthiness of the business.

➤ *See also* Accounting, Financial Statement, Loans, Tax

Zoning

Most cities and towns impose regulations on the uses to which various areas under its jurisdiction can be put. Thus, some sections or streets may be *zoned* for residential use only, others for retail or light manufacturing or heavy industry. Zoning regulations sometimes specify the number or size of buildings in relation to land area. This is done to preserve the character of a community and to protect residential areas, for example, from the noise of heavy industry. A grandfather clause in most zoning regulations permits activities which existed prior to the establishment of the regulations to continue. That's why you might find a gas station or a drug store on a street otherwise zoned for residential use only.

Zoning regulations can sometimes have an important impact on the conduct of a theater company. Many municipalities have enacted zoning ordinances for the purpose of regulating certain entertainment activities. For example, some ordinances prohibit erotic or nude dancing in establishments outside a "tenderloin" zone, while others prohibit a concentration of adult entertainment. Several jurisdictions have enacted laws establishing geographical areas which are intended to house adult entertainment.

Most zoning regulations have provisions for granting an exception, known as a *variance*. This is process is begun when you petitions for a variance. Hearings are held in which you present your case and your neighbors or such agencies as health, building, or fire departments have an opportunity to state their objections. The neighbors may simply object to the additional traffic.

Before you make major alterations in your building, be sure they conform with the zoning regulations. Violations can be very expensive to correct.

Some jurisdictions have enacted special laws which permit artists and entertainers to work in their residences. Other jurisdictions have allowed artists to live in commercially-zoned studios. The first of these laws was passed in the SoHo district of New York City, where the Volunteer Lawyers for the Arts' first major project was to draft and successfully lobby through a law permitting artists to live in manufacturing lofts where their studios were located. A number of other jurisdictions have enacted comparable laws. California, for example, has adopted enabling legislation permitting local municipalities to pass special zoning laws for entertainers and visual artists.

➤ *See also* Lease

Appendix A

Organizations

TRADE UNIONS AND ASSOCIATIONS

Actors' Equity Association (AEA)
165 West 46th Street
New York, NY 10036
(212) 869-8530
Represents live theatrical performers
(principals, chorus, and extras), stage
managers, and assistant stage managers.

American Federation of Musicians of
  the U.S. and Canada
600 Paramount Building
1501 Broadway
New York, NY 10036
(212) 869-1330
Represents any musicians in a production.

American Federation of Television
  and Radio Artists (AFTRA)
260 Madison Avenue
New York, NY 10016
(212) 532-0800
Represents performers (including actors,
announcers, narrators, sound effects
artists, and featured or group singers)
appearing on live radio or television pro-
grams (including programs recorded by
equipment used in connection with live
broadcast programming).

American Guild of Musical Artists
  (AGMA)

1727 Broadway
Second Floor
New York, NY 10019
(212) 265-3687
Represents vocalists in live musical
performances.

American Society of Composers,
   Authors, and Publishers (ASCAP)
One Lincoln Plaza
New York, NY 10023
(212) 595-3050
Organization of composers of music,
writers of lyrics, and music publishers, that
offers the services of licensing, on a non-
exclusive basis, small performing rights in
musical compositions written and pub-
lished by members. Also polices users of
small performing rights on behalf of writer
and publisher members to ensure that
users have licenses, and commences copy-
right infringement suits on behalf of mem-
bers whose music is used without license.

Associated Actors and Artistes of
   America (4 A's)
165 West 46th Street
Room 500
New York, NY 10036
(212) 869-0358
Umbrella organization chartered by the
AFL-CIO for unions representing per-
formers in movie, television, and live the-
ater. Issues charters to the various unions,
including AEA, AFTRA, AGMA, and SAG.

The Association of Performing Arts
   Presenters (APAP)

1112 16th Street, NW
Suite 400
Washington, DC 20036
(202) 833-2787

Association of Theatrical Press
   Agents and Managers
165 West 46th Street
New York, NY 10036
(212) 719-3666
Represents press agents, company
managers, and house managers.

Broadcast Music Inc. (BMI)
320 West 57th Street
New York, NY 10019
(212) 586-2000
Originally formed by major radio stations
and networks to offer competition to
ASCAP; now an independent organization
performing the same functions as ASCAP.

The Dramatists Guild
234 West 44th Street
Eleventh Floor
New York, NY 10036
(212) 398-9366
The guild is not a union, but represents
authors, composers, lyricists, and book-
writers.

International Union of Operating
   Engineers
1125 17th Street NW
Washington, DC 20036
(202) 429-9100
Represents those involved with the opera-

tion and maintenance of the physical plant, including the heating and air conditioning systems.

Legitimate Theatre Employees
  Union
Local B183
319 West 48th Street
New York, NY 10036
(212) 586-9620
Represents ushers, doormen, ticket takers, and the backstage doormen.

National Artists Equity
1285 Avenue of the Americas
New York, NY 10019
(212) 265-1976

National Association of Performing
  Arts Managers and Agents
c/o Ingrid Kidd, President
Main Stage Management Int'l., West
3532 Katella Avenue
Room 111
Los Alamitos, CA 90720
(310) 493-5690

Screen Actors Guild (SAG)
5757 Wilshire Boulevard
Los Angeles, CA 90036
(213) 954-1600
Represents performers (including actors, professional singers, stunt artists, airplane and helicopter pilots, and puppeteers) for movie and television productions produced on film within the U.S. or by producers with a base in the U.S.

Society of Stage Directors and
  Choreographers (SSDC)
1501 Broadway
Thirty-first Floor
New York, NY 10036
(212) 391-1070
Represents directors and choreographers of live theatrical productions.

Theatrical Protective Union, IATSE
1515 Broadway
New York, NY 10036
(212) 730-1770
Represents the house crew, including carpenters, electricians, those handling the properties, and curtain and sound personnel.

Theatrical Wardrobe Attendants
  Union
151 West 46th Street
Eighth Floor
New York, NY 10036
(212) 221-1717
Represents wardrobe supervisors and dressers.

Treasurers and Ticket Sellers Union
1500 Broadway, Room 2011
New York, NY 10036
(212) 302-7300
Represents treasurers and other box office personnel.

United Scenic Artists
575 Eighth Avenue
New York, NY 10018
(212) 581-0300

247

Represents set designers, costume designers, and lighting designers.

Writers Guild of America (WGA)
8955 Beverly Boulevard
Los Angeles, CA 90048
(310) 550-1000
Represents writers in movies and the entertainment portion of motion pictures produced for initial release in the U.S. on television.

LIST BROKERS

Dependable Lists, Inc.
257 Park Avenue South
New York, NY 10010

R. L. Polk & Co.
551 Fifth Avenue
New York, NY 10017

Fred Woolf List Co.
309 Fifth Avenue
New York, NY 10016

Alan Drey Co., Inc.
600 Third Avenue
New York, NY 10016

Fritz S. Hofheimer, Inc.
88 Third Avenue
Mineola, NY 11501

Noma List Services
2544 Chamberlain Road
Fairlawn, OH 44313

Names Unlimited, Inc.
183 Madison Avenue
New York, NY 10016

VOLUNTEER LAWYERS FOR THE ARTS
A non-profit organization providing legal services and information for the arts community since 1974.

CALIFORNIA
California Lawyers for the Arts
(formerly Bay Area Lawyers for the Arts and Volunteer Lawyers for the Arts-Los Angeles)
San Francisco Office
Fort Mason Center
Building C, Room 255
San Francisco, CA 94123
(415) 775-7200

Oakland Office
247 4th Sreet
Suite 110
Oakland, CA 94607
(510) 444-6351

Santa Monica Office
1549 11th Street
Suite 200
Santa Monica, CA 90401
(310) 395-8893

DISTRICT OF COLUMBIA
Washington Volunteer Lawyers for
   the Arts
Attn: Joshua Kaufman
918 16th Street, NW

Suite 503
Washington, DC 20006
(202) 429-0229

Washington Area Lawyers for the
   Arts (WALA)
1325 G Street, NW
Lower Level
Washington, DC 20005
(202) 393-2826

ILLINOIS
Lawyers for the Creative Arts (LCA)
213 West Institute Place
Suite 411
Chicago, Il 60610
(312) 944-2787

NEW YORK
Volunteer Lawyers for the Arts (VLA)
One East 53rd Street
Sixth Floor
New York, NY 10022
(212) 319-2787

WASHINGTON
Washington Lawyers for the Arts
   (WLA)
219 First Avenue S.
Suite 315-A
Seattle, WA 98104
(206) 292-9171

*Contact these groups for refernces to other
local VLA groups.*

OTHER RESOURCES

American Arbitration Association
140 West 51st Street
New York, NY 10020
(212) 484-4000
Alternative dispute resolution.

Americans for the Arts
927 15th Street, NW
Twelfth Floor
Washington, DC 20005
(202) 371-2830

Arts, Crafts, and Theater Safety
   (ACTS)
Director, Monona Rossol
181 Thompson St., #23
New York, NY 10012
Publishes Arts Facts, *a monthly news-
letter updating regulations and research
affecting the arts.*

College Art Association
275 Seventh Avenue
New York, NY 10001
(212) 691-1051

Dome Publishing Co.
Providence, RI 02903
Business forms and bookkeeping systems.

Federal Trade Commission
Pennsylvania at 16th Street
Washington, DC 20580
(202) 326-2222

First Nation Arts
69 Kelly Road
Falmouth, VA 22405
(703) 371-5615

Idaho Shakespeare Festival
P.O. Box 9365
Boise, ID 83707
(208) 336-9221

Ideal System Co.
P.O. Box 1568
Augusta, GA 30903
Business forms and bookkeeping systems.

National Association of Campus
Activities
13 Harbison Way
Columbia, SC 29212-3401
(807) 732-6222

National Endowment for the Arts
(NEA)
1100 Pennsylvania, NW
Washington, DC 20506
(202) 682-5400
TDD (202) 682-5496

National Endowment for the
Humanities
1100 Pennsylvania, NW
Room 402
Washington, DC 20506
(202) 606-8400

National Fire Protection Association
1 Batterymarch Park
Quincy, MA 02269

(703) 516-4346
Publications: (800) 344-3555

National Institute of Occupational
Safety & Health (NIOSH)
(800) 356-4674

Occupational Safety and Health
Administration (OSHA)
(202) 523-9667

Office of Student Financial
Assistance
U.S. Department of Education
Washington, DC 20202

Opera America
777 14th Street, NW
Suite 520
Washington, DC 20005
(202) 347-9262

Oregon Shakespeare Festival
P.O. Box 158
Ashland, OR 97520
(503) 482-2111

Seattle Shakespeare Festival
1904 Third Ave., Suite 327
Seattle, WA 98104
(206) 624-7151

Small Business Administration
Washington, DC 20416

Small Business Administration
Publications
P.O. Box 30
Denver, CO 80201-0030

Small Business Administration
  Answer Desk
(800) 368-5855; (202) 653-7561

Stage and Screen (formerly known as
The Fireside Theatre)
Subscriptions:
6550 East 30th Street
P.O. Box 6370
Indianapolis, IN 46209-9493
"The Book Club for the Performing Arts."

U.S. Copyright Office
Library of Congress
Washington, DC 20559

U.S. Customs Service
1301 Constitution Avenue South
Washington, DC 20229

Appendix

Printed References

Agricultural Cooperative Service
U.S. Department of Agriculture
*Several excellent booklets on the principle
of cooperatives and how to organize them.*

ABCs of Borrowing
Publication FM1
Small Business Administration
   Publications
P.O. Box 30
Denver, CO 80201-0030

Art Law in a Nutshell, 2nd Ed.
by Leonard D. DuBoff (1993)
West Publishing Co.
P.O. Box 65426
St. Paul, MN 55164-0526

(612) 228-2778

*Behind the Scenes: Practical
   Entertainment Law*
by Michael I. Rudell (1984)
Harcourt Brace Jovanovich
757 Third Avenue
New York, NY 10017

*Be Your Own Boss: The Complete,
   Indispensable, Hands-On Guide
   to Starting and Running Your
   Own Business*
by Dana Schilling (1984)
Penguin
375 Hudson St.
New York, NY 10014

(212) 366-2000
(800) 331-4624

Business Forms and Contracts (In Plain English)® for Craftspeople, 2nd Ed.
by Leonard D. DuBoff (1993)
Foreword by Lammot duPont
  Copeland
Interweave Press
201 East Fourth Street
Loveland, CO 80537
(303) 669-7672; (800) 272-2193

Copyright Directory
Copyright Information Services,
  a division of Association for
  Educational Communications
  and Technology
1025 Vermont Avenue, N.W.
Suite 820
Washington, DC 20005

Cultural Business Times
bi-monthly publication of
Fred B. Rothman & Co.
10368 W. Centennial Road
Littleton, CO 80127
(303) 979-5657, (800) 457-1986

The Deskbook of Art Law, 2nd Ed.
by Leonard D. DuBoff and Sally
  Holt Caplan
Oceana Press
75 Main Street
Dobbs Ferry, NY 10522
(914) 693-8100

Entertainment Law, 2nd ed.
Shephard's/McGraw-Hill Inc.
P.O. Box 35300
Colorado Springs, CO 80935-3530

Fire Safety Fact Sheet
Publications 91-41 and 3088
OSHA Information,
Room N-3647
U.S. Department of Labor
Washington, DC 20210

Form Book of Art Law
by Leonard D. DuBoff (1996)
Fred B. Rothman and Co.
10368 W. Centennial Road
Littleton, CO 80127
(303) 979-5657, (800) 457-1986

Foundation Directory
Columbia University Press
136 S. Broadway
Irvington, NY 10533

General Information Concerning Patents
Superintendent of Documents
U.S. Government Printing Office
Washington, DC 20402

Insurance and Risk Management for Small Business, 2nd Ed.
Small Business Management Series
No. 30
Superintendent of Documents
U.S. Government Printing Office
Washington, DC 20402

*Insurance Checklist for Small
    Business*
Small Marketer's Aid #148
Small Business Administration
Washington, DC 20416

*Law and Business of the
    Entertainment Industries*
Auburn House Publishing Company
Dover, MA 02030

*The Law (In Plain English)® for
    Photographers*
by Leonard D. DuBoff (1995)
Allworth Press
10 E. 23rd Street
New York, NY 10010
(212) 777-8395

*The Law (In Plain English)® for
    Small Businesses, 2nd ed.*
by Leonard D. DuBoff (1991)
John Wiley & Sons
605 Third Avenue
New York, NY 10158-0012
(212) 850-6000

*The Law (In Plain English)® for
    Writers, 2nd ed.*
by Leonard D. DuBoff (1992)
John Wiley & Sons
605 Third Avenue
New York, NY 10158-0012
(212) 850-6000

Martindale-Hubbell® Law Directory
Martindale-Hubbell
121 Chanlon Road

New Providence, NJ 07974
(908) 464-6800

*Performing Arts Management and
    Law*
by Joseph Taubman (1972)
Law-Arts Publishers, Inc.
New York, NY

*The Photographers Business and
    Legal Handbook*
by Leonard D. DuBoff (1989)
Images Press, Inc.
22 E. 17th Street
New York, NY 10003
(212) 675-3707

The Sondheim Review
Attn: Department S-Z
P.O. Box 11213
Chicago, IL 60611-0213
(800) 584-1020

*Sound Cash Management and
    Borrowing*
Publication FM9
SBA Publications
P.O. Box 30
Denver, CO 80201-0030

Tax Guide for Small Business
Publication 334
Internal Revenue Service
U.S. Government Printing Office
Washington, DC 20402

Ventilation: A Practical Guide
by Nancy Clark, Thomas Cutler,

Jean-Ann McGrane
Center for Occupational Hazards
Five Beekman Street
New York, NY 10038
(212) 227-6220

Your Social Security
Social Security Office
See U.S. Government listings in telephone book for local office.

Allworth Books

Allworth Press publishes quality books to help creative individuals and small businesses. Titles include:

Booking and Tour Management for the Performing Arts
by Rena Shagan (softcover, 6 × 9, 272 pages, $19.95)

Stage Fright: Health and Safety in the Theater
by Monona Rossol (softcover, 6 × 9, 144 pages, $16.95)

An Actor's Guide: Your First Year in Hollywood
by Michael Saint Nicholas (softcover, 6 × 9, 256 pages, $16.95)

Writing Scripts Hollywood Will Love
by Katherine Atwell Herbert (softcover, 6 × 9, 160 pages, $12.95)

How to Pitch and Promote Your Songs, Revised Edition
by Fred Koller (softcover, 6 × 9, 192 pages, $18.95)

Artists Communities by the Alliance of Artists' Communities
(softcover, 6¾ × 10, 208 pages, $16.95)

Arts and the Internet: A Guide to the Revolution
by V. A. Shiva (softcover, 6 × 9, 208 pages, $18.95)

The Internet Publicity Guide
by V. A. Shiva (softcover, 6 × 9, 208 pages, $18.95)

The Internet Research Guide
by Timothy K. Maloy (softcover, 6 × 9, 208 pages, $18.95)

The Business of Multimedia
by Nina Schuyler (softcover, 6 × 9, 240 pages, $19.95)

The Copyright Guide
by Lee Wilson (softcover, 6 × 9, 192 pages, $18.95)

Please write to request our free catalog. If you wish to order a book, send your check or money order to Allworth Press, 10 East 23rd Street, Suite 210, New York, NY 10010. Include $5 for shipping and handling for the first book ordered and $1 for each additional book. Ten dollars plus $1 for each additional book if ordering from Canada. New York State residents must add sales tax.

If you wish to see our catalog on the World Wide Web, you can find us at Millennium Production's Art and Technology Web site:
http://www.arts-online.com/allworth/home.html
or at **http://www.interport.net/~allworth**